I0813810

CASEMATE | ILLUSTRATED | SPECIAL

GERMAN LOGISTICS 1939–45

SIMON FORTY &
RICHARD CHARLTON TAYLOR

CISS0021

Published in 2025 by
CASEMATE PUBLISHERS
1950 Lawrence Road, Havertown, PA 19083, USA
and
47 Church Street, Barnsley, S70 2AS, UK

Print Edition: ISBN 978-1-63624-518-8
Digital Edition: ISBN 978-1-63624-519-5

© 2025 Simon Forty and Richard Charlton Taylor
Simon Forty and Richard Charlton Taylor have asserted their right to be identified as authors of the work.

All rights reserved. No part of this book may be reproduced or transmitted in any form or by any means, electronic or mechanical including photocopying, recording or by any information storage and retrieval system, without permission from the publisher in writing.

Design by Eleanor Forty-Robbins
Printed and bound in the Czech Republic by FINIDR s.r.o.

CASEMATE PUBLISHERS (US)
Telephone (610) 853-9131
Fax (610) 853-9146
Email: casemate@casematepublishers.com
www.casematepublishers.com

CASEMATE PUBLISHERS (UK)
Telephone (0)1226 734350
Email: casemate@casemateuk.com
www.casemateuk.com

Author's note: All photos credited on the captions. The authors thank all those who have contributed, in particular Ruth Sheppard, Chris Cocks, and Lizzy Hammond at Casemate for helpful and constructive assistance, Eleanor Forty-Robbins (design), Mark Franklin (artwork), and for their help with illustrations and other material: Neil Powell at Battlefieldhistorian.com, Ian Spring of Pixpast.com, Marc Romanych of Digitalhistoryarchive.com, and last but not least, the generosity of Akira Takiguchi. If we've omitted anyone in error, please let us know through the publisher.

We'd like to recommend the following websites that helped greatly with our research: allworldwars.com/German-English-Military-Dictionary.html; feldgrau.com; kfzderwehrmacht.de; kriegsfunker.com; lexikon-der-wehrmacht.de; lonesentry.com; axishistory.com; panzerworld.com; track-link.com; waralbum.ru; and wwiidaybyday.com

A note on measurements: three types of ton appear in the book: tonne/metric ton = 2,205 lb; short (U.S.) ton = 2,000 lb; ton (imperial/long ton) = 2,420 lb.

Cover photo credits: Front: Ian Spring/Pixpast.com (top), RCT (bottom three). Back from top: Akira Takiguchi, RCT, Kfz70 baku13/WikiCommons/CC BY-SA 3.0, Tanis.

Title page: As the late-war loss of the *Wilhelm Gustloff* showed, the potential for disaster was ever-present when troop movements were made by ship—one reason why the Allies made so much use of fast liners. (SF Collection)

Right: The first Class 52 Kriegslok taking a photo call in the Berlin Machine Building Corporation factory in Wildau. (Bundesarchiv)

Above right: Men of 118. Jäger-Division rest during the advance toward Zadar in Dalmatia on September 22, 1943. In the foreground is an NSU 501 OSL motorbike. The motorcycle troops worked well in the West on good roads; in the East, on poor surfaces, they struggled. (NAC)

The Publisher's authorised representative in the EU for product safety is Authorised Rep Compliance Ltd., Ground Floor, 71 Lower Baggot Street, Dublin D02 P593, Ireland.
www.arccompliance.com

Contents

Introduction

Battlefield logistics provide the blade to the cutting edge of the armed forces and do so under fire. It's not very glamorous and Hollywood doesn't make movies about it, but successful logistics are the key to successful wars. To fight a battle, you need to have the right people and equipment at the right place at the right time. Those people need to have the food, ammunition, and backup necessary to fulfill their mission. Tactical logisticians must worry about keeping front-line units supplied. If the antitank gunner doesn't have a suitable round to hand, he won't be able to stop a tank; if a machine-gunner has no ammunition, he can't lay down covering fire; if an infantryman doesn't have a grenade, urban fighting suddenly gets a lot more difficult; if there are no boats and no bridging equipment, even small rivers can hold up an attack irreparably.

Field post was an essential element in a soldier's life, and the post must get through ... even in the snow. Each unit had its own *Feldpostnummer* and the field post office was usually to be found with other supply units (ammunition, clothing, and food) at transport hubs. Postcards and letters up to 100 g and packets up to 200 g were free of charge as were postcards, soldiers being able to send two of the latter per man per week. (NAC)

Even ambulances get bogged down. Here a team of horses is used to free an ambulance from the *Rasputitsa.* (Dutch Archives)

To get the front-line soldier what he needs, a successful supply chain must know what is needed, where it's needed, and when it's needed. Operational logistics act as the bridge between homeland industry and supply depots and the front line, bringing men and materiel close enough to the front to allow the combat units to access them. This is the realm of long-distance transport: of railroads and roads, of traffic control and security patrols, and—in the case of the German Army—often horse-drawn columns inching their way toward the front. Operational logistics must manage success—the distance that advancing armies can get from their railheads—and failure: in the Soviet Union that could mean partisans, snow, or the dreaded *Rasputitsa*, the muddy period that made roads impassable. If soldiers don't prepare for cold weather, when it's cold their guns don't fire, their engines don't start, and they freeze to death. If mud makes the roads impassable, supplies don't get through to the front. Horses starve or are killed to keep men alive. Without fuel, advancing armies must stop and await replenishment.

The biggest problem, however, facing any country at war is strategic logistics: what to build and when to build it, how to guarantee the availability of raw materials and fuel, how to direct the economy and industry to provide the weapons needed: aircraft or tanks, warships or artillery?

Nazi Germany was a militaristic society whose aggressive leadership was ready to plunge the country into war from the first. Indeed, *Mein Kampf* identifies the main reasons for war: lebensraum. Quite simply, Hitler believed that Germany needed to annex swathes of land in the east to be autarkical (self-sufficient and independent of all other nations). The concept was older than Nazism, but the problems caused by the British and Allied naval blockade of Germany during World War I were a significant factor. The Nazis remembered the suffering that shortages had led to during the war and wished no repeat of them. Just as the United States had felt its "manifest destiny" was to stretch from the Atlantic to the Pacific, so Nazi Germany felt it needed to expand into Russia. The breadbasket of Ukraine would feed the German people, the oilfields of the Caucasus would provide motive power, the Urals and Russian forests would provide raw materials.

The trade agreements between the Nazis and the Soviet Union saw oil and raw materials head to the Reich. Here a driver of a Soviet oil train talks to a German soldier on the border at Przemyśl. (NAC)

Through a mixture of punchy politics and brinkmanship, Hitler managed to set the German economy on a path for a war he anticipated would come in the early 1940s. In a confidential memorandum of August 1936, he ordered that:

> I. The German Army must be operational [*einsatzfähig*] within four years.
>
> II. The German economy must be fit for war [*kriegsfähig*] within four years.

Although the Nazis did away with the secret training installations, testing grounds, and engineering facilities set up in the Soviet Union under the 1922 Treaty of Rapallo (such as the flight school at Lipetsk and tank training area at Kazan), they did appreciate the resources that were available from the East. Clever commercial deals with the Soviet Union helped provide raw materials and fuel. But everything changed when Hitler rushed into war with Poland in 1939, triggering a response from Britain and France that saw Europe once again embroiled in a major war.

From a logistics point of view, World War II started well for the Germans. The benefits—particularly military equipment—that had come from the *Anschluß* and the annexation of Czechoslovakia helped Germany to rearm. Poland fell quickly enough and when the Wehrmacht invaded Western Europe, it did so with sufficient men and equipment to challenge the powerful French and British defenders. When the dust cleared, the Wehrmacht was on the Channel coast. The defense had disintegrated, and German tactical nous was able to achieve what its World War I counterparts had not. The German economy and war machine benefited enormously as the Germans availed themselves of the booty—industry and agriculture, weapons and war materiel, gold and treasures, and, of course, the labor of the conquered countries' workforces.

In many ways, the speed of the campaigns in the West—and subsequently in the Balkans and Greece—masked any operational logistic problems. The industrialized West with its excellent rail and road communications was easily within range of German aircraft and gave few opportunities for Britain to flex its major muscle: the Royal Navy (RN). German industry coped with the wartime requirements without any problems and Germany itself was far enough removed from the action to be able to enjoy the fruits of military success. The chilling excesses that started against the Jews and Polish intelligentsia weren't too visible and at this stage the "Final Program" seemed more intent on parceling the Jews off to the Holy Land or Madagascar than what it became.

Arrogant in victory, faced by what they saw as Slav subhumans, the attack on the Soviet Union was expected to result in a victory as swift as that in the West. The German high command was aware of the problems of distance, terrain, and climate, just as it was of the different rail gauge and the problem of supplies. But there was a plan: a vile and ideological decision to ensure the armies should live off the land in a way that was expected to result in starvation and death for the many conquered civilians. The ridding of the land of most of its people would leave only enough of them to work as slaves for the German settlers who would take over. The invasion of the Soviet Union may not have started with the intention to exterminate Jews and Slavs, but very quickly that became the rationale.

The trouble was that even as millions of Soviet PoWs were starved to death, Jews rounded up and killed, and civilians treated like animals, the Red Army proved steadfast in its defensive resolve. Finding out quickly what would happen to the people and the land when taken over by the Germans, the Red Army kept fighting.

And then the logistical problems hit: awful road conditions and too few trucks, the destruction of railroad infrastructure, too few trains, and the last straw, the winter. The Wehrmacht ground to a halt. *Panzer* divisions became *Panje* divisions as only horses could provide transport—and not the big European and German horses the Wehrmacht had commandeered from conquered nations or bred itself, but sturdy Russian ponies. The German Army clung to its positions by its frostbitten fingertips and—only just—weathered the storm; indeed, rebuilt by great effort, as *Fall Blau* was launched in summer 1942 and the troops sped toward the Caucasus and its oilfields, there was a moment when everything seemed on track again.

It was a chimera. Overextended, too dependent on allies who lacked the necessary weapons and training, enmeshed in the largest urban battle of all time, the wheels came off. There were too few transport aircraft to sustain 6. Armee in Stalingrad because the strategic decision on which aircraft to build had been forced on Hitler by the actions of the Allied bombers over the Reich. He had fighters aplenty but too few transports—and even fewer after the siege ended. At Kursk—a battle delayed so as to rush mighty new AFVs to the theater—the Soviets made good use of the extra time by building further layers of defense. The German attack was blunted, and the Soviets gained the initiative. In the West, so did the Allies as they drove the German forces in North Africa into an ever-diminishing area of Tunisia. German logistics poured reinforcements in, but it was too little, too late. Even worse was to come in 1944 when the vaunted Atlantic Wall—created by pouring millions of cubic feet of reinforced concrete, from the Arctic Circle to the Pyrenees—was blown away within hours of the Normandy landings. A few days later, in the East, Operation *Bagration* knocked great holes in the so-called Panther Line and pushed the Wehrmacht out of the areas of the Soviet Union it had taken in 1941.

Henceforth, tactical logistics might improve as their lines of communication reduced but strategically, the Germans were dead men walking. They prolonged the war despite Allied bombing of their industry, lack of fuel, and the numbers ranged against them. Thousands of slave laborers were imported into the Reich to be worked to death and production levels peaked in 1944; secret rocket weapons were indeed produced and used to affect Allied civilian morale. But it was to no avail. Allied air superiority became air supremacy over the battlefield. Allied industrial output vastly exceeded the German. German lack of fuel saw many of their best weapons immobilized and destroyed by their own crews. As the Allies advanced into the Reich, they did so at the end of logistical supply chains that had been the major reason for their success.

Strategic Logistics

It is often said that armies prepare to fight the last war rather than the next one. Certainly, the building blocks of military warfare tend to be based on decisions made years before, often by politicians rather than military men. National identity, ideology, and history play their part in the decisions that planners make. So too does overconfidence. If something is working, why change it? It is all too easy to underestimate how quickly requirements can change in war.

As 1942 dawned, over two years from the start of the war, the German people were still in the main part ignorant of the dangers they faced. There was, however, a growing sense of unease. The war in the East that they thought would be over by Christmas 1941 was still dragging on; more and more losses were being reported and men mobilized. Nevertheless, the powers-that-be in general, and the Führer himself, didn't seem overly concerned. Used to Nazi military success, most believed the propaganda that the Soviets were already beaten.

As if to show their lack of concern, even at this stage of the war German munitions production had not reached peak output and was still not as significant a part of Nazi Germany's GNP or total industrial output as might be expected. The reason for this surprising lack of activity was due to some extent to the complacency brought on by the successes since the reoccupation of the Rhineland in 1936. Political success had led to military success. As the United States Strategic Bombing Survey points out:

> It is easy to ascribe Germany's failure to expand her munitions output to the confidence bred of easy victories in the west.
>
> That the General Staff should also have been victim to such overconfidence is less easy to understand, yet there is evidence that the military authorities considered the prevailing rate of output generally sufficient for the successful invasion of Russia.

Apart from possible complacency, there were other reasons why military spending hadn't ramped up. It was already a considerable proportion of the German economy:

> Of the growth in total national output in Germany between 1935 and 1938 almost half (47%) was accounted for directly by the increase in the Reich's military spending. If we add investment … the share rises to two-thirds (67%). … Of the goods and services purchased by the Reich, the Wehrmacht accounted for 70% in 1935 and 80% the year after. [Adam Tooze]

The acquisition of new territories saw large amounts of weaponry captured: over 2,000 French AFVs, huge numbers of British vehicles at Dunkirk and elsewhere, massive amounts of Soviet weapons including artillery and antitank guns in the first months of 1941. As well as capturing physical stocks there was the industrial output, too—of Czechoslovakia in particular, but also France and the Low Countries. One immediate result of this was that the German armies that took part in *Unternehmen Barbarossa* included several divisions equipped either wholly or in part with the PzKpfw 35(t) and 38(t)—the (t) meaning they were of Czech origin, although each now included a radio as was required for command and control in all German AFVs. These designs had been at least as good as anything available in 1938, although by 1941 they were obsolescent. Friedrich Sander went to war in Russia in a PzKpfw 35(t) and said in late summer 1941:

> We only take note of the special events. And for the old Skoda drivers, these events are usually linked to the ever-increasing ailments of our "Skoda Super Sports." I hope we get rid of the old bangers soon. I stand in awe when I see the admirable and difficult work our maintenance and repair services are doing. The old Skodas in particular cause a huge amount of work.

Blockade Busting

The Russo-German agreements of 1939–40 are best known for the agreement to invade and partition Poland. What is perhaps less well-known is the huge trade deal that took place and was augmented in 1940 by a commercial agreement that saw Germany agree to send 650 million RM's worth of machinery, manufactured goods, and technology in return for a similar value of raw materials, foodstuffs, and oil (see table). The Soviet Union also agreed to secretly help Germany circumvent the blockade by undertaking the purchase of goods from third parties on Germany's behalf. Note the key products: oil and grain.

Soviet Exports to Germany, 1939–June 1941 (in RM millions)*

Type	1939	1940	Jan.-Jun. 1941
Oil products	5.1	617.0	254.2
Grains	0.2	820.8	547.1
Manganese ore	6.2	64.8	75.2
Phosphates	32.3	131.5	56.3
Technical oils & fats	4.4	11.0	8.9
Chromium	0.0	26.3	0.0
Copper	0.0	7.1	7.2
Nickel	0.0	1.5	0.7
Legumes	10.9	47.2	34.8
Tin	0.0	0.8	0.0
Platinum	0.0	1.5	1.3
Chemicals: finished	0.9	2.9	0.2
Chemicals: unfinished	0.9	2.6	1.0
Oil cake	0.0	29.0	8.6
Raw textiles	9.0	99.1	41.1
Wood products	171.9	846.7	393.7

* German figures; these don't include products in transit when *Barbarossa* started.

Another reason that the *Beutepanzer*—lit. booty tanks—and Czech industrial output helped was that the outbreak of the war prompted an immediate fall in German industrial production, thanks to a loss of manpower to the Wehrmacht. In 1939 there were five *Wellen* or waves of mobilization that added over 60 divisions to the German Army. This reduced the civilian workforce by 10%, a loss that wasn't made up until 1941.

However, while all appeared calm as Germany entered 1942, the writing was on the wall. In the Soviet Union, logistics problems had led to enormous problems over the winter period. Losses there meant that production had to be increased, but another important factor came into play on March 28/29, 1942, when 234 British aircraft bombed the port of Lübeck. Then, on May 30, 1,046 bombers destroyed Cologne. The increasing number of Allied air raids meant that air defense, whether by aircraft or antiaircraft artillery, was vital.

An important catalyst of this change of tempo was the arrival on the scene in February 1942 of Albert Speer, who became minister of weapons and ammunition after the death of the incumbent, Fritz Todt, in an air crash. Today, the appreciation of Speer's role in the increase of German munitions production in 1942–44 has been rowed back. At the time and in the immediate postwar period he was seen as being a miracle worker, but most of his claims have since been seen as propaganda and many of the statistics he published were inflated. He was ambitious and was given great powers, first over army munitions production; later production for both the Kriegsmarine (in October 1943) and Luftwaffe (June 1944) came under his aegis. Rather than being a result of Speer's "revolution," German industry had just started to iron out its own problems, had got used to being on a war footing, and Speer benefited from the concomitant improvements. His later attempts to increase production—for example, by prefabricating sections of U-boats—proved specious. Additionally, to the detriment of the beleaguered Ostheer desperately needing more men, Speer did what he could to retain his workforce and loosen the tightening of the deferment rules that had helped revive the army before *Fall Blau*.

Whether a result of Speer's work or not, the increases in production from 1942 were significant. In 1940–42, armament production was around 10% of GNP. By 1944 that had risen to 18%. In 1942 the armament industry accounted for 25% of industrial production, by mid-1944 over 40%. The allocation of finished steel increased from 10.3 million tons in 1940 to 17.3 million tons in 1943. Workers in the armament industry also increased: from 2.7 million in June 1941 to 3.9 million in mid-1944. With over six million men drafted into the Wehrmacht, other personnel were also brought into service. Fritz Sauckel, the general plenipotentiary for labor deployment from March 1942, by April 1943 provided Speer for his armaments factories over 1.5 million extra hands, mainly forced labor, prisoners of war, and concentration camp prisoners.

It wasn't all plain sailing. There were production bottlenecks for components and parts, and design and testing of the heavy tanks that appeared 1942–43 saw *Panzer* production curtailed to work on the new vehicles. To compensate, various *Panzerjäger* expedients were produced on existing but obsolete chassis, particularly the Marders, using the PzKpfw II and 38(t) chassis. Many of these stopgap weapons made use of captured Soviet guns rechambered to take German ammunition.

Panzerjäger Expedients		
Type	Principal weapon	Date introduced
Marder II (SdKfz 132) on PzKpfw II	7.62 cm PaK 36 or 7.62 cm PaK 36(r)	From March 1942
Panzerjäger 38(t)/Marder III (SdKfz 138) on PzKpfw 38(t)	7.62 cm PaK 36 or 7.62 cm PaK 36(r)	From May 1942
Marder I (SdKfz 135) on Lorraine 37L Schlepper	PaK 40, 7.5 cm	From July 1942
Marder II (SdKfz 131) on PzKpfw II	PaK 40, 7.5 cm	From July 1942

The lack of suitable tanks also led to increasing use of the *Sturmgeschütz*, designed for infantry support, in the *Panzerjäger* role. The StuG may have proved an effective tank killer but, as *Generalinspekteur der Panzertruppen*—inspector general of armored troops, from March 1, 1943—Heinz Guderian kept pointing out, a *Sturmgeschütz* could not be a substitute for a tank as the spearhead of an attack when the StuG had such a small amount of traverse (24° compared to 360°) and was thus vulnerable to attacks from the flanks and rear. Even with a close-defense weapon, lack of decent all-round vision defined the *Sturmgeschütz* as an infantry support weapon that required an infantry escort. The reason it was considered at all was the lack of availability of proper tanks.

The process of tank procurement and the vagaries of a system so dominated by its leader show major flaws in the performance of German logistics on a strategic level. A good, if extreme, example is the arrival of the Panther at Kursk.

The Panther started life with a design brief dated November 25, 1941. It led to a competition between MAN and Daimler-Benz whose designs were submitted on May 13, 1942. The MAN design was chosen. The prototypes were delivered for testing at the end of the year. Problems pushed the in-service delivery date back, but at Hitler's insistence they were hurried into service in time for *Unternehmen Zitadelle*, which led to little time for crew training. Additionally, *Zitadelle*'s start date had to be delayed to accommodate the use of the Panther and the new Ferdinand *Panzerjäger*. For *Zitadelle*, Panzerabteilungen 51 and 52 had, nominally, 200 Panthers available for action. However, as XLVIII. Panzerkorps' war diary for July 2, 1943, said:

The PzKpfw V Panther was undoubtedly an excellent AFV but its introduction to combat left a great deal to be desired. It was a complicated vehicle that performed well with seasoned crews but lacked side vision and was easily flanked in tight conditions such as the hedgerows of the bocage country of Normandy. (Dutch Archives)

> They hadn't conducted tactical training as a complete Abteilung and radio sets hadn't been tested. Since their assembly areas were so close to the front, permission couldn't be granted for them to test and practice with the radio sets.

This undoubtedly compounded the extreme problems of automotive unreliability. Five days into the operation, on July 10, only 10 Panthers were operational at the front, although this did increase to 43 by the 13th. Fuel pump deficiencies saw 56 Panthers burnt out beyond repair.

A report prepared by Panther regimental commander Major Mainrad von Lauchert after Kursk highlighted a long list of defects: that the taper on the pistol port needed to be strengthened because, were the port to take a direct hit, the cover would be blown into the turret, killing the loader and commander; that frontal armor needed strengthening because the mantlet deflected shots down and through the roof into the fighting compartment; more protection was needed against mines—40 Panthers were put out of action by mines, and in one case the mine ignited ammunition under the turret cage; that training had been too short, which Lauchert stressed was the cause of a large percentage of technical and tactical failures; and the smoke pots were quickly destroyed by enemy fire, and a new way of producing smoke needed to be found.

Problems would continue to dog the Panther in service, and it was rare to find as many as 50% operational in any unit. For example, between August 20 and September 20, 1943, Panzerabteilung 51 started with 28 of 74 Panthers operational and ended with eight of 56; between October 20 and November 20, operational vehicles in the *Abteilung* went from 13 of 59 to one of 49. The Panther may have earned a reputation for its gun, gunsight, and lethality, but lack of initial training and spare parts meant that it didn't perform as effectively on the battlefield in 1943 as the *langrohr* (with the longer 7.5 cm KwK 40 main gun) PzKpfw IVs.

It wasn't just the teething problems of new, more sophisticated and better equipment that was the problem but an endemic issue with repair and spare parts. While much of the postwar historical output of the German generals needs to be treated cautiously, General Burkhart H. Müller-Hillebrand's (lead author) pamphlet about tank spare parts provides a catalogue of issues but the theme is a common one. First, the actual lack of sufficient spare parts:

> From the very beginning, the number of spare parts actually delivered was by no means equal to the demand. Some tanks required spare parts immediately after their first test run. The limited stocks of spare parts on hand were often insufficient to meet the demands. Supplementary requisitions for certain parts were placed in good time with the Ordnance Office, but deliveries to the parts depots usually suffered long delays. The rapid expansion of the armored forces may have had a considerable effect on the manufacturers' capabilities of delivering spare parts on schedule. Most industrial enterprises were overloaded with military and civilian orders.

Müller-Hillebrand then outlines the supply problems:

> When the Germans launched their summer offensive in 1942, more than 75% of their total tank strength was employed in the southern part of the Russian theater. Within a short time, hundreds of tanks were disabled and a major backlog of repairs accumulated because the necessary spare parts were not available. Most of the disabled tanks could have been quickly restored to service since the repairs involved only the replacement of defective parts. Less than 80% of the damaged tanks required welding or time-consuming labor. Had parts been in stock or available at a nearby depot, most of the repairs involving the replacement of defective parts could probably have been accomplished within 2 weeks. However, at this time the spare-parts problem had become so critical that it had a paralyzing effect on the simultaneous thrusts toward Stalingrad and into the Caucasus.

Another example of problematic procurement is that of APCR antitank ammunition. The Germans had tungsten-cored APCR ammunition available for use by PaK and KwK in September 1940. However, as

Barbarossa started, less than 6% of the ammunition available to these weapons was APCR and availability of these rounds dwindled as the war progressed.

The usual reason given for this is the German lack of tungsten. From the start of the war, Germany was faced with the problem of procuring raw materials—as it had in World War I—thanks to the blockade by the Royal Navy. One of the key factors in Britain's refusal to accept peace terms in 1940 was that the government felt confident it could strangle German industry through such a blockade. Indeed, British intelligence sources in 1939 thought that Germany would be unable to fight a prolonged war and would run out of raw materials within 18 months of the blockade taking effect. The main metals used in the manufacture of weapons—chromium, copper, nickel, and tungsten—were highlighted. This lack is often cited as a reason for Germany's Blitzkrieg approach to warfare: that Hitler knew he couldn't win a long war and that the German tactics developed accordingly.

In fact, there's every indication that this isn't entirely correct. The Germans had every expectation that the war would not be a short one. Blitzkrieg is a term used with hindsight after the complete success of the attack on the West: something that surprised the attackers as much as the defenders. German analysts spent a great deal of time and effort considering the problem of availability of critical materials and had thought carefully about what they'd need to conduct a long war and where they could procure what they couldn't produce themselves. They became adept at substitution—for example, using aluminum instead of copper for power lines—and carefully rationing the use of key materials to extend the lifetime of their reserves. Their success at this was carefully concealed—so well that British intelligence massively overestimated German consumption at the end of the 1930s; by 67% in the case of tin, by 33% in the case of copper, and by 26% in the case of nickel.

As an example, tungsten—which the Germans bought from China until war was declared after Pearl Harbor in 1941, then Spain until 1944 when they threatened Spain with an oil embargo—was at no stage in critical demand in Germany. They built up large stocks through legal and illegal methods. Additionally, it *was* available in Germany itself through mining. In 1942, the Reichsamt für Bodenforschung thought that German tungsten mines were as rich as those of Portugal and Spain and could provide 700 tons per annum, around one-third of German tungsten consumption in 1943. However, though Germany never ran out of tungsten, it was in short enough supply to force decisions about what it was used for—machine tools rather than hardening steel plating (vanadium was substituted)—and to restrict its use for ammunition mainly to 5 cm shells. This meant that APCR rounds were always at a premium.

While Germany certainly expected a longer war in the West than took place, it's also worth pointing out that, when compared to British munitions output, German output "clearly indicates the inadequacy of Germany's military preparations in the early war years." (United States Strategic Bombing Survey)

Output of Selected Munitions, Germany and United Kingdom, 1940–42

Munitions	Germany 1940	UK 1940	Germany 1941	UK 1941	Germany 1942	UK 1942
Aircraft, excluding trainers	9,498	9,924	10,887	13,479	14,386	17,731
Tanks, including SPGs	1,643	1,397	3,790	4,844	6,180	8,611
Artillery, ground and AA (7.5 cm and over)	5,499	1,872	7,082	5,314	11,988	6,086
Artillery ammo (per million rounds)	27	13	27	29	57	59

The Poor Bloody Infantry

A few minutes' rest and then the advance continues. (NAC)

The trouble with the lack of motorized transport was that the infantry had to walk—always chasing the tanks to complete the great encirclement battles in 1941 and 1942 and hurrying to escape the pursuing Red Army from mid-1943. For marching the Wehrmacht used benchmarks, an average march would be 21–30 km a day; an express march 30–35 km; a forced march 40–50 km, although the latter was an unsustainable rate. In practice, weather, road conditions, and availability of rations—other than the "Do not touch" iron rations—played an important role. Carrying heavy cumbersome kit, around 10–20 kg, more with ammunition boxes, enduring hot and sweaty or wet and cold weather, uncomfortable days were followed by the excruciating violence of combat. If possible, potential rest areas were recced in advance: usually one at the beginning of a march after a couple of kilometers when a short rest allowed readjustment of clothing and loads. Thereafter, for long marches halts were every two hours or so: long enough for feeding and drinking including animals. In summer, location—shade for all—was essential as was proximity to water.

A heavily armed group at rest waiting for rations to be delivered—they can be seen in the background. The group includes auxiliaries, Hiwis, who had little or no love for the Soviets. The second figure up from the bottom is a Hiwi who carries a K98k rifle. The two pairs of boxed 7.92 mm MG rounds belong with the MG 34 crew; there will be other boxes. The section commander sits to the left with his MP 40 on the ground in front of him. (NAC)

German infantry march past a group of Soviet PoWs. Short term, the odds are stacked against the Soviets who will almost certainly die of starvation or brutality as did most of those captured in 1941. Longer term, the boot would be on the other foot for the Germans. Infantry warfare has always been a mincing machine, high on casualties. Manpower become an issue for both sides. (NARA)

An exhausted MG 34 crew sleep in as much shade as a paling fence can provide. The boxes each hold 250 rounds of 7.92 mm ammunition in five 50-round belts. The key function of the crew was to feed the MG and always have spare boxes at hand. Note the Model 24 stick grenades. Contrary to Hollywood these were offensive weapons, used in the attack and relying on blast to disorient the enemy. The stick allowed a longer throw which gave the attacker time to follow up the effect of the blast. The pebble-dash effect on several of the helmets is there to deflect sunshine and stop flashes of light. (NAC)

As the table on p. 13 shows, in the early war years British industry—before the huge output the United States brought to the party—outproduced the Germans in all major military components save artillery. On top of this, German production of ammunition and motor vehicles deteriorated: the latter would become a critical problem in the fighting in the East. If one looks at German light vehicle manufacture, the disparity between the Allies and the Axis becomes even more stark. Between 1934 and 1944, German industry built around 840,000 trucks, of which a substantial number were for civilian usage and export. In comparison, over 800,000 CMP (Canadian Military Pattern) trucks and light wheeled vehicles alone were built from 1939–45—most by Ford, GM, and Chrysler of Canada. The United States produced similarly huge numbers of trucks: between them the two countries' output ensured the mobility of the United States and British and Commonwealth forces, while also providing substantial numbers to the Soviet Union.

There are many reasons why the Germans didn't build more trucks in this period: lack of roads, the importance of other war materiel such as tanks and aircraft, and the need to reserve fuel and rubber for the military. The result was that the Germans had to press captured equipment into service. By the time of *Barbarossa* this meant they had some 2,000 different types of vehicles with all the spare parts and logistics issues that that entailed. The wear and tear of the campaign exacted a heavy toll. By June 1942, a year after *Barbarossa* started, the Wehrmacht had lost nearly 130,000 MT vehicles and many, many more were under repair. Remarkably, given the manpower constraints as the pool of adult men was bled white to fill the ranks of the fallen in the East, German industry was able to produce a similar number of vehicles to those lost. Slowly, the trucks the Ostheer needed for *Fall Blau* arrived in the East.

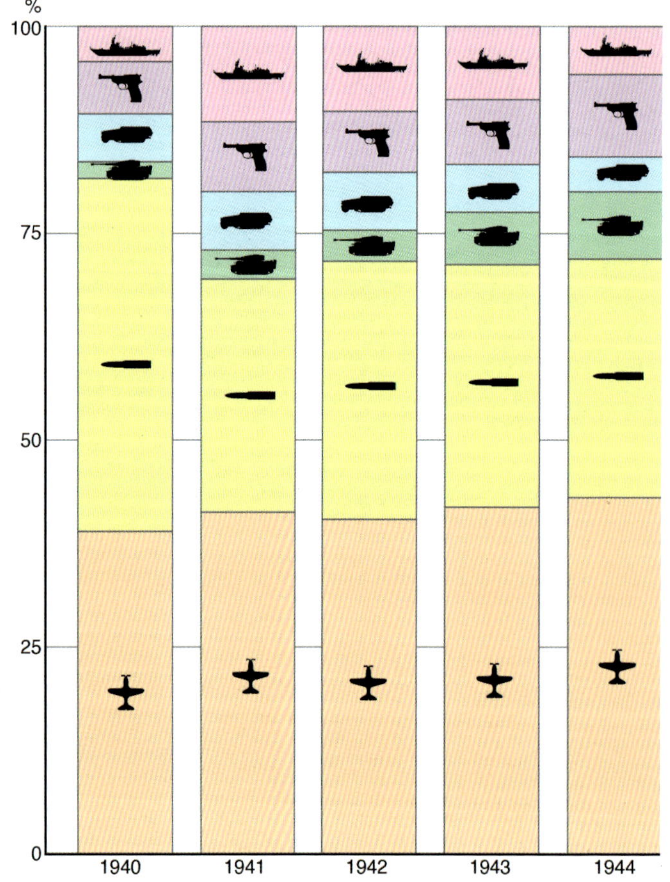

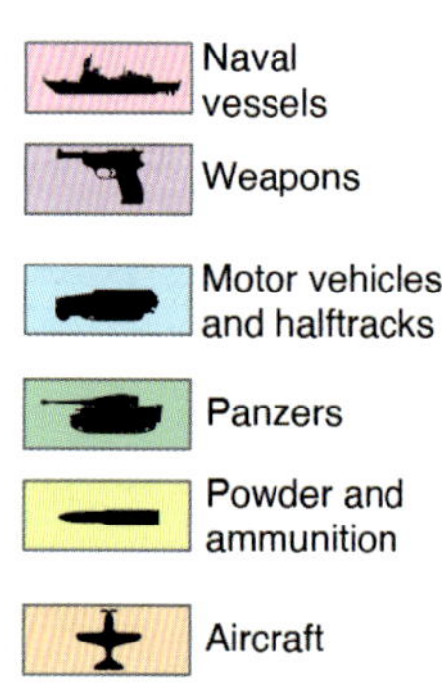

Percentage distribution of armaments production annually, 1940–44. (CBO German manufacturing stats)

German Truck and Passenger Car Production for the Armed Forces, the Civilian Economy, and Export, 1934–44				
Year	Number of trucks produced	% armed forces	% civilian economy	% export
1934	28,452	6.2	85.9	7.9
1935	45,213	15.6	75.3	9.1
1936	70,040	10.4	80.1	9.5
1937	79,126	16.1	66.1	17.8
1938	87,661	26.0	58.3	15.7
1939	101,745	32.0	52.0	16.0
1940	87,888	60.7	24.6	14.7
1941	86,147	59.3	25.2	15.5
1942	80,512	72.1	21.2	6.7
1943	92,959	79.8	15.9	4.3
1944	77,177	87.3	9.8	2.9
TOTAL	836,920			

With Speer at the helm and German industry beginning to get its act together, munitions production increased. Among the reasons for this was a sensible review of the numbers of weapon types produced. Rationalization and standardization were something the Western Allies were very good at promoting. The Germans—especially when one considers the booty of their conquests—less so.

On the negative side, during 1943 Allied bombing began to affect production directly (see table below). As the United States Strategic Bombing Survey noted,

> Raids on single-engine fighter plants began in July 1943; and although relatively light, they caused an estimated 13% loss of aircraft production for the period July through December. Only part of this loss was the direct result of the raids; part of it was due to the dispersal measures undertaken in anticipation of further raids.

Changes in Output of Total Munitions and Main Munitions Categories, October 1942–July 1944 (in RM millions)				
Munitions	October 1942	May 1943	December 1943	July 1944
Aircraft	527	863	739	1,446
Ammunition	471	572	653	719
Weapons	107	170	186	278
Panzer	57	147	165	234
Naval vessels	130	211	138	135
Motor vehicles	72	93	74	72
Half-tracks	23	41	44	48
Powder	44	80	66	63
TOTAL	1,432	2,158	2,065	2,995

The Schell Plan

The German auto industry lagged behind other Western nations. Passenger cars increased in number from around half a million in 1933 to 1.3 million in 1938, but truck numbers grew more slowly from around 150,000 to 250,000 in the same period. The main reason for this was the excellent rail network that allowed most goods to be transported by rail. (In 1939 70% of all freight traffic was carried by railroads, 20% by inland waterways, and the rest by coastal shipping and roads.)

Hitler, however, was greatly enamored with roads and road transport and on September 23, 1933, turned the first sod of the first of the *Reichsautobahnen* (they'd become known as the *Straßen des Führers*—the Führer's roads). However, by 1939 only around 2,000 miles had been completed—less than 2% of the German road network and only half of the *Autobahnen* were declared *kriegswichtig* (war important). Surprisingly, they had also been built haphazardly and provided little strategic assistance—they didn't, for example, provide any of the key economic areas of the Ruhr, Silesia, and the Saar with road transport links. An opportunity to provide an alternative to Germany's creaking railroad system was lost.

German auto manufacturers were artisans and there were a lot of them—but what the Wehrmacht needed was mass production of standardized vehicles. Luckily, to hand was a man who was clever enough to know what was needed and, more importantly, able to convince Hitler:

Hitler loved the German motorways and was personally linked to them as is shown with this postcard. It remembers the groundbreaking ceremony of September 23, 1933, and that 1,000 km had been prepared by the same date in 1936. The length and the location of the *Autobahnen* rendered them less useful than that sounds. (WikiCommons/ Asurnipal, CC BY-SA 4.0)

Oberstleutnant Adolf von Schell. On November 1, 1938, he had been appointed head of the Weapons Department of the armored forces, cavalry and army motorization in the OKH (*Leiter der Waffenabteilung der Panzertruppe, Kavallerie und Heeresmotorisierung*) and soon after undersecretary of state in the Reich Ministry of Transport and put in charge of the development of the Reich's motor vehicle system as *Generalbevollmächtigter für das Kraftfahrzeugwesens* (General Plenipotentiary for Motor Vehicles).

The result was the Schell Plan—the Program for the Restriction of Motor Vehicle Types—presented in mid-March 1939. It outlined the way ahead: reducing the number of vehicles (motorbikes, trucks, and cars):

Schell Plan Type Restrictions

Vehicle	1939 number of types	Future number
Motorcycles	150	26
Passenger vehicles	52	30
Trucks	114	19
Truck trailers	1,367	8

There was also standardization within truck weights to 1.5 ton, 3 ton, 4.5 ton, and 6.5 ton.

Oberstleutnant Schell's plan came into force on January 1, 1940, the first of several attempts to structure the German economy. The problem—as was so frequently the case in the labyrinthine Nazi power structure—was all the vested interests ranged against the plan, mainly from within the industry. These were successful in undermining Oberstleutnant Schell. On January 16, 1942, Hitler's old friend and Daimler-Benz board member Jakob Werlin was appointed general inspector of the Führer for motor vehicles. On September 10, 1942, Schell was placed on the Führer reserve.

In 1944/45 the Luftwaffe had to disperse its aircraft to reduce the risks from bombing or Allied *Jabos*. Here, Ju 88s make use of a forested section of motorway. (Library of Congress)

The improvement to production levels continued in 1944, reaching their peak in July—a 45% improvement on 1943—but the gains were selective. Aircraft, although often obsolescent types, and AFVs were, understandably, at the top. Motor vehicles and ammunition suffered, as did ship deliveries (mainly because of changes to manufacturing methods for new types of submarines, which proved to be a disaster). However, after July, munitions output dropped 18% by December because of strategic bombing. From then till the end of the war, the combination of bombing and Allied advances led to the final collapse of German industrial production.

The United States Strategic Bombing Survey identified in 1944 that

> Panzer production, previously interrupted only by area raids, was subjected to systematic attacks from August through October, in the course of which all assembly plants and several of the main engine plants were successfully bombed. The resultant damage not only set back the industry's ambitious and soundly based expansion program but actually lowered production, though the latter recovered in November and December when bad weather put a halt to the air offensive. The loss of output for the whole period is estimated at 20 percent.
>
> The systematic attack on the motor vehicle industry began at the end of June 1944. The industry had been attacked before but only sporadically and with negligible effect on output. The heavy raids beginning in June were very effective; they halved truck production at the Büssing, Daimler-Benz, and Opel truck plants, while the raid on the Volkswagen plant at Fallersleben cut passenger car production to a sixth of the preraid level. The total loss of motor vehicle production for the half year was about 20 percent.

What did all this mean for the German serviceman? Nazi strategic decisions about arms procurement in the 1930s concentrated perhaps too heavily on Kriegsmarine surface ships. As Gregory Liedtke points out (in *Enduring the Whirlwind*),

> Perhaps the greatest drawback was that the resources required to produce these warships also impaired the growth of the pre-war U-boat fleet by tying up scarce shipyard space and raw material allocations. As a result, by September 1939 the German Navy possessed a mere 57 U-boats, of which only 32 were capable of operating on the high seas. In exchange for the 200 million RM spent on the battleship Bismarck alone, the Kriegsmarine could have possessed an additional 30–50 U-boats, which cost between six and four million RM each. Considering the havoc inflicted upon Allied shipping lanes during the first years of the war by Germany's existing submarine fleet, the impact of these additional U-boats would most likely have been very significant.

Additionally, the steel had to come from somewhere and other things had to give: building battleships meant the production of PzKpfw IIIs and IVs suffered accordingly. Germany entered the war with a fleet of PzKpfw Is and IIs and only 98 PzKpfw IIIs and 211 PzKpfw IVs. What is remarkable is how well the German Army used the tanks it had. By the time of the attack on France, the numbers had increased to 381 PzKpfw IIIs and 290 PzKpfw IVs, the majority of which—along with 106 35(t)s and 228 38(t)s—were used in the attack.

After the battle in the West had been won, on June 23, 1940, Hitler decided to reduce the army to 120 divisions. Five weeks later, he changed his mind and decided to attack in the East, that the army should be increased to 180 divisions, and production increased. This meant that when *Barbarossa* started, the percentage of PzKpfw Is and IIs involved had dropped from 57% to 31% and the number of StuG units had expanded considerably. One of the ways that industry manpower was beefed up to enable the increase of AFVs was by sending the bulk of 18 infantry divisions to work on armaments. They were recalled into their divisions in February 1941.

While production increased in 1941, looking at AFV and aircraft numbers, the change between 1942 and 1944 was even more substantial. Certainly, the AFVs built and shipped to the East ensured that *Fall Blau* could

Panther tank turrets in carriages at Aschaffenburg, southeast of Frankfurt. Allied bombing of the railroads affected every element of the logistics chain. The growth of armaments production between February 1942 and May 1943 that had seen monthly growth of 5.5% stagnated as the bombing campaign disrupted production and the transport system. (NARA)

start with a decent complement of AFVs. It's also important to remember the qualitative shift between the start of the war and 1943/44. This is best portrayed by the difference between the PzKpfw I and the PzKpfw VI Tiger which was introduced into service in late 1942. The PzKpfw I was 13 ft 2 in (4 m) long, weighed 6 tons (5,443 kg), had a 59 hp (44 kW) engine, 7–13 mm of armor, and was armed with two 7.92 mm MG 13 machine guns. The Tiger was 27 ft 9 in (8.45 m) long with barrel to the front, weighed 60 tons (54,432 kg), had a 690 hp (515 kW) engine, 25–120 mm of armor, and was armed with an 8.8 cm KwK L/56 main gun and two 7.92 mm MG 34s.

Perhaps of equal importance to the Tiger was the first of 8,400 StuG Ausf Gs that also appeared in 1942. It was 22 ft 2.5 in (6.77 m) long with gun, it weighed 23.3 tons (23,900 kg), had a 300 hp (224 kW) engine, 16–80 mm armor, and was armed with a long-barreled 7.5 cm Sturmkanone (StuK) 40 L/48. The StuG had started out as an infantry support vehicle. It also became the highest-scoring tracked *Panzerjäger* in the German inventory.

German War Production, 1940–45, Ground and Air Munitions (in thousands)

Weapon	1940	1941	1942	1943	1944	1945	TOTAL
Rifles, carbines	1,352	1,359	1,370	2,275	2,856	665	9,877
Machine pistols	119	325	232	234	229	78	1,217
Machine guns	59	96	117	263	509	111	1,156
Guns	6	22	41	74	148	27	318
Mortars	4.4	4.2	9.8	23.0	33.2	2.8	77.4

AFV Production 1939–45				
Date	All AFVs	PzKpfw	*Sturmgeschütze/Panzerjäger*	*Selbstfahrlafetten*
1939				
TOTAL	247	247	–	–
1940				
TOTAL	1,643	1,459	184	–
Monthly average	136	121	15	–
1941				
TOTAL	3,790	3,245	545	–
Monthly average	316	270	46	–
1942				
TOTAL	6,180	4,137	824	1,219
Monthly average	516	345	69	102
1943				
TOTAL	12,063	5,996	3,323	2,744
Monthly average	1,005	500	277	229
1944				
TOTAL	19,002	8,344	9,286	1,372
Monthly average	1,583	695	774	114
1945				
TOTAL	3,932	998	2,847	87
GRAND TOTAL	46,857	24,426	17,009	5,422

Number of German Aircraft Produced by Type Annually, 1939–44						
Year	Fighters	Bombers	Transports	Trainers	Others (incl. gliders)	TOTAL
1939	1,856	2,877	1,037	1,112	1,413	8,295
1940	3,106	3,997	763	1,328	1,632	10,826
1941	3,732	4,350	969	889	1,036	11,776
1942	5,213	6,539	1,265	1,170	1,369	15,556
1943	11,738	8,589	2,033	2,076	1,091	25,527
1944	28,926	6,468	1,002	3,063	348	39,807
TOTAL	54,571	32,820	7,069	9,638	7,689	111,787

An Sd Kfz 7 (mittlerer Zugkraftwagen 8t—medium towing motor vehicle) with an assorted load on top of the enclosed ammunition storage compartment. It is towing an 8.8 cm FlaK 37 with protective shield on the twin-wheeled bogies of the Sonderanhänger 202 (special trailer). Note the barrel has been screwed down to the barrel-locking collar. (NAC)

Towing vehicles

Originally starting life as a Renault 35R light tank, around 110 of the vehicles seized by the Germans in 1940 were converted to become artillery tractors—Umbau von Panzerkampfwagen 35R (f). They were used to tow 15 cm sFH 18 howitzers, the 17 cm Kanone 18 in Mörserlafette, and 21 cm Mörser 18. This one is towing the cradle section of the 17 cm Kanone 18; the barrel would be towed separately. (SF Collection)

Hungarian SdKfz 7 with a road tarmacadam-laying machine, the forerunner of today's machines. Next to it are two small bulldozers. The war effort required such machines for building and maintaining roads for military transport. This vast network of roads stretching across occupied Europe was a key element of the German war machine, allowing the movement of tanks, artillery, and other heavy vehicles to deliver the needs of the forces. (Fortepan/Hungarian Archives/Lissák Tivadar)

Number of U-boats Produced Annually, 1935–45 (www.uboat.net/technical/shipyards/)			
Year	Total	Year	Total
1935	14	1941	199
1936	21	1942	238
1937	1	1943	286
1938	9	1944	229
1940	50	1945	91

Total figure depends on how achieved: 1,174 were launched, 1,153 commissioned, 14 captured and employed by Kriegsmarine. Of these, 173 of 1,000–1,600 tons; c. 863 of 500–1,000 tons; 120 of 250–500 tons. Additionally, c. 700 midget submarines (202 × two man; 350 × one man; 144 × radio-controlled).

These production figures don't consider losses, and in 1943–44 these were high. For example, during the war, 765 of the 1,156 U-boats in service were lost; of these, two-thirds were lost in this period: 241 in 1943 and 234 in 1944. The bare statistics also hide some pertinent facts: that the Germans had no strategic air arm and a significant lack

A PzKpfw III moves off the factory grounds. Tank production became more difficult as the war went on as the weight, size, and complexity of the vehicles, their weapons, and armor were modified. The Germans won the technical arms race but lost out on availability and numbers. (Bundesarchiv, Bild 183-B22419/Reichelt/CC BY-SA 3.0 de)

A Steyr Raupenschlepper Ost (RSO) towing a Soviet 122 mm H38 light howitzer and gun crew. Based on the Steyr 1500A light truck, 23,000 of all versions of the RSO were built, entering service in 1942. (SA-Kuva, Finnish Archives)

17,500 of the SdKfz 10 (leichter Zugkraftwagen 1t) were built; it was used as a versatile towing vehicle for light artillery guns—the 2 cm FlaK 30, FlaK 38, 7.5 cm leIG 18, or 3.7 cm PaK 36—and their crews. Here, it's carrying a signals detachment. (RCT)

A feared "Acht-Acht"—this one a FlaK 36 on its SdAh 202—and its SdKfz 8 towing vehicle: both are well camouflaged and waiting to travel. (RCT)

Railroads were a vital cog in the manufacturing and logistics chain, taking parts to central construction points or finished articles to depots. These are He 111 fuselages—some 6,500 were built of this medium bomber that was also used as a cargo container-drop aircraft. (RCT)

of transport aircraft. The former meant that Soviet production was untouchable once it moved east; the latter proved extremely limiting—at Stalingrad and elsewhere. However, it's fair to say that the Germans didn't run out of AFVs or aircraft. They ran short of equipment, but it wasn't the lack of weapons that was the Third Reich's biggest problem. The strategic logistics of munitions production—raw materials and manufacture—was not the Reich's weakest link: keeping the AFVs and aircraft moving, manned, and fueled was.

Fuel: Oil and Coal

The first and most obvious difference between the armies of the Western Allies and Germany was the latter's dependence on the horse and all that that entailed. Germany had not been heavily motorized prewar—there were only nine motor vehicles for every 1,000 Germans, whereas Britain had 43 and the United States 200—but Hitler knew that it was fuel that made the modern military machine go round and this would be Germany's biggest headache. Lacking colonies that could provide oil and not being involved in one of the seven oil companies (five American and two European) that controlled the global supply of oil, Germany had to come up with alternatives. Exploration in Germany itself found some oilfields in the Northwest, especially Reitbrook and Heide-Meldorf. The oil produced there was best suited to lubricating oils and was used as such until Allied bombing curtailed operations.

Until *Barbarossa*, two trade and commercial agreements saw the Soviet Union providing a great deal of oil and some access to world markets, but this was always going to be short term. The German high command obviously hoped that the Wehrmacht would take Soviet oilfields. Nevertheless, it was ironic in June 1941 that the Germans invaded the Soviet Union fueled by Soviet oil and eating bread made from Ukrainian grain.

The level of the fuel problem is summed up in the diary entry for August 7, 1941, (47th day of *Barbarossa*) of General Franz Halder, chief of staff of the OKH:

> Motor fuel situation:
>
> As of 1 Oct. we shall have available:
>
> | | |
> |---|---|
> | From own production: | 380,000 tons a month |
> | Imports: | 320,000 tons a month |
> | Total: | 700,000 tons a mouth |
>
> Current requirements of the Armed Forces and domestic economy
>
> | | |
> |---|---|
> | (without operations): | 570,000 tons a month |
> | For countries in our orbit: | 125,000 tons a month |
> | For Italy: | 130,000 tons a month |
> | Total | 825,000 tons a month, |
> | i.e.,. a deficit of | 120,000 tons a month. |
>
> It is hoped to make up for the missing 120,000 tons by:

> cutting civilian consumption by — 10,000 tons
> stepping up production in Germany by — 40,000 tons
> cutting Italy — 30,000 tons
> cutting other countries — 15,000 tons
> cutting safety margins — 25,000 tons
> Total — 120,000 tons
>
> On this basis the Armed Forces are in no position to embark on any large-scale operation.

Romanian oilfields also provided helpful amounts to Germany, although prewar they were dominated by the British and French oil companies. A trade agreement between Romania and Germany in May 1940 changed the balance of power there: Romania agreed to deliver 200,000 tons of oil to the Reich each month in exchange for armaments. Romania went on to become Germany's largest supplier, reaching nearly three million tons in 1941.

However, Hitler's autarkic policies also ensured that with oil in mind, another course was pursued: synthetic oil. This option was particularly sensible for Germany. It had vast coal deposits (coal supplied 97% of its energy consumption) and the amount of coal available to the Third Reich increased during the war, thanks to the captured coalfields of Poland and Czechoslovakia. Because of this, German coal production reached 268.9 million tons in 1944, and it was obvious that making oil from coal could make a sizable contribution to Hitler's military requirements. The method of doing this had been developed by Franz Fischer and Hans Tropsch at the Kaiser-Wilhelm Institute for Coal Research in Mulheim in 1925. Chemical company IG Farben opened a processing plant in Leuna in 1927.

The biggest drawback to this approach was the cost: the average manufacturing cost for a barrel of synthetic oil at the time was around $15, while a barrel of crude was being traded in December 1939 at 93 c.

Fuel train being unloaded at a railhead. Always a critical commodity, Hitler's dash to the oilfields of the Caucasus was a move he felt was forced upon him. "If I do not get the oil of Maikop and Grozny then I must end this war," he said to officers of Heeresgruppe Sud on June 1, 1942. (Bundesarchiv, Bild 101I-186-0166-04A/Fremke, Heinz/CC-BY-SA 3.0)

Horses are carefully unloaded from a "Kassel" covered goods wagon. Mounted and horse-drawn units had a small reserve of replacement horses in their combat train, but the number wasn't sufficient to cover losses in the Soviet Union. Wherever possible, replacements came up by train, but some had to make long marches from Germany. (RCT)

Hitler, however, was pragmatic. What good was the money if the army couldn't move? He was willing to pay the price and by September 1939, annual German synthetic production was some 16.7 million barrels. In 1943 this annual production reached 42 million barrels. This allowed stocks of aviation fuel—97% of which had been created synthetically—to reach 219.5 million gallons. They didn't last long, however, and the Luftwaffe shared the same problems with fuel that the army encountered as the war progressed, particularly when the Allies' bombing campaign began to target aviation fuel refineries.

Another drawback was that coal, although available in plenty from European mines, was also a problem: moving it from the pits was difficult because the railroads were short of tracks and locos, especially after those in the conquered West had been confiscated for use elsewhere. Indeed, coal production fell by nearly 20% in France from 1940 with all the knock-on effects—things like steel production—as well. This reduction was caused by many factors: the effects of the fighting, a subsequent lack of food, and the need to put men into the army after the invasion of the Soviet Union all militated against improving the levels of coal production. Using foreign labor was a part answer—but unless they were fed properly, they couldn't hope to work effectively in the mines. Food production was already an issue in Germany; after the fighting, it was a problem throughout Europe.

Home production of synthetic fuel had another drawback for the Luftwaffe. It was not able to enjoy a breakthrough made in the Unites States in 1935 that allowed production of 100-octane gasoline. This edge for the USAAF and RAF led to the development of more powerful engines which meant the Western Allies' aircraft flew 15% faster, 1,500 miles farther, and 10,000 feet higher than the Germans'. Among other things this meant that the Luftwaffe didn't develop a strategic bombing arm that could attack Soviet industry in the Urals, or Canadian and American manufacturing in North America.

Fuel usage—especially by the Luftwaffe—was a major reason why Hitler thrust toward the Caucasus in summer 1942. The object of the attack—on top of destroying Red Army units—was oilfields: those of Maikop and Grozny which the British Ministry of Economic Warfare estimated were each producing approximately 18.3 million barrels of oil annually, and Baku, one of the world's most productive oilfields, capable of producing 176 million barrels a year, more than enough to solve Germany's fuel problems and sound the death knell to the Soviet Union's ability to keep fighting. As we know, it didn't happen. The only oilfield of the three that the Wehrmacht took was Maikop and they had to retreat before they could achieve their aims.

Lack of fuel for the Luftwaffe had widespread effects: it restricted training flights that then had an obvious knock-on effect on pilot quality (as did the regular combing of training units for serviceable aircraft because they were so desperately needed—this is covered in a separate section). In early 1944 the Allies began bombing Luftwaffe aircraft factories in Operation *Argument* and in May the Combined Bomber Offensive turned its sights on the oil industry. The Luftwaffe was forced to respond and, in doing so, lost over half its fighter aircraft. Speer urged Hitler to dedicate more aircraft for home defense:

> I implored Hitler in my memorandum to "reserve a significantly larger part of the fighter plane production for the home front." I repeatedly asked him in the most urgent terms whether it would not be more useful "to give sufficiently high priority to protecting the home hydrogenation plants … [not doing so] makes it a certainty that in September or October the Luftwaffe both at the front and at home will be unable to operate because of the shortage of fuel. … Again and again, I had explained to him that it would be pointless to have tanks if we could not produce enough fuel."

It made no difference. Germany couldn't defend itself effectively against the CBO. Around 75% of the Luftwaffe's fuel came from 16 synthetic oil production plants, which turned German coal into oil. In January 1944, synthetic petroleum output was around 3.6 million barrels; in June, it dropped by a third; by the end of 1944 another third. In 1945, it was negligible. On the ground, German tanks were being destroyed by crews for want of fuel. Without it, the defenses crumbled.

The Sandman, a B-24 Liberator piloted by Robert Sternfels, over the Astra Romana refinery, Ploesti, Romania, August 1, 1943. The Romanian oilfields were the Third Reich's fuel lifeline. Without them, the Reich struggled. (USAF)

Sources of German Oil 1938–43 (in thousand tons)						
Year	Imports	Domestic crude oil production	Occupied countries crude oil production[1]	Synthetic oil production[2]	Synthetic oil captured[3]	Synthetic oil from existing stocks[4]
1938	4,957	552	–	1,600	–	–
1939	5,165	888	–	2,200	–	–
1940	2,075	1,465	–	3,348	745	–
1941	2,807	1,562	332	4,116	112	1,140
1942	2,359	1,686	370	4,920	–	134
1943	2,766	1,883	–	5,748[5]	140	139

Notes

[1] U.S. intelligence estimate for 1938 and 1939.

[2] Unknown for 1938, 1939, and 1942. Captured oil during *Fall Weiß* amounted to 10,800 cu m of fuel, eight train wagons of diesel oil, three train wagons of machine oil, and 1,000 l and two train wagons of lubricating oil.

[3] Unknown for 1938, 1939, and 1940.

[4] Unknown for 1938, 1939, 1940, and 1943.

[5] 3,822 in 1944 and 62 in 1945.

German successes in the West added to their problems as they now were in command of countries—particularly France—that depended on high levels of fuel to function. Tooze reflects on the effects of the occupation:

> From the summer of 1940 France was reduced to a mere 8% of its prewar supply of petrol … the results were dramatic … just one example, thousands of litres of milk went to waste in the French countryside every day, because no petrol was available to ensure regular collections.

Fuel rationing in Germany was so strict that (Tooze again):

> The Wehrmacht was licensing its soldiers to drive heavy trucks with less than 15 km of on-road experience, a measure which was blamed for the appalling attrition of motor vehicles during the Russian campaign.

Hamburg was the main refining center for gasoline in Germany using imports from Mexico and Venezuela before the war. These were stopped by the blockade and the indigenous fields of Reitbrook, Heide, Neinhagen, and Austria took over. The Rhenania-Ossag oil refinery at Harburg, near Hamburg, was flattened by 1,800 tons of bombs dropped by 732 heavy bombers of the U.S. Eighth Air Force in August 1944. The effect of the CBO on Germany's fuel production would have immediate and severe ramifications for the Wehrmacht's logistics. (NARA)

Yearly Fuel Production and Consumption: German production, imports, consumption, and exports 1940–44 (in thousand tons)			
Fuel Type	Production	Consumption	Stock, year end
1939			
Aviation fuel	–	–	511
Motor gasoline	–	–	280
Diesel	–	–	150
1940			
Aviation fuel	966	863	613
Motor gasoline	2,130	1,811	599
Diesel	1,482	1,335	296
1941			
Aviation fuel	910	1,274	254
Motor gasoline	2,284	2,504	379
Diesel	1,726	1,856	164
1942			
Aviation fuel	1,472	1,426	324
Motor gasoline	2,023	2,089	313
Diesel	1,493	1,519	138
1943			
Aviation fuel	1,917	1,825	440
Motor gasoline	2,223	2,101	436
Diesel	1,793	1,744	244
1944			
Aviation fuel	1,105	1,403	146
Motor gasoline	1,471	1,805	118
Diesel	1,260	1,435	121
TOTAL			
Aviation fuel	6,370	6,791	–
Motor gasoline	10,131	10,310	–
Diesel	7,754	7,889	–
GRAND TOTAL	24,255	24,990	–

Steel

Probably the most important of all the strategic military commodities, steel is made from iron ore, carbon, and alloying elements like chromium, manganese, nickel, or vanadium. Critically, Germany had to import most of its iron ore as its own deposits were small. The main source was the mines of the Gällivare–Kiruna region of northern Sweden. This was a significant factor in the Norwegian campaign for both the Germans and British. German success in Norway and a trade agreement with Sweden ensured that the flow of iron ore continued through the war, much of it going through the port of Narvik.

However, during the disruption of the military campaign, domestic production of iron ore was important—and had been carefully analyzed by the Nazis before the war. In 1937 the Reichswerke Hermann Göring was established to source domestic iron ore (mainly from Salzgitter in Lower Saxony)—extraction that didn't make money but fulfilled the need for steel. Later the company took over the mining concerns absorbed by the *Anschluß*, the occupation of Czechoslovakia, and the conquest of Poland, France, and the Soviet Union. German domestic coal reached almost as much as 18 million tons in 1939, but fell back by 1943, by which time the percentage share of imported iron ore going to the Ruhr broke down to Scandinavia 56.3%, France 35.9% (from Lorraine, Normandy, and Brittany), Soviet Union 2.9% (mainly Krivoi-Rog in Ukraine), and Spain 2.5% for a total of 15.2 million tons. Domestic production to the Ruhr was a very respectable 5.6 million tons. In 1943, crude steel production reached 38 million tons.

As far as the other metals are concerned, nickel came from a Finnish mine at Petsamo and went to the refineries the Germans took over in Norway; manganese was mined at Nikopol in Ukraine.

Swedish iron ore was crucial to the Reich's steel production, accounting for 43% of its 1933–43 procurement. Of high quality, it was transported by rail to ports in eastern Sweden for shipping through the Gulf of Bothnia to German ports when the sea was unfrozen; in the winter months it was sent to Narvik and used the *Skjaergaard*—the Norwegian corridor—before heading for Germany. If landed at Lübeck or Stettin the ore again traveled by train to the Ruhr; if at Hamburg or Bremen it could be shipped using the inland waterway system. (NAC)

Rubber

A hugely important strategic commodity, rubber was needed for soldiers' footwear, clothing, and equipment; around 1,000 lb was needed for building an aircraft; 2,000 lb for a tank; and over 10% of the weight of a U-boat was from rubber. The first large-scale industrial production of synthetic rubber was at Elberfeld in 1915. Hitler urged German industry to make the country self-sufficient, and it was IG Farbenindustrie AG who started producing Styrene-butadiene artificial rubber—Buna-S, best for tire production—in Schkopau in Saxony from 1937. Other large plants were set up near Marl, Ludwigshafen, and most notorious of them all, at Auschwitz. Under the supervision of the SS, the Auschwitz prisoners provided slave labor and were literally worked to death. Life expectancy of the camp inmates was on average three months and those who couldn't work hard enough were sent to be gassed. Around 35,000 camp inmates worked there; more than 25,000 died. Vile though the means were, German synthetic rubber production was substantial: 40,000 tonnes in 1940; 70,000 tonnes in 1941 (that year the United States produced but 8,000 tonnes). Of all the strategic commodities, rubber certainly wasn't the biggest problem for the Reich although in the East the difficulties with the roads didn't help. Halder's diary for August 7, 1941: "Rubber: We have in stock about 7,000 tonnes. Very little for our submarine and automotive program. Situation very tight."

Manpower

Of all the commodities used in warfare, the human component is, of course, the most important and the least replaceable. German armed forces employed some 18 million people during the war, the official numbers boosted by upward of a million foreign volunteers and conscripts, *Hiwis* (*Hilfswillige*—"volunteer" helpers), *Ostlegionen*, and others, along with half a million *Wehrmachtshelferinnen* (women Wehrmacht helpers). In the final months of the war, the Volkssturm saw any male aged 16 to 60 not serving elsewhere put into arms. Numbers are difficult to establish but anywhere up to 1.5 million men joined the Volkssturm, of whom it seems that around 500,000 saw action and 78,000 died. (Overmans)

German Armed Forces Strength, 1939–45 (in millions)

Service	1939	1940	1941	1942	1943	1944	1945
Heer	3.737	4.55	5	5.8	6.55	6.51	5.3
Luftwaffe	0.4	1.2	1.68	1.7	1.7	1.5	1.0
Kriegsmarine	0.05	0.25	0.404	0.58	0.780	0.81	0.7
Waffen-SS	0.035	0.05	0.15	0.230	0.450	0.6	0.83
TOTAL	4.22	6.05	7.234	8.310	9.48	9.42	7.83

Of the 18 million Germans who saw service, Rudiger Overmans suggests some 5.3 million died (a number after the war in Soviet prison camps)—the bulk, 3.3 million, in 1944–45. Of the total: 4.8 million were Wehrmacht (including 4.2 million Heer, 433,000 Luftwaffe, 138,000 Kriegsmarine) and 0.5 million Waffen-SS and others (Volkssturm, police, etc.).

After the restrictions of Versailles were repudiated by the Nazis, the Wehrmacht was able to conscript 35 divisions between 1935 and 1938 and another 60 or so in 1939. By May 1, 1940, mobilization provided a strength of 135 infantry, 10 *Panzer*, four motorized infantry, three mountain, and one cavalry division—153 in total. Many of these received a high level of training and most were ideologically in tune with the Nazis and prepared to fulfill their oath to Adolf Hitler and die for the cause. There is no doubt that the German system of conscription, training, and employment of its armed forces was excellent—and a prime reason for the successes in 1939–41—but the system began to creak as the war went on and casualties mounted. In 1941 for *Barbarossa* the Germans raised 84 new divisions (having disbanded 43) to take the total to 202, while at the same time the Kriegsmarine doubled in size and the Luftwaffe increased from 1.1 to 1.5 million. By June 15, 1941, the army had reached 5.2 million and the Wehrmacht 7.3 million. Better still, provision was in place for losses. Liedtke again:

> [The] Ersatzheer was able to accumulate a considerable pool of 471,600 replacement personnel with at least three months' training and thereby stood ready to replace casualties in the field forces as necessary. In addition, 114 of the 151 divisions committed to Barbarossa possessed a field replacement (Feldersatz) battalion as part of their internal structure that was intended to provide them with an immediate reservoir of replacement manpower in the field ... this meant that the German Army had the capability of sustaining 561,600 casualties ... 85 percent of all German males between the ages of 20 and 30 were already in the Wehrmacht.

The first serious problems for German manpower came toward the end of 1941 as battlefield losses, the onset of winter, and the remarkable tenacity of the Soviets to keep fighting began to erode the Wehrmacht's morale. Exhausted by the continuous heavy fighting—and, for the infantry, the fact that many of them had walked most of the way—having lost so many of their best young, trained NCOs and subalterns, it's unsurprising that the colossus wobbled.

It didn't fall, however. Losses by summer 1942 had reached two million dead, wounded, and sick. The Luftwaffe had lost 2,500 aircraft. AFV complete losses had passed 3,200 by January 1942. But the Soviets were in an even worse state, and the Germans had managed to find the manpower for new divisions: 44 between October 1941 and June 1942. On top of that were supporting divisions from the Germans' allies: 24 divisions by late June 1942. By the time *Fall Blau* started on June 28, 1942, manpower wasn't at full complement, but it was much better than it had been at the start of the year.

There were various reasons for the improvement: the number of *Hiwis* employed in rear echelon duties (from laborers to cooks), the return to service of many sick and injured men from convalescence, and a tightening of the deferment rules. In May 1942 this was put in the hands of Generalleutnant Walter von Unruh, who,

> armed with the authority to order irrevocable transfers to the Eastern Front, had been combing the rear areas as Hitler's personal representative. Unruh, whose visits generally met with dismay if not terror and who earned the nickname "General Heldenklau" (hero snatcher), had succeeded in paring down some of the rear echelon staffs; but after three or four months it had become apparent that the results, though worthwhile, would not be decisive. [Ziemcke]

Units were disbanded or combined; Liedtke quotes an April 3, 1942 report from VII. Armeekorps noting that three of its infantry divisions had disbanded a total of 11 (out of 27) infantry battalions, nine artillery batteries, and two antitank companies. HQ, logistics, and artillery personnel were used as front-line infantrymen. On occasion, so were tank crewmen, much to their chagrin. Using soldiers trained for a role like this—or, as another example, signalers—shows how bad the circumstances had gotten. The soldiers in question didn't make good infantrymen, and if wounded or killed deprived the army of important trained specialists. The shortage of combat units also forced the command to commit training battalions as temporary combat units. During the last stage of the war, training and replacement divisions as well as army service schools were often called into action in emergencies. As a result, training organizations that had been built up under great difficulties were repeatedly torn apart and destroyed.

Indeed, Liedtke's analysis suggests that by July 1, 1942, the Wehrmacht had increased in strength by 1.1 million, and the army by half of that to 5.75 million. *Fall Blau* blew the Soviet opposition away, inflicting huge losses of men and materiel as they thrust into the Caucasus but then they deviated from the plan, attacking toward Stalingrad and the rest is history. Fighting on two fronts front from late 1942 after the Allied landings in Africa, in 1943 German manpower took the double hit of the fall of Tunisia and the surrender at Stalingrad. Earl Ziemcke:

> On September 8, 1942, the Organizational Branch, OKH, reported, "All planning must take into account the unalterable fact that the predicted strength of the Army field forces as of November 1, 1942 will be 800,000, or 18 percent, below established strength [approximately 3,200,000] and that it is no longer possible to reduce those numbers."

Of course, many more Germans could have been released into the army if they had made better use of not only Red Army PoWs, but the people in Belarus and Ukraine whose political ties to communism had been corroded by 20 years of Stalin's regime of terror. Had it not been for the murderous barbarism of the German forces there may have been opportunities to reduce the manpower issues. Instead, genocide and slave labor ensured that few wanted to work with the Germans and the Wehrmacht had to contend with increasing numbers of partisans. On March 21, 1942, Thuringian Gauleiter Fritz Sauckel became *Generalbevollmächtigter für den Arbeitseinsatz* (general plenipotentiary for labor deployment) and he certainly increased the number of foreign and Eastern workers in the German Reich—but they weren't voluntary. Around a million PoWs were employed in German industry and around four million conscripted laborers—these rounded up from the rear areas administered by the *Reichskommissariats* and the *Korück* (rear army areas). Others working for the Germans—over a million on the railroads in 1942, plus around half a million *Hiwis* in the Heer and Luftwaffe—did so because they knew the alternative: death by starvation. They got paid in food: no work, no eat.

Part of the problem was the political complexity of the Nazi regime, the power struggles within the top echelons of the party that had a chaotic effect on the recruitment, training, and deployment of troops. Good examples of this are the creation of the *Luftwaffefelddivisionen* (Luftwaffe field divisions) and the Volkssturm. The latter was created late in the war and control of it became a political football between Martin Bormann and Heinrich Himmler—although quite why either thought it mattered is hard to understand.

The *Luftwaffefelddivisionen*, however, were a different matter. The Luftwaffe's *Fallschirmjäger* more than proved themselves in every theater. The AA units, particularly those used in the antitank role, performed excellently as in North Africa, for example, or against Operation *Goodwood* in Normandy. The "Acht-Acht" was greatly feared by all the Allies and with good reason: by 1943 there were two Luftwaffe *Flak-Korps* supporting the Ostheer. However, when OKW suggested transferring Kriegsmarine and Luftwaffe personnel to the army, Hermann Göring refused and suggested to Hitler that the Luftwaffe provide the units. This went ahead and 22 *Luftwaffefelddivisionen* were created, involving as many as 250,000 men. They started service on the Eastern Front in winter 1942/43. They were poorly trained, lacked experience, and while they often fought bravely, were no match for Red Army regulars. The lower ranks of the Ostheer labeled them "*Luftwaffen-Fehlkonstruktions-Divisionen*" or "mistakenly constructed air force divisions." Late in 1943 they were amalgamated into army units.

The catastrophe evolving at Stalingrad forced Hitler to act. Troops and weapons flooded to the East and Manstein, while unable to relieve the surrounded 6. Armee, was able to hold the line and halt the Soviet advances. At home, on December 19, 1942, Hitler ordered that the 5.4 million men exempt from service be trimmed. This would add 1.6 million to the Wehrmacht by mid-1943. On January 13, 1943, the Führer decree on the full employment of men and women in the defense of the Reich was issued. Where possible, male factory workers should be replaced by women aged between 17 and 50. For all men aged 16–65, compulsory service was decreed. On January 27, an ordinance from Fritz Sauckel ordered men and women to register themselves for service. On February 4, the Reich Labor Ministry closed businesses and restaurants that weren't essential for the war effort. Working hours were increased.

As far as women went, this was a major volte face by the Nazis who had preached home and child-rearing as the role for females—although they had hedged their bets in the 1935 Military Service Act by saying, "In war, in addition to compulsory military service, every German man and woman is obliged to serve the fatherland." As early as summer 1940 half a million *Helferinnen der Wehrmacht* were employed at home and abroad. Most volunteered, some were drafted. As well as army auxiliaries the police, Gestapo, and SS had auxiliary corps, the latter volunteers. The German Red Cross had 400,000 nurses and nurses' helpers. Toward the end of the war, 450,000 women were heavily involved with antiaircraft work as *Flakbehelfspersonal.*

As well as women, between November 1942 and December 1943 foreign workers increased in number, not just the Europeans—French, Dutch, and Belgian—but Russians as well. As many as 1.5 million additional workers were brought to the Reich. A good reason for the extra hands was the impetus to munitions-building taking place. The Adolf Hitler Tank Program was proposed by the Führer in late 1942: by 1944, he wanted 1,400 AFVs produced a month, to include 600 Panthers, 50 Tigers, 300 *Sturmgeschütze*, and 300 SP guns.

It was a good idea and in January 1943 Hitler pushed Speer about it. As might be expected, Speer and others explained how impossible the idea was for the newer, more complicated vehicles. Hitler wasn't assuaged and on January 22 decreed that all necessary steps should be taken—even if this adversely affected other industries. The decree also prohibited taking the technicians away in the draft. Unfortunately for the Reich, while the numbers improved, Hitler's orders proved unachievable—especially when Alkett's Berlin plant was bombed and output was cut. It is suggested that production was curtailed by as many as 400 vehicles as a result.

The Ostheer had taken a beating in winter 1942/43. On July 1, 1943, Liedtke identifies 664,632 combat losses and 336,551 estimated sick. Germany's allies had had 378,459 casualties. On top of that the Wehrmacht had lost 4,505 tanks, assault guns and *Panzerjäger*, 3,883 artillery pieces, 3,307 antitank and 6,017 antiaircraft guns, 9,012 mortars, and 119,838 trucks.

However, Hitler's tank program and replacement drive had made a significant difference: there had been 782,100 personnel replacements and new production of 5,272 tanks, assault guns and *Panzerjäger*, 7,358 antitank guns, 12,173 antiaircraft guns. Motor vehicles, however, hadn't received the same attention and only 32,057 trucks had been constructed (a shortfall of 87,781).

By May 1943, 20 of the 27 divisions destroyed in the Eastern Front were reconstituted as were five of the seven divisions lost in Tunisia. This meant that when the battle of Kursk took place, the German forces were if not at full strength, then close to it. The improvement in numbers, however, didn't improve the strategic position, but they made Hitler confident enough to attack at Kursk when he should, perhaps, have improved his defenses. From then on, however, the strategic initiative was passed to the Soviets and the Western Allies. The personnel and materiel problems would get worse, but there was one benefit to retreat: it made the lines of communication shorter and improved logistic distances. The Ostheer was able to withstand continuing and heavy attacks through the whole of 1944: the Dnieper–Carpathian offensive (December 24, 1943–May 6, 1944) cost over 250,000 and possibly as many as 380,000 casualties. It was the first of what the Soviets named Stalin's "Ten Blows" that saw the Ostheer battered as Leningrad, Ukraine and the Crimea, Poland, the Baltic states, Budapest, and Belgrade were liberated, and the Red Army stood on the borders of Germany itself.

Death on the Eastern Front, 1941–44

Year	Total dead
1941	302,000
1942	507,000
1943	701,000
1944	1,233,000

Looking after the dead, burying them, and marking their graves is important, particularly to soldiers in far-off lands. As the casualties rose, however, and retreating became more frequent, identifying casualties and giving them proper burial became difficult.

At home, death cards were produced by the family and appeared in newspapers and other publications or were printed and given out at funerals or memorial services.

"In memory of my dear husband, our good son, brother, brother-in-law and uncle Josef Schmidbauer, driver from Tegernsee, Stabsgefreiter in a mountain infantry regiment, holder of the E. K. II, Ostmedaille, and Kriegsverdienstkreuz mit Schwertern [War Merit Cross with Swords]. He died a hero's death on September 25, 1944, after five years of war service in Nisch (Serbia) at the age of 41."

Gebets-Andenken
an meinen
lb. Gatten,
unseren
guten Sohn,
Bruder,
Schwager und Onkel
Josef Schmidbauer
Kraftfahrer von Tegernsee,
Stabsgefr. in einem Gebirgsjäger-Regt.,
Inhaber des E. K. II, Ostmedaille,
Kriegsverdienstkreuz mit Schwertern,
Er starb am 25. September 1944 nach
5jähr. Kriegseinsatz in Nisch (Serbien)
im Alter von 41 Jahren den Heldentod.

Ach, es ist ja kaum zu fassen,
Daß du nie mehr kehrst zurück,
So jung mußt du dein Leben lassen,
Zerstört ist unser aller Glück
Ein jeder, der dich hat gekannt
Und auch dein treues Herz,
Der drückt uns nur noch stumm die Hand
In diesem tiefen Schmerz.
Du gutes Herz, ruh' still im Frieden,
Ewig beweint von deinen Lieben.

Buchdruck: K. Kübler Eggenfelden 0477

Stabsgefreiter
Josef Schmidbauer
gef. am 25. September 1944
in Serbien

Scheiden, welch ein bitt'rer Schmerz,
Für das arme Menschenherz.
Doch, die Christi Wege geh'n,
Hoffen auf ein Wiederseh'n.

HCoM

309

Oh, it's hard to believe,
that you will never return home,
that you must leave your life so young,
destroying the happiness of us all.
Everyone who knew you
and your faithful heart too,
can only offer a silent embrace
for this deep pain.
You good heart, rest in peace,
forever mourned by those who loved you. (RCT)

Stabsgefreiter Josef Schmidbauer who fell on September 25, 1944, in Serbia.

Parting, what bitter pain,
For the poor human heart.
But those who walk the paths of Christ,
Hope for a reunion.

From early 1940 women were recruited to become Nachrichtenhelferinnen des Heeres (Army Women's Signals Helpers) and as *Luftwaffehelferinnen*. By mid-1944 there were 450,000 *Flakhelferinnen* in the Luftwaffe antiaircraft gun auxiliary working searchlights (as above right) and sound-ranging equipment. Their special arm badge is evident as is (at right) a single chevron indicating the rank of *Helferin*. (Library of Congress)

German manpower was also stretched by the sheer geographical breadth of the war. In 1943 the Allies attacked Sicily and then Italy, knocking that country out of the war. Half a million Germans fought a long delaying action from defensive line to defensive line up Italy. Then in 1944 the Normandy landings opened a major third front.

By late 1944 the various methods to bulk up the Wehrmacht had all been used and couldn't hope to cover the high losses in the East and West. Ziemcke:

> The manpower shortage was affecting most the old and experienced divisions. In the period September 1 to December 31, 1944, one-third of the replacements for all fronts, 500,000 men, went into new or completely rebuilt divisions. At the end of the same period the old divisions had over 800,000 unfilled authorized spaces—after a 700,000-space reduction in the 1944 tables of organization.

Soon, the Germans were grasping at straws as men as old as 60 were called up to join the Volkssturm. While raising a people's army to fight—as the Prussian Landsturm had done against Napoleon—fitted well with the Nazi ethos, it lacked practicality in modern warfare. Over 1.25 million Germans died in the final four months of the war, half soldiers, half Volkssturm.

The will to keep on fighting, so evident in the Red Army in 1941, was certainly still apparent in the German Army of 1944–45 despite its obvious battlefield predicament. This was not just a question of morale and discipline—although neither of those can be questioned to any great extent, it's worth pointing out that some 20,000 German servicemen would be executed during the war for desertion, cowardice, or for saying the wrong thing in the wrong place. While this is small compared to the 100,000+ Soviets, it's a great deal more than the single U.S. soldier, Eddie Slovik, who suffered the same fate. The brutal regime was quite happy to use the threat of *Sippenhaft*—shared familial responsibility—to ensure that men's actions in the field didn't lead to state actions against their families. Morale in the armed forces toward the end could best be described as fatalistic, and the paramount concern was to head west to surrender to the Western Allies rather than the Red Army and face the retribution for their actions in the East.

Pockets

While it had been the Red Army on the receiving end during the early months of *Barbarossa*, the Soviet counterattack at the end of 1941 saw the start of a series of similar envelopments of German troops—the most famous being 6. Armee at Stalingrad. Earl Ziemcke graphically describes the feeling of being surrounded:

> A sudden encirclement of a modern army is a cataclysmic event, comparable in its way to an earthquake or other natural disaster. On the map it often takes on a surgically precise appearance. On the battlefield it is a rending, tearing operation that leaves the victim to struggle in a state of shock with the least favorable military situation: his lines of communications cut, headquarters separated from troops, support elements shattered, and front open to attack from all directions. The moment the ring closes every single individual in the pocket is a prisoner. Death is in front of him and behind him; home is a distant dream. Fear and panic hang in the air. Escape is the first thought in the minds of commanders and men alike, but escape is no simple matter.

After the relief of the Cherkassy pocket in February 1944, Manstein sent the survivors to Poland to recover. Ziemcke:

> First Panzer Army reported, "It must ... be recognized that these troops were encircled since January 28 and, consciously or subconsciously, had the fate of Stalingrad before their eyes." It observed that the "inner substance" was still there, but added, "One must not fail to recognize that only the few soldiers who possess inborn toughness (as opposed to that which might be instilled by military discipline) would be able to withstand such strain more than once."

Another important factor in the morale of encircled forces is the likelihood of casualties surviving, as was emphasized in *Operations of Encircled Forces*:

> One of the most important logistical problems is that of evacuating casualties. Whether or not the wounded are taken along has a profound effect upon the morale of the encircled troops. Any measure from which they might derive the slightest indication that wounded personnel are to be left behind will immediately reduce their fighting spirit ... In such situations the commanders are under the strongest moral obligation to take the wounded along and must bend every effort to make this possible.

Food

As we know, weapons and fuel only play part of the story: an army moves on its stomach. German armies were no different and, to make feeding them more difficult, many fought a very long way from home.

Germany had suffered cruelly in World War I: the winter of 1916/17 was the turnip winter; then in 1918/19 saw most of Germany go hungry. Hitler was in Munich at the end of the war and knew how hunger affected a people's will to fight. He felt that self-sufficiency was the answer, but the problem was that there was little chance of that being successful in Germany when it came to food. When the Nazis came to power, Walther Darré, minister for food and agriculture from June 1933, set up the Reichsnährstand. This organization controlled and administered every aspect of food nutrition and production, from growing to distribution. Farmers were protected from imports by tariffs. Darré's ministry had some success as the yield of crops such as potatoes, sugar beet, cabbage, and rye increased but it couldn't get round the need for imported fodder and other foodstuffs. Food shortages and high prices contributed to inflation.

Hitler's "Confidential Memo on Autarky" (August 1936) outlines his views succinctly:

> We are overpopulated and cannot feed ourselves from our own resources.
>
> In so far as this consumption falls upon the foodstuffs market, it is not possible to satisfy it from the domestic German economy. For, although numerous branches of production can be increased without more ado, the yield of our agricultural production can undergo no further substantial increase.
>
> The final solution lies in extending living space of our people and/or the sources of its raw materials and foodstuffs. It is the task of the political leadership one day to solve this problem.

Hitler's views were also espoused by Herbert Backe, a state secretary in the Reich Ministry of Food and Agriculture from October 27, 1933. Increasingly influential, Backe's name is associated with what has become known as the Hunger Plan. Simply put, this proposed that the German armies in the Soviet Union should as far as possible live off the land and not care about the resulting hunger that the local population would experience, and further that the produce of Ukraine that wasn't needed to feed the troops should be sent to Germany. The anticipated human loss was expected to be over 30 million—but this had the added benefit of reducing the number of people who would have to be sent east of the Urals to make way for German farmers. This shocking approach for civilians went even further when the decision was made to turn the final solution to the Jewish problem into genocide. Killing "useless" people meant not having to feed them.

Fortunately, the Nazis were unable to follow through completely with their plans. While the killing of Jews, Poles, Slavs and other "undesirables" got underway from 1940, providing the numbers of German settlers proved more difficult—and those who did resettle in Poland found conditions were not nearly as fruitful as they had been led to believe. As far as the German armies were concerned, living off the land also proved easier said than done. Some areas initially provided reasonable amounts of food. Lizzie Collingham:

> Between September 1941 and August 1942 Belorussia provided Army Group Center with 60 per cent of its bread grain, 90 per cent of its potatoes, 65 per cent of its meat and 10 per cent of its fat. But by January 1943 the strain on the agricultural system was beginning to show and its contribution to the army's needs had fallen and accounted for only 17 per cent of its grain and 11 per cent of its meat. The deficits had to be made up by transports of food from the Ukraine or the Reich.

An additional problem was that once they had eaten the Soviet farmers' food, the soldiers then ate the draught animals. Without food or horses, the farming system broke down.

The treatment of the population had another damaging effect: it fostered a stronger bond between people who could have been turned away from communism and the Soviet command system. The partisans not only

Daily Food Rations for the Feldheer

Foodstuff	Ration
Bread	750 g
Or crispbread	500 g
Fresh meat	250 g
Or salted bacon	200 g
Or tinned meat	200 g
Rice, pearl barley, semolina	100 g
Fresh vegetables	200 g
Or canned	100 g
Or dried	60 g
Fat	50 g
Marmalade	40 g
Salt	15 g
Sugar	80 g
Coffee	10–25 g
Tea	3 g
Brandy	0.375 l
Smoking tobacco	
Cigars	2
Cigarettes	7
Calories	4,253

The table can only provide a rough guide because:

1) the quantities stated were sometimes only used as a basis for invoicing and a portion was paid out in cash;

2) there were different portions for different missions;

3) some foods could be replaced by others;

4) individual portion sets changed frequently in short periods of time.

With its cooking vessel steaming away, this horse-drawn Hf. 13 is taking hot food to the troops. (SF Collection)

Soldiers resting on the Eastern Front. Some write letters, some read the newspapers. Visible in the background, cooks are preparing food for two *Feldküchen*. (NAC)

had a military function—particularly the harassment of German supplies by rail and road—but also had an important political function. The commissars and leaders sent out to the partisans were not only able to exert control over the groups but also ensured that they stayed on the right political message.

Lack of the right food leads to health problems. The nutrition inspector of the Waffen-SS, Sturmbannführer Ernst Günther Schenck, reported on the conditions of the soldiers of the Leibstandarte SS Adolf Hitler, who spent the winter of 1941/42 in the Taganrog area:

> The troops' rations were inadequate. "The necessary amounts of protein, fat and carbohydrates and therefore the required number of calories were not administered. The vitamin supply was also inadequate." In addition to the severe emaciation of the men, a visible expression of the increasing malnutrition was "an enormous reduction in resistance to disease, which manifested itself in constantly increasing losses due to illness (mostly jaundice, pneumonia and diphtheria) and took on alarming symptoms at the beginning of January 1942." [Barbara Maiwald]

Elsewhere, in Western Europe food production was also an issue. The British naval blockade caused significant problems; having to feed the conquered population of Western Europe also raised difficulties. Reducing the calorific intake could only go so far and had the byproduct of increasing the size of the already flourishing black market. It is unsurprising that even countries in Western Europe hovered on the edge of starvation—and overstepped the mark in early 1945 and the "hunger winter."

Other Rations

Much against Hitler's views—on March 12, 1943, he said, "It is not right to believe that the soldier cannot live without smoking. It was a mistake … to give every soldier so many cigarettes every day" (Barbara Maiwald)—tobacco was an important component of rations and soldiers were daily issued with cigarettes (or cigars, smoking or chewing tobacco). Tobacco wasn't just important for smokers. Nonsmokers used their rations as barter. As an aside, Western PoWs received only inferior tobacco; Soviets were expressly excluded from the tobacco supply.

Alcohol was also part of the field rations, often supplemented on special operations. It was certainly also supplemented by soldiers wherever possible, even though there were harsh penalties. Some of these extras were with the connivance of higher command:

> According to a secret order issued by the OKH on 30 June 1943, for example, bonuses in the form of alcohol were issued for the recovery of serviceable Russian T-34 tanks and usable spare parts. There were 40 bottles for a tank, six bottles for an engine, transmission or complete optics, and one bottle for a battery or air purifier. According to the instructions of the Intendant responsible for the salvage troop section, the bottles were issued by the sutler in the nearest army catering station. [Barbara Maiwald]

The sutler had a variety of products on offer: food and luxury foods as well as everyday necessities (such as toiletries, stationery, pocketknives, etc.) and, of course, Pervitin (methamphetamine).

Much has been written about the overuse of drugs by German servicemen. While Pervitin—a methamphetamine—wasn't officially available (free sale was banned in 1941) it was still available from medical units: 200 tablets were included in each set of troop medical equipment (*Army Ordinance Gazette* of August 1, 1944).

Another use of rations to promote morale was the *Führergeschenk für Fronturlauber* (Führer's gift for soldiers from the front on leave) issued from May 1941 to those who didn't have their own ration cards—members of the Wehrmacht, RAD (Reichsarbeitsdienst—Reich Labor Service), and SS. A soldier on home leave for a week received 2,250 g bread, 250 g meat or meat products, 140 g butter, 70 g margarine, 175 g jam, 200 g sugar, 150 g food, 60 g coffee substitute, 60 g cheese, and an egg. Additionally, after the fall of Stalingrad, they could receive a *Reichskarte für Urlauber* (Reichs card for this on leave) of 5,000 g of wheat flour, 1,000 g of sugar, 2,000 g of nutrients or pulses, 500 g of butter, and 1,500 g of jam.

In spring 1943 an additional *Führerpakete für Osturlauber* (Führer parcel for those on leave from the East) was provided: "A small thank you from the Führer to his soldiers," a 10 RM note and an additional ration card, which was valid until May 31, 1943. For Christmas 1943, Himmler did the same for the SS.

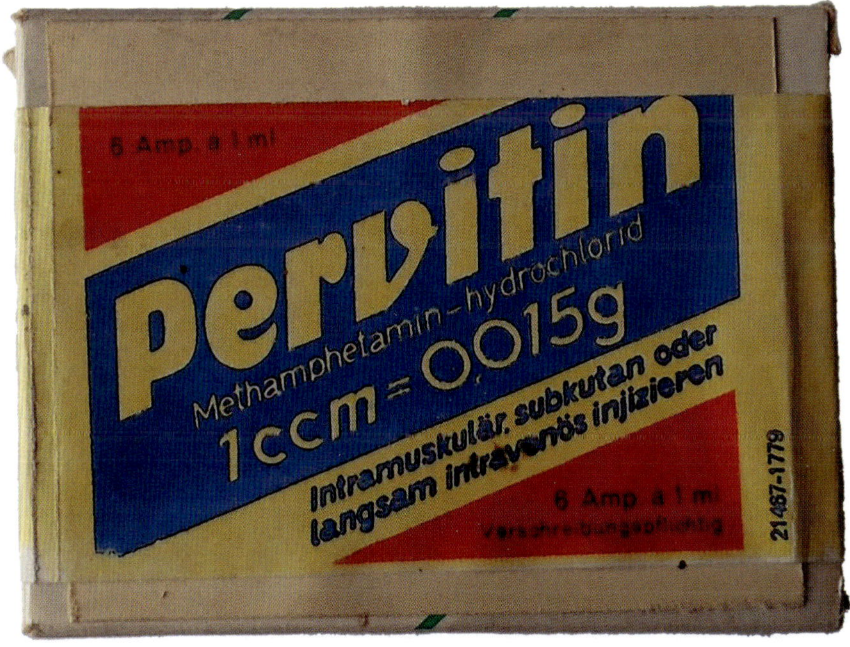

1940s packaging containing six Pervitin (methamphetamine hydrochloride) ampoules. (Komischn/WikiCommons, CC BY-SA 4.0)

While most field kitchens were towed, a number were—as above—mounted inside vehicles: light LKW 1.5-tonne or light and medium trucks 2.5–3 tonne, and often the light all-terrain 2.5-tonne Einheits LKW. (NARA)

Ohne Mampf, kein Kampf! (No food, no fight!)

The field kitchen (*Feldkuche*)—lovingly known as the *Gulaschkanone* (goulash cannon)—was as popular in the German Army as in any. The German Army's food supply relied on a combination of rations cooked by the field kitchen and local produce. Each soldier carried a day's worth of iron rations (*Halbeiserne Portionen*) which consisted of 200 g of *Fleischkonserve* (preserved meat) and 300 g of *Zwieback, Hartkeks,* or *Knackebrot* (various types of hard cracker). They could be opened only with permission, if there was no opportunity to get field rations. The field kitchen held a full iron ration (*Eiserne Portionen*) for each man. This was the half pack above with additions:

• 150 g *Gemuse* (preserved or dehydrated vegetables) or *Erbswurst* (lit. pea sausage—a sausage made from pea flour, pork belly, and hard fat which produced a nutritional soup. It was invented in 1867 by a Berlin cook, Johann Grüneberg; the Prussian state sold the patent to Knorr in 1889).

• 25 g *Kaffee-Ersatz*—coffee substitute. One of the effects of the blockade in World War I was to cut back the amount of real coffee that was available. Cue the creation of a range of substitutes that used anything from acorns to chicory. An acquired taste, German soldiers consumed large amounts of *Kaffee-Ersatz* often accompanied by condensed milk.

• 25 g *Salz* (salt).

Above and Opposite, Below: The Hf. 13 *grosse Feldkuche* (large field kitchen) was the standard cooking wagon in both world wars. The two-wheeled wagon had a 200 l double-lined stewpot and next to it a 90 l coffeemaker dispensed by tap. On the other side a stove plate for sausages, potatoes, or whatever else was available. Each company had one and the standard procedure was for the troops in line to pass with their mess tins at the ready. One unit could feed up to 200 men. They were built in large quantities. (Akira Takiguchi/waralbum.ru)

Production of General Cooking Equipment 1943/44

Type	1943	1944
Large and small field kitchens	13,100*	13,200*
Field cookers and RAD cookers	16,800	18,700
RAD cooking kettles	57,000	48,500
Food transport containers	Unknown	13,270

* This corresponds to an average monthly production of around 1,100 field kitchens. A comparison with World War I is remarkable: between August 1914 and July 1917, monthly production was between 500 and 600 large field kitchens.

Someone's got to do it. Spud bashing for the squad was sometimes a punishment, sometimes a social activity, but always an important part of food preparation no matter the location. (RCT)

Below: Getting hot rations to troops in cold conditions is essential. The *Essenträger* (food carrier) system was versatile but—despite its double skin—not hugely effective if the distance between pot and soldier were too far or under fire. (Note the snowshoes.) The 1942 *Taschenbuch für den Winterkrieg* said:

> All commanders and all units concerned with rations should always be conscious of the fact that they have the very responsible task of keeping their troops healthy. In the winter the troops should receive warm food and hot drinks more often than in summer. Hot soups should be served frequently with breakfast and supper. Always have hot water ready for preparing warm drinks. The colder the weather, the more fat should be included in the food. Food, especially cold cuts, must not be served if its temperature is under 50°F. Cold easily causes deterioration or reduction of nutritive value; therefore, special attention should be given to the transportation, storage, and care of food which is susceptible to cold. [NAC]

Bread and water distribution in the desert. (Battlefield Historian)

Food in the desert was not straightforward and involved army refrigeration centers to allow transportation in high temperatures over the long distances from Benghazi harbor to the front. Troop doctors also criticized both the monotony of the diet and the fact that it was too high in calories for the climatic conditions. Often tinned food was inedible when it reached the troops: diarrhea, stomach, and intestinal colic were the consequences. Fresh meat, fruit, and vegetables were just as rare on the menu as potatoes, semolina, or rice. Reheating the rations also proved difficult because of the lack of fuel tablets for the Esbit Model 9 cookers. Made from zinc-coated steel, these cookers burned Esbit—an acronym for Erich Schumm (the inventor) and *Brennstoff in Tablettform* (fuel in tablet form). This photograph shows a field kitchen in the desert with large numbers of water (white cross) jerrycans. (SF Collection)

The Allied Bombing Campaign

As has been seen throughout this chapter, Germany lacked many strategic necessities for the continuance of its war from the start—from raw materials to oil—but there's no doubt that Allied airpower played a significant role in adding to these logistical problems at every level. The bombing of German military locations started in 1939 but after the indiscriminate bombing of London during the Blitz, the Allies moved from targeted attacks to more widespread area bombing, usually of industrial cities where civilian casualties would include the industrial workforce. As Richard Overy says in *Why the Allies Won*:

> The air offensive was one of the decisive elements in Allied victory ... There has always seemed to be something fundamentally implausible about the contention of bombing's critics that dropping almost 2.5 million tons of bombs on tautly-stretched industrial systems and war-weary urban populations would not seriously weaken them.

One of the main factors in the restriction of the Allies' bombing campaign was imprecision. During World War II, bombing was hindered by a considerable lack of accuracy and reports of "precision bombing" were pipedreams—or the result of clever marketing by Norden of its bombsight. In 1944 the USAAF's Fifteenth Air Force ORS reports looked at the accuracy of bomber attacks on bridges. Between April 1 and June 4, 1944, 706 bombers dropped 1,906 tons of bombs on bridges. Their accuracy in good weather was 41% of bombs within 1,000 ft; in bad weather, 26%. Of 22 bridges attacked, seven received hits. So, around 100 bombers had to drop

Allied bombing of German industry hit its peak in late 1944 and 1945 when the Luftwaffe had been almost cleared from the skies by a combination of attrition and lack of fuel. Until then, the Allied air forces paid a heavy penalty for their missions. The numbers of aircraft and AA weapons needed, however, meant that the Germans lost the air parity or superiority they had enjoyed, particularly over the Eastern Front. The mainstay of the USAAF's daylight operations were the bombers of VIII Bomber Command (from February 1944 Eighth Air Force)—the B-17 Flying Fortresses (as seen here) and B-24 Liberators based in Britain's East Anglia. (NARA)

270 tons of bombs for each hit. And this was a major improvement! In 1943, it took 190 bombers to produce one hit.

Even more important than accuracy in the reduction of Allied bombing efficiency was the attrition: its own losses. The RAF and USAAF lost over 16,500 bombers and 137,000 crew in the campaign. Until escort fighters were developed with suitable range, the Luftwaffe defenders—in the air and from the ground—took a heavy toll on aircraft and crew. However, by putting large numbers of aircraft—May 30/31, 1942, saw the first of the 1,000-bomber raids on Cologne—carrying large bombloads over German industrial areas night after night and day after day, the Allies severely affected German industrial capabilities and communications, logistics, and output. They also ensured that 75% of the Germans' most effective antitank gun, the famous "Acht-Acht" 8.8 cm, had to be used for its original AA purpose. While German production increased in 1944, disruption to transport systems meant that they took a long time to reach the front lines and often lacked fuel when they got there.

Examples of the effects of the bombing campaign can be seen at every logistical level. At the strategic, the Wehrmacht had to spend time and money on air defense that it would have preferred to spend elsewhere. Fighter production increased, as did the number of deaths of experienced pilots. By the time of the D-Day landings, the paucity of the Luftwaffe's strike element meant that the Allies' logistical buildup was virtually unhindered. While the Germans proved adept at overcoming some of the problems caused by bombing by dispersing construction sites, building them underground, careful camouflage, and increased use of slave labor, the effects of the bombing were massive. In Germany as a whole, Speer estimated the loss in industrial production due to bombing as 20–30%. That could well have been a war-winning deficit.

Also important was the difficulty in moving anything out of Germany. The Allied offensive against transportation in 1944–45 had a catastrophic impact on German industry and military communications:

Leipzig was an important industrial location and was bombed heavily from 1943—the destruction, however, wasn't limited to industry. When American troops entered the city in April 1945, they found 40–60% of the buildings had been damaged or destroyed. Major targets were the Erla Ironworks and the Erla Maschinenwerk aircraft factory where Bf 109s were built. Around 65% of the latter was destroyed during Operation *Argument*—Big Week—February 20–25, 1944. This photo shows the roundhouse at Leipzig after bombing. Over 140,000 people lost their homes and nearly 3,500 died. (NARA)

> Freight cars loaded in the Reich totalled 900,000 for the week ending August 19, 1944. From there the total dropped to 700,000 per week by October 31. A further drop to 550,000 by December 23 was followed by a catastrophic decline to 214,000 by 3 March 1945. [Bombing Survey]

At the operational level, Allied airpower contributed significantly to the logistical problems of the Axis forces. The attacks on the oil refineries were crippling and exacerbated German fuel problems, so much so that operations such as the attack in the Ardennes in late 1944 had to be predicated on capturing Allied fuel dumps. In the Middle East, operating out of Malta and Egypt in close conjunction with Royal Navy assets, resupply of the German forces was hindered greatly. As an example, From June to the end of October 1941, the Axis lost 40 ships. After 15. Panzer-Division reached Africa in July, the monthly army supply requirements were 30,000 tons and the Luftwaffe's 8,000 tons, before taking reserves into account. For Rommel's offensive in November, planners estimated that 24,000 tons would be needed in Tripoli and 35,000 tons in Benghazi. In October, some 50,000 tons of supplies were sent by sea: around two-thirds were sunk. The story was the same in November: of 37,000 tons sent, only 8,500 tons reached Africa. The bulk was sunk from the air or by submarines.

In April 1943, Operation *Flax* hastened the end in Tunisia by starving the Axis of any airborne resupply, taking a great toll on its aircraft over North Africa and bombing its Italian airfields. By May 5 the Luftwaffe had almost run out of aircraft and the Allies were able to force the ground troops—some 250,000—to surrender. Rommel later wrote:

> Anyone, even those with the most modern of means, who attempts to fight against a foe who has complete air superiority, is fighting like a bushman against modern European forces—with the same chances and under the same conditions.

There are numerous other direct examples of Allied air superiority affecting Axis tactical logistics—particularly after 1944. Perhaps the most extreme was at the end of the battle of Normandy in August 1944 in the lanes around Moissy, Trun, and Mont Ormel where the retreating Germans were harried from land and air. The carnage saw 10,000–15,000 German dead, 40,000–50,000 taken prisoner along with 500 tanks and assault guns lost and 10,000 horses killed. Many of the AFVs—as high a proportion as 77%—were destroyed by their crews as escape became impossible thanks to the lack of fuel and inability to effect repairs caused by Allied airpower. Eisenhower said of it:

> The battlefield at Falaise was one of the greatest "killing fields" of any of the war areas. Forty-eight hours after the closing of the gap I was conducted through it on foot, to encounter scenes that could only be described by Dante. It was literally possible to walk for hundreds of yards at a time, stepping on nothing but dead and decaying flesh.

General Spaatz, commander of the United States Strategic Air Forces in Europe, highlighted the three major accomplishments of the Allied bombing campaign:

1) achieving air supremacy;
2) the destruction and dislocation of the German war economy;
3) the disruption of movement of vital commodities and weapons through the transportation campaign against railroads and canals.

To sum up Allied air operations, two quotes from Germans who were in the thick of it. Generalfeldmarschall Gerd von Rundstedt, Commander-in-Chief Western Front, said:

> Additional divisions could never have compensated for the lack of gasoline during the defensive operations in Normandy, and this was equally true east of Paris, in the Siegfried Line, and after the breakthrough to the Rhine. Additional divisions in a traffic desert are always a liability.

The threat of invasion was a British concern in 1940–42 and the RAF made frequent attacks on concentrations of shipping in the Channel area. This one was reported in the press on Thursday, August 21, 1941:

> RAF DAYLIGHT ATTACK ON SHIPPING AT ROTTERDAM
> Blenheim aircraft of Bomber Command of the RAF made a daring low-level daylight attack upon a large concentration of German shipping in Rotterdam docks. In all, seventeen ships of an estimated tonnage of 90,000–100,000 tons were put out of action, while on land two warehouses and a factory were left in flames. Approaching thewir targets, the Blenheims flew low over Dutch Territory in formation, which was taken as a victory symbol by the Dutch who waved to the RAF as they swept into the attack. British bomb bursts in background on dock at Rotterdam. Tail of aircraft is seen in foreground. [NARA]

On October 7, 1944, it was the turn of Krupp-Grusonwerk AG in Buckau/Magdeburg, about 80 miles southeast of Berlin, to get the treatment. The USAAF's Eighth Air Force started numerous fires at the factory that had become the sole producer of the Sturmgeschütz IV following the bombing raids on the Alkett factory in Berlin in November 1943. An even larger attack took place on the night of January 16/17, 1945, when the RAF destroyed up to 44% of the city's built-up area. By the time the Red Army entered the city, 80% of the Grusonwerk was destroyed. (NARA)

Air Power

Air power was a dominant feature of the German early-war Blitzkrieg. Stuka dive-bombers (1) ensured that ground forces were supported in attack. As Soviet and Allied air forces gained the upper hand, the boot was on the other foot as these photographs of Allied interdiction in Normandy show (2 and 3). Interdiction is to destroy an enemy's transport system and materiel en route to and at the front—reinforcements, assembly areas, ammunition and other dumps, lines of communication, fuel, coastal shipping (4), and rail networks (5).

As the Falaise Gap narrowed, so the pocket became a killing ground—much as the Soviet pockets had been in 1941. Around Moissy (6), the lanes were clogged with the German dead and discarded equipment. The effectiveness of Allied airpower was, however, overstated. A report on the results of operational rocket attacks on ground targets during April and May 1944 concluded that under combat conditions the 50% zone for rockets was 75 yards. That meant that the chances of an eight-rocket salvo from a Typhoon securing a single hit on a tank within an area 200 sq ft, was about 0.7%. More severe than the physical damage, however, was the effect of the attacks on the enemy troops' morale. (1 Battlefield Historian/2–6 NARA)

6

5

3

4

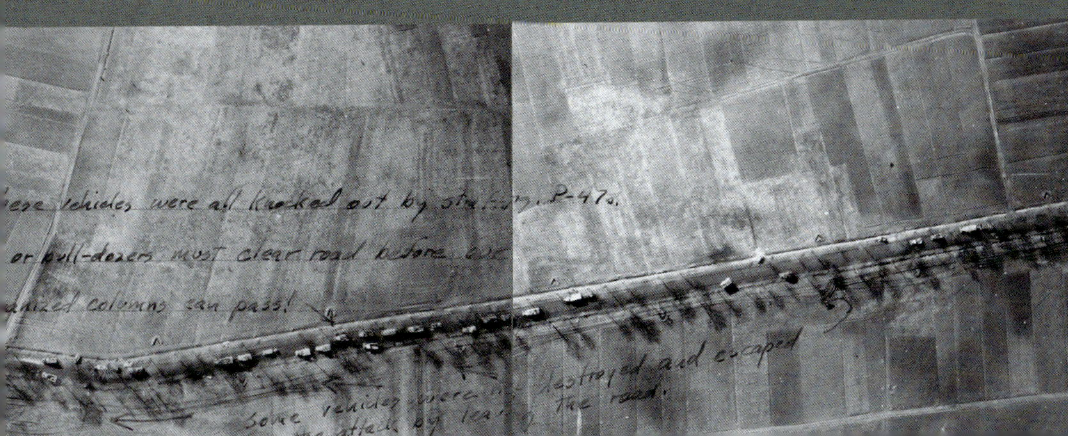
vehicles were all knocked out by
P-47s.
or bull-dozers must clear road before
columns can pass!
destroyed and escaped
Some vehicles were
the road.
attack by

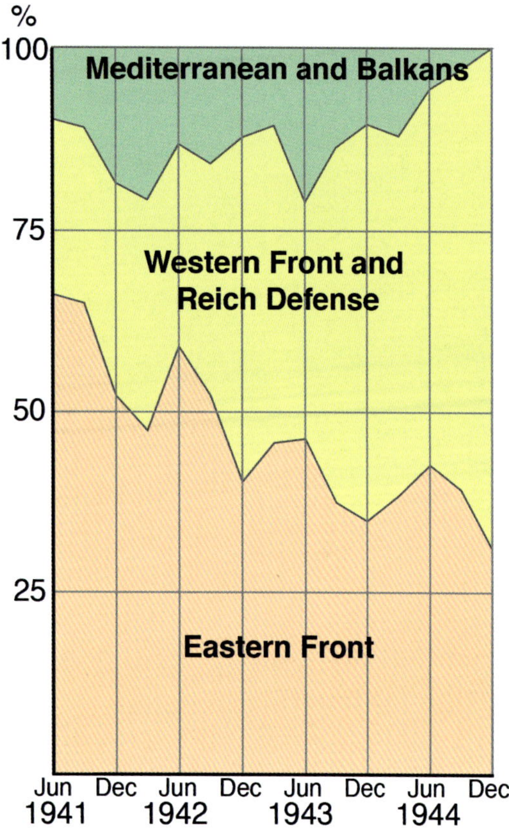

Distribution of Luftwaffe on different fronts June 1941–December 1944. (*The Strategic Air War Against Germany*)

Rundstedt's senior logistician, Oberst Hans Hoeffner, *General des Transportwesens West*, said of the air offensive: "We could not have conducted this offensive better ourselves."

However, it is also worth pointing out that despite the bombing, the Germans were exceptionally good at working around problems and in the face of Allied airpower were still able to extemporize crossings over the Seine in August to save many of their troops. Their losses were great and their flight headlong back to the Reich perilous, but by use of ferries and hastily constructed pontoon bridges (particularly that at Poses) 240,000 men, 14,000 vehicles, and as many as 135 tanks made it to safety. In a further escape, 15. Armee on the Channel coast was able to escape across the Scheldt, again despite Allied air attacks. Using ferries from Breskens and Terneuzen while an Absperrlinie (holding line) kept the advancing Canadians at bay, between September 5 and 23, 1944, 86,100 men, 616 guns, 6,200 vehicles, 6,200 horses, and 6,500 bicycles escaped.

In Conclusion

Discussion about Germany's success on the field of battle in 1939–41 often glosses over the problems that it experienced in the 1930s and those that warfare brought on. Yes, its troops were all-conquering and were able to secure the booty it needed from the conquered lands which were denuded of goods, raw materials, and what were, in effect, slaves—much the same approach that Rome had used centuries before. In the short term, that hid the cracks in the system. Lacking so many of the essential raw materials for a modern war—steel, fuel, food—the problems for the Third Reich were significant before the Allies began to bomb its means of production, its logistical means of moving raw materials to factories, and the factories themselves. Constant wartime requirements led to severe rationing not just at home but also in the field. Armies were unable to advance because they lacked fuel. Manpower resources dwindled. The industrial output of the Allies and their huge manpower reserves, the reach of their strategic forces, and the effectiveness of their sea blockade and bombing campaign meant that Germany lost the strategic logistical battle.

Operational Logistics: Depots and Distribution

Strategic logistics ensured—as far as possible—that industry had sufficient raw materials to produce the necessary equipment and weapons for the Wehrmacht. Controlling the stockpiles and distribution of the supplies to the front was a fundamental requirement of the logistical chain. This is the area so disregarded by most students of military history and of many field commanders—it's a criticism often leveled at one of Germany's military icons, the Desert Fox himself, Erwin Rommel.

The *Versorgungstruppen*—the service troops—were the men who worked mainly behind the lines to keep the fighting troops equipped and fed. The main divisions within the service troops were administration, supply, medical, veterinary, field vehicle, motor pool, water supply, police, and field post.

There was a clear distinction between the service troops and the fighting troops. This distinction—and the number of service troops needed to keep the armies in the field—has long been a military conundrum. Too few front-line troops often led to thinning out of service troops to reduce the "tail." If not handled carefully, that could lead to supply problems.

Distribution of Army Supplies

Economic production in Nazi Germany was completely under governmental control. Three ministries were involved: the Reichsminsterium für Rüstung und Kriegsproduktion (Reich Ministry of Armament and War Production) controlled war materiel and ammunition production; the Reichswirtschaftsministerium (Reich Ministry of Economy) controlled other industrial production; and the Reichsministerium für Ernährung und Landwirtschaft (Reich Ministry of Food and Agriculture) controlled food production.

The organization of army supply from industry was under the control of the *Chef der Heeresrüstung und Befehlshaber des Ersatzheeres* (chief of army equipment and commander of the replacement army). He handled procurement, storage, and distribution. In particular, he identified what should be sent to the Feldheer (field army) and what should go to the elements behind the front (such as training units).

Control of the supply lines to the Feldheer was the province of the *Generalquartiermeister* (Quartermaster General—General Eduard Wagner until his suicide after the July 1944 bomb plot) who was the chief of supply and administration. He requisitioned what the army needed and was responsible for storing and dispensing supplies in the field. The *Generalquartiermeister* was also responsible for the evacuation of the wounded and PoWs, controlled stocks of materiels—including captured materiels—and mobile supply trains. Important repair centers were also under his control. Down the chain of command, the next significant player was each *Armee*'s *Oberquartiermeister* who organized ordering supplies, oversaw them once they arrived, maintained the dumps and depots in which they were stored, and distributed them down the chain. Most of the supplies went from *Armee* to division, although the *Korps Quartiermeister* was an important link in the chain: it was to him that the various division supply officers directed their requisitions.

In a perfect world, everything expended each day of combat would be replaced immediately. While there was certainly flexibility in the German system, much depended on battlefield exigencies. Key to timely resupply was that requisitions were sent for the correct amount of supplies up the chain to the *Armee* in time for them to be processed, ordered if necessary, and fulfilled.

Distribution to the Feldheer could be direct from the factory but was usually through ammunition depots, equipment parks, SS depots, or special OKW depots. The main army depots came under

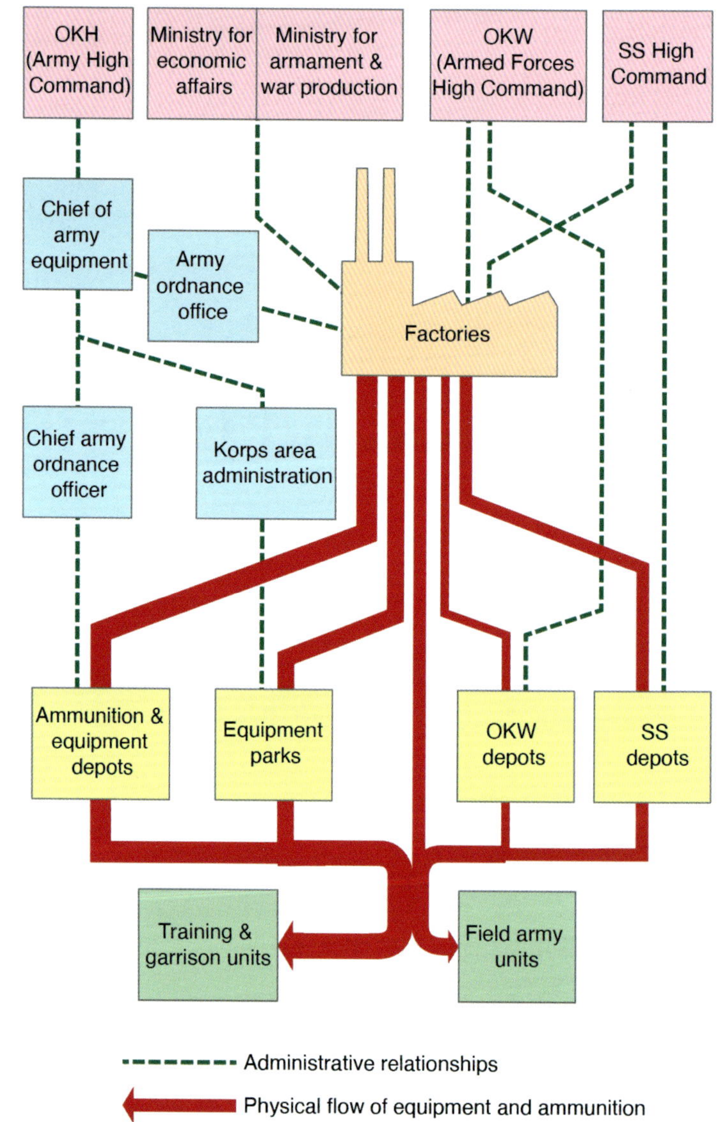

Above: Key elements of supply chain administration. (*TM-E 30-451*)

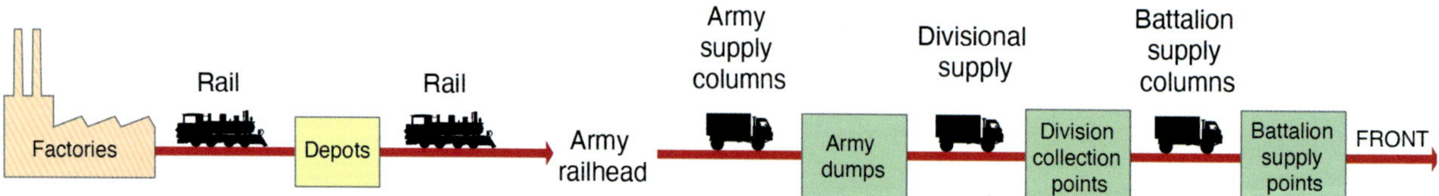

Above: Key elements of supply chain from factory to front.

the Feldzeuginspektion (Ordnance Inspectorate) headed by the *Feldzeugmeister* (chief army ordnance officer). Its duties were to store and then supply the army with weapons, equipment, and ammunition, and to train armorers and those dealing with weapons. This branch also controlled the repair of vehicles too badly damaged to be repaired in the field and the salvaging of equipment, ammunition, and materiel.

At the start of the war, the Feldzeuginspektion controlled the *Feldzeug-Inspizienten* (field equipment inspectors). The initial three of these were expanded to five in 1939:

- Fz.Inspizient 1 and 3 for weapons and equipment
- Fz.Inspizient 2 and 4 for ammunition
- Fz.Inspizient 5 motor vehicles, expanded in 1940 to include armored vehicles

The *Feldzeug-Inspizienten* were reorganized from July 2, 1941, into three *Feldzeuggruppen* (regional ordnance groups) with headquarters in Berlin, Kassel, and Munich, and Feldzeug-Inspizient 5 became K.

Beneath the *Feldzeuggruppen* were the *Feldzeugkommandos* (ordnance/field equipment commands) which were housed in every *Wehrkreis*. There was also a special Feldzeugkommando XXX (in charge of ammunition depots in central Germany) and from 1943 the Panzer-Feldzeugkommando was created to centralize the supply of all types of armored fighting vehicles and their spare parts.

Under the command of the *Feldzeugkommandos* were a total of 19 *Heereszeugämter* (army equipment offices), 94 *Heeres-Neben-Zeugämter* (auxiliary army equipment offices) with 350 equipment depots, 65 army ammunition depots, 120 auxiliary army ammunition depots, and the Metz and Strasbourg field equipment staffs with six vehicle depots.

After the reorganization of July 1941, the Feldzeuginspektion was structured as follows:

- *Waffenmeister-Schulen* (weapons master schools) I and II.
- *Feuerwerker-Schulen* I and II: these taught the safe handling and use of ammunition and explosives.
- *Feldzeuggruppe 1*: Fz.Kommandos I, II, III, VIII, XX, XXI, and the *Feldzeugwesen* (ordnance units) in the occupied northern and eastern territories.
- *Feldzeuggruppe 2*: Fz.Kommandos VI, IX, X, XI, XII, XXX, and the *Feldzeugwesen* in the occupied western territories.
- *Feldzeuggruppe 3*: Fz.Kommandos IV, V, VII, XIII, XVII, XVIII, and the *Feldzeugwesen* in the Protectorate of Bohemia and Moravia.

By 1 July 1944, that had again changed and the Feldzeuginspektion had the following departments:

- Heeres-Waffenmeisterschule I
- Heeres-Feuerwerkerschule I
- Feldzeuginspizient des Ersatzheeres
- Feldzeuginspizient K für Kraftfahrzeuge im Gesamtbereich
- 21 *Feldzeug-Kommandos* associated geographically (see below)
- The *Panzer-Feldzeugkommando*
- The independent FzKdo XXX

Ordnance Commands—*Feldzeugkommandos*

Of the 21 *Feldzeugkommandos*, 17 were linked with the *Wehrkeise/Armeekorps*. These were FzKdos I–XXI (less XIV, XV, XVI, XIX—see Glossary for details). There were also *FzKdos* for the Generalgouvernement (set up June 1, 1942, in Warsaw—later it moved to Jüterbog) and for the Protektorat Böhmen und Mähren and the independent FzKdo XXX (Kassel). There were also two *Feldzeug-Arbeitsstaben*—Elsaß (Alsace, set up October 4, 1940, in Baden-Baden, based in Strasbourg and subordinate to FzKdo V), and Lothringen (Lorraine, set up October 4, 1940, in Wiesbaden; it was based in Metz and subordinate to the FzKdo XII).

Army Equipment Offices—*Heereszeugämter* and *Heeresnebenzeugämter*

Subordinate to the *Feldzeugkommandos* were *Heereszeugämter* (army equipment offices), *Heeresnebenzeugämter* (army auxiliary equipment offices), army ammunition centers, army auxiliary ammunition centers, equipment depots, ammunition depots, army clothing, and army auxiliary clothing offices. The *Panzer-Feldzeugkommando* (Armored Field Equipment Command) was also in charge of the *Heerespanzerzeugämte* and *Heerespanzernebenzeugämter* (army armored/army auxiliary armored equipment offices) and army armored workshops.

The *Heereszeugämter* service centers approved the products manufactured in their area by industry, comparing the end product against the order and checking tolerances and functionality. If accepted, the product received an acceptance stamp and was then stored preparatory to being sent into the field. While stored, the *Heereszeugämter* added any missing weapons, ammunition, and equipment necessary including crew weapons, radios, tools, and accessories. Reports were sent to the OKH, and distribution was catalogued. Delivery to front-line units was usually by rail.

The *Heereszeugämter* also handled repairs that couldn't be sorted out in the field. Each had two sections: storage depot (*Lager*) and workshop (*Werkstatt*). The former was subdivided into specialist departments (*Bezirke*) for different equipment.

Equipment Parks

Complementing the *Heereszeugämter*, there were equipment depots in the *Wehrkreise* to handle motor transport, engineer equipment, the distribution of horses, veterinary equipment, and medical equipment for its allotted area—but the *Wehrkreis* was also charged with the supply and maintenance of units of the Feldheer.

The *Wehrkreise* were divided into *Heimatkraftfahrbezirke* (home motor transport districts). From December 1942 these were renamed *Kommandeure der Kraftfahrpark-Truppen* (MT troop commands). Within the districts were several *Heimatkraftfahrparke* (HKP—home motor transport parks). These worked on motor vehicles other than (a) tanks and armored vehicles and (b) newly manufactured vehicles. Most of the vehicles repaired in the HKPs were from the Wehrmacht and the SS. The size of the HKPs varied. *TM-E 30-451* quotes the three HKPs in Berlin held as many as 1,000 vehicles and repaired 30 daily. However, most HKPs outside the capital were a tenth that size. Also, as the vehicles reaching the HKPs were often in very bad condition, many had to be scrapped and cannibalized. The number of HKPs in a *Wehrkreis* varied greatly: *TM-E 30-451* identifies nine in Wehrkreis VI, while Wehrkreis V had only four.

Supplies of spare parts and tires were procured from *Zentralersatzteillage* (ZEL—central spare parts depots) and *Reifenlager* (tire depots), both controlled by the HKP, but some also came direct from factories.

Tracked vehicles needed extensive maintenance, more so than wheeled. In this photo a Marder IIIM's 7.5 cm gun is having work done on the gun cradle. When the war began, the Panzerwaffe had a centralized maintenance system. Minor repairs were made in the field and major ones at the factory of origin. As the war progressed and the army moved farther away from Germany, spare-parts depots were established closer to the front. This led to many tanks being stripped for parts to keep other less-damaged vehicles in the field. (Dutch Archives)

The *Heeres-Kraftfahrbezirke* (the army motor vehicle districts) in the occupied territories were renamed *Kraftfahrzeug-Instandsetzungs-Regimenter* (motor vehicle repair regiments) in 1943–44. In addition to the tire retreading and repair squadrons, the MT troops also included the replenishment squadrons for tires.

In the field, the main MT unit was the *Heereskraftfahrpark* (HeKP or Army Motor Transport Park). Usually, several HeKPs were established in each *Armeegruppe* area. Unlike the HKP, as far as possible, the HeKP handled the repair of damaged vehicles coming from *Armeekraftfahrparke* (individual *Armee* motor transport parks) itself. HeKPs also held reserves of new vehicles. One of the most important of the HeKPs' functions was to set up fuel stations along the *Rollbahnen* and other important roads.

The maintenance of armored vehicles was a key area of the logistics chain. Damaged tanks were kept on the books and repaired where other countries might have sent them for scrap. The chain started in the field where the *Kraftfahrzeuge-Instandsetzungsdienste*—powered vehicle repair units—were

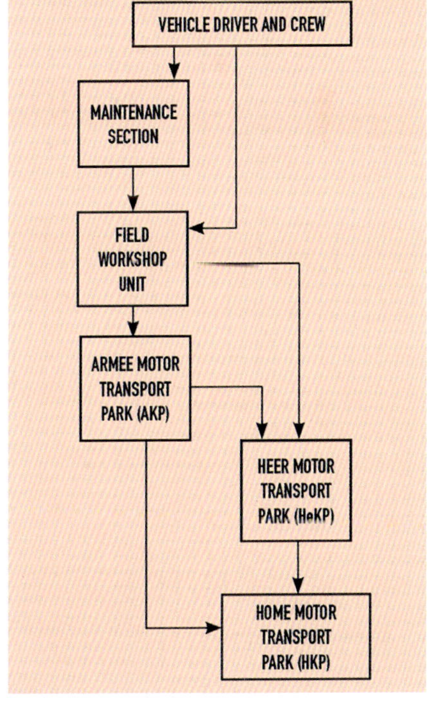

Motor vehicle repair and maintenance. (*TM-E 30-451*)

split into those that handled wheeled and halftracked armored vehicles and the *Panzer-Instandsetzungsdienste* (tank repair services). If an AFV couldn't be repaired in the field—or if there were too many to repair—it was sent up through its *Armee* to stationary workshops at either army group level or back to the *Heimat* home depot maintenance units. There were representatives of various manufacturing companies who could provide some assistance, and some of the vehicles were cannibalized rather than sent home to the *Heereszeugämter*. From October 15, 1942, there were various changes to the organization which ended with the *Panzer-Instandsetzungsdienste* transferred to the newly named *Panzertruppen* on April 1, 1943 (hitherto they had been *Schnelle Truppen*).

Also under Feldheer control were spare parts depots (*Ersatzteillager*), tire depots (*Reifenlager*), track depots (*Gleiskettenlager*), tank spare parts depots, (*Panzerersatzteillager*), armored car spare parts depots (*Panzerspähwagenersatzsteillager*), and tractor spare parts depots (*Zugkraftwagenersatzteillager*). The depots furnished supplies to maintenance sections, workshop units, army parks, and Feldheer parks.

Other depots included *Heimatpionierparke* (home engineer parks), *Heimatfestungspionierparke* (home fortress engineer parks), and *Gasschutzgeräteparke* (gas defense equipment parks) each of which, as their names suggest, handled storage, training, and distribution of men and equipment.

The problem of lack of spare parts led to difficulties and depots and supply dumps. Müller-Hillebrand:

> Since the advance dumps and army group depots were usually out of those parts for which there was a heavy demand, the tank maintenance companies began to send details to the depots to represent their interests. Upon the arrival of a supply train carrying spare parts, each detail tried to secure the parts its company needed most urgently ... the depots became the scenes of fierce struggles for priority items. ... During the latter part of the war some of them [maintenance company commanders] even resorted to bribery. ... Occasionally, even tactical commanders took part in the hunt for parts when the number of serviceable tanks at their disposal began to dwindle. It happened in several instances that a private or noncommissioned officer escorting a rail shipment of laboriously acquired spare parts would suddenly be confronted by a field grade officer of some other regiment or division who simply ordered him to surrender the entire cargo.

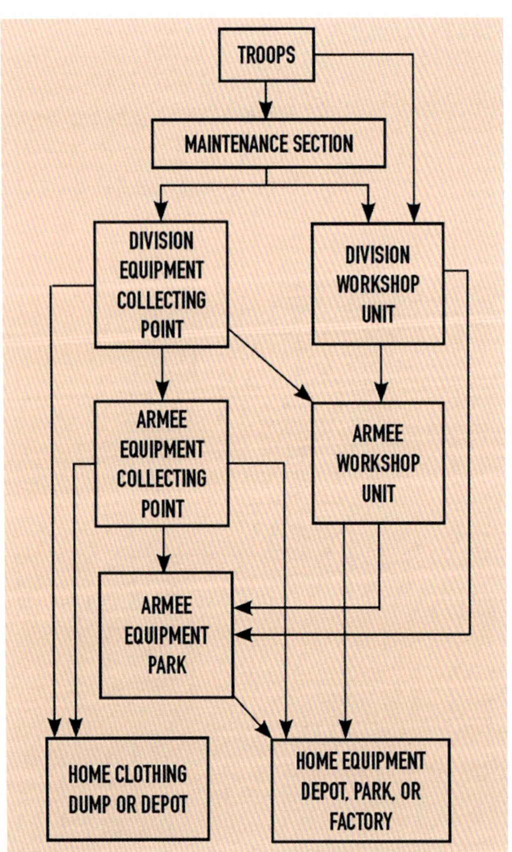

Repair of equipment and clothing. (*TM-E 30-451*)

Clothing Depots

The Wehrmacht Procurement Office for Clothing and Equipment (Wehrmachtbes-chaffungsamt Bekleidung und Ausrüstung) handled procurement under the aegis of the Allgemeines Heeresamt/Stab/Bekleidung (General Army Office/Staff/Clothing). The raw materials were then issued to the relevant clothing depot:

Receiving Units of Medical Supplies

Receiving units	Place of receipt
Division units	Division surgical hospitals or main dressing stations (established by the division medical companies) which received two sets of "Class B" medical equipment from the stocks of the division surgeon.
Divisions, division surgeons, corps troops, and corps medical troops	Corps medical supply point, usually attached to corps billet hospital, receiving about 10 tons of medical equipment which the army medical depot sent only to corps.
Corps, corps surgeons, army troops, army medical troops	Army medical depot or branch depot.
Army, army surgeons, army group troops, and army group medical troops	General medical depot.
Army groups and army group surgeons	*Wehrkreis* medical depots and central medical depot.

the army's were the *Heeresbekleidungsämter* (HBA—army clothing depots). These manufactured and supplied the clothing and controlled the testing and repair sections (*Verwaltungs und Instandsetzungabteilungen*) which repaired damaged or captured clothing for reissue. From the HBAs the clothing went out to army clothing dumps and branch dumps (*Heeresbekleidungslager und Nebenlager*) within each *Wehrkreis*.

Medical and Veterinary Parks

Again, the *Wehrkreise* played an important role within the medical and veterinary systems. The *Wehrkreissanitätsparke* (WSP—*Wehrkreis* medical parks) were subordinate to the HSP (*Hauptsanitätspark*—main medical park), latterly set up in Berlin-Lichtenberg in 1943. They collected surgical apparatus, drugs, bandages, etc. from factories and handled distribution to hospitals in the *Wehrkreise* and to *Sammelsanitätsparke* (medical collecting parks) for the field forces. The HSP also had a testing function and was responsible for supplying "disinfestants"—mainly in the form of Zyklon B—to the camps which used it. *TM-E 30-451* also mentions *Sanitätsbeutesammelstellen*—medical booty collecting points—centers for the collection and testing of captured medical equipment, which was then sent out into the field if appropriate.

The veterinary equivalent of the *Wehrkreissanitätsparke* were the *Heimatveterinärparke* (home veterinary parks). They were also subordinate to a main veterinary park (Heereshauptveterinärpark)—the Central Procurement Agency for Veterinary Equipment.

Two other important collecting establishments existed: *Heeresremontëamter* and *Heimatpferdeparke*. The army remount-purchasing commissions (*Heeres-Remontierungskommissionen*) procured young horses. These commissions were outside the *Wehrkreis* structure and directly subordinate to the OKH. The horses were stabled and maintained by *Heeresremontëamter* (army remount depots), independent of the remount purchasing commissions, that trained purchased horses for field use. After training they either went to *Wehrkreis* riding schools, to home units, or to *Heimatpferdeparke* (home horse parks) from where they went into units.

A stack of wooden artillery boxes with the appropriate information labels and stencils serves as a suitable place for a smoke. (SF Collection)

In extremis, the woven straw step-in overboots served a different purpose. (SF Collection)

Partially camouflaged supply dump. The importance of these dumps cannot be underestimated. Food and water were a small part of the supply chain: ammunition, fuel, and replacement/spare parts provided the bulk. As an upgrade of Napoleon's "an army runs on its stomach," add a fuel tank. The smoke in the background implies that the front is close. (SF Collection)

Promoted to *Generalmajor* at the start of the war, Rudolf Gercke was the head of transport in the OKH. Of note was the brilliant deployment of troops to the start lines for *Barbarossa*, accomplished in great secrecy. Even more remarkable was the movement of troops to the Ardennes in late 1944 under the noses of the Allies, allowing the attack to achieve complete surprise. This photo shows him in September 1943 after being awarded the Ritterkreuzes des Kriegsverdienst-kreuzes mit Schwertern (Knight's Cross of the Cross of the Order of Merit with Swords). (Bundesarchiv, Bild 183-J15556/ CC-BY-SA 3.0)

Engineering and Railroad Depots

After the Polish campaign, several *Eisenbahn-Pionier-Park-Kompanien* (railroad engineer park companies) were set up to provide for the various railroad engineer units materials, machines, and technical equipment for track construction and to carry out repairs. They were linked to specific *Armeegruppen* and managed the *Eisenbahn-Pionier-Parke* (railroad engineer supply depots). Here, the material was catalogued and measured carefully before being sent out on demand. There was liaison between the units and the DRB to allow coordinated routing of inward- and outward-bound trains. When they needed extra hands, the *Eisenbahn-Pionier-Park-Kompanien* could call on local PoWs, civilian construction platoons, Organization Todt, and units of the Ersatzheer for help.

As far as the organization and command structure was concerned, railroad troops answered ultimately to the OKH's *Chef des Transportwesens*, Generalleutnant Rudolf Gercke. They were army troops and the chain of command from the OKH ran to the *Befehlshaber der Eisenbahntruppen*—usually shortened to *Bedeis* (Commander of the Railroad Troops)—then to the *Heeresgruppe Kommandeure der Eisenbahnpioniere* (usually shortened to *Grukodeis*—the Army Group Railroad Engineer Commander) and then on to the *Kommandeure der Eisenbahnpioniere* (*Kodeis*—Railroad Engineer Commander) who had the equivalent rank to a *Bevollmächtigten Transportoffizier* (BvTO—authorized transport officer).

A busy scene in Poland: note in the background the three lines of track, flat cars, and stake wagons. (SF Collection)

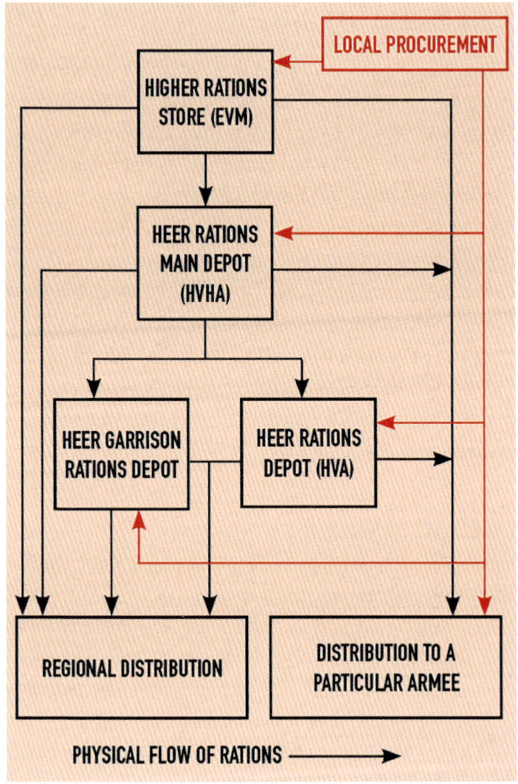

Supply of rations. (*TM-E 30-451*)

With the establishment of the *Generale des Transportwesens* (generals of transport) in February 1942, tactical command in the *Heeresgruppe* area was transferred to them, but the position of the *Grukodeis* in their area of responsibility did not change in practice.

Ration Depots

Because of the number of horses in the Wehrmacht, human and horse rations were handled by the same agencies. The Wehrmacht's rations were procured and supplied by the OKH's Amtsgruppe Verpflegang und Beschaffung (Rations and Procurement Group). Some of these rations came from local producers, sometimes purchased by the *Ersatzverpflegungsmagazine* (EVM—Ration Depot). Where possible, the troops lived off the land.

There were various levels of organization with the ration depots, the EVM being the most important. Each was expected to maintain one month's rations for 300,000 men; this would amount to over 10,000 tons of food. The EVM usually had a bakery and—where possible—good rail facilities; lower depots often lacked both.

Units contacted the nearest rations depot and were automatically attached to a depot for their supply of rations. For the supply of rations to the Feldheer, a group of EVMs was needed for each army, which sent the EVM an estimate of the probable rations' strength 28 days in advance. Having done that, the EVMs had to be able to supply 10 days of rations. The amount needed is given in *TM-E 30-451* as:

Rations Required for Different Duties	
Character of fighting in area	Total lb per man per day
Inactivity	5–10
Mopping-up	15–20
Defensive fighting (but not against a major Allied push)	20–25
Heavy defensive fighting	25–50
Offensive fighting	25–50

A soldier's daily ration in theory consisted of three meals, the main meal by size being lunch. Troops in combat were supposed to receive more than those in garrison or in the *Wehrkreise*, but combat exigencies and other wartime issues affected when and what was served. On the Eastern Front, soldiers were expected to live off the land.

Animal rations also had to be carefully organized: if horses aren't fed properly, they can't pull gun carriages. In theory, heavy draft horses received a maximum allowance (i.e., when conditions demanded it) of 5.65 kg oats, 5.3 kg hay, and 5.75 kg straw (including bedding straw).

Rations Carried in an Army for Each Man

Where carried	Full rations	Iron rations
With the man	–	1 (half)
On a combat vehicle	–	1
In the field kitchen	1	1
In the unit ration train	2	–
In the division train	1	–
In the army dumps and train	c. 3	–

Ordinarily there are two full and two iron horse rations carried either on the horse or in unit supply columns. Other rations are carried by the army and the division. For staff planning purposes, the weights of rations were computed by the Germans as follows:

Weights of Rations

Type of rations	Weight (g)	Weight (lb)
Human rations:		
Standard ration with packing	1,500	3.3
Iron ration with packing	825	1.82
Iron half-ration with packing	535	1.18
Horse rations:		
Standard ration	10,000	22
Iron oat ration	5,000	11
Iron hay ration	5,000	11
Iron straw ration	2,500	5.5

Armeeverpflegungslager (army ration dumps)—and sometimes corps ration dumps (*Korpsverpflegungslager*)—supplied the divisional rations distributing point (*Verpflegungsausgabestelle*). Supplies were received at this point and distributed to units such as butchery platoons and field bakeries. *TM-E 30-451* suggested butchery platoons could process the following number of animals per day:

Butchery Platoon Daily Processing Numbers

Number of animals	Type	Meat ration equivalence
40	Beef cattle	40,000
80	Pigs	24,000
240	Sheep	19,000

Layout of Motorized Bakery Company Type E (mot) (KStN 1277 of 1941)

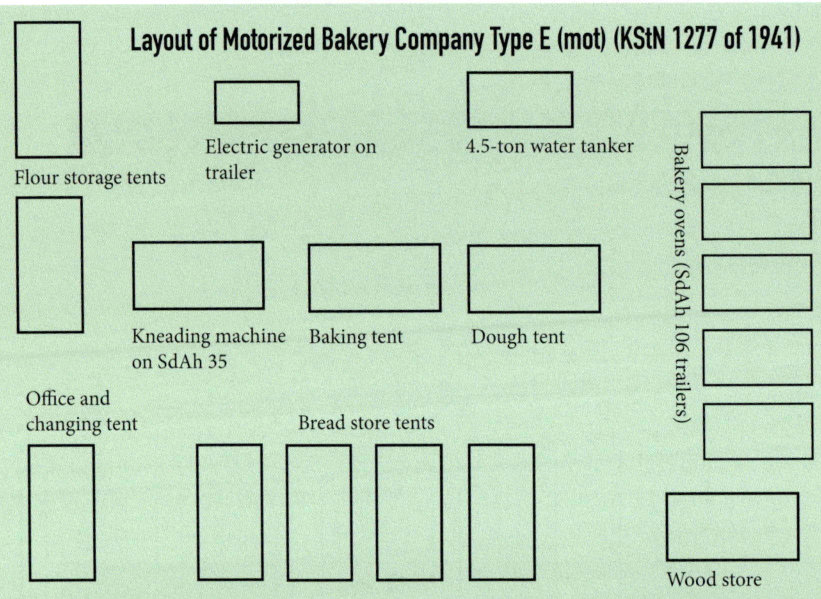

Flour storage tents

Electric generator on trailer

4.5-ton water tanker

Bakery ovens (SdAh 106 trailers)

Kneading machine on SdAh 35

Baking tent

Dough tent

Office and changing tent

Bread store tents

Wood store

Parking for vehicles

Company HQ
- 1 × medium PKW
- 2 × motorcycles

Platoon 1
- 1 × motorbus (28 bakers + driver)
- 2 × medium LKW (3 ton)
- 2 × medium LKW (3 ton) to pull bakery oven trailers
- 1 × medium LKW (3 ton) to pull kneading machine trailer
- 1 × medium LKW (3 ton) to pull generator

Platoon 2
- 3 × medium LKW (3 ton)
- 1 × motorbus (28 bakers + driver)
- 3 × medium LKW (3 ton) to pull bakery oven trailers

Company train
- 2 × medium LKW (3 ton)
- 1 × water tanker
- 1 × light PKW
- 1 × light LKW (1.5 ton) for rations
- 1 × light LKW (1.5 ton) for fuel
- 1 × motorbus (28 bakers + driver)

Motor maintenance section
- 1 x motorcycle and sidecar
- 1 x Kfz 2/40 repair vehicle

Above: Typical layout of a motorized bakery company in the field. (Info from *Handbook of German Administration and Supply 1944*)

Right: The German soldier's rations were carefully calculated—but depended on combat exigencies. Here tank men of Großdeutschland queue to collect hot food for their crews. (SF Collection)

The key component of a baking company: four SdAh 106 Backanhänger bakery ovens. They ran on either coal or wood needing around 120 kg of coal or 180 kg of wood and 8,000–9,000 l of water for use over a 24-hour period. (RCT)

It goes on:

> A field bakery company can produce between 15,000 and 19,200 bread rations, according to the weather and the time of year. After passing through the rations supply points of the division units, the supplies finally reach field kitchens and troops. Field kitchens of two types are found: large, with a capacity for supplying 125 to 225 men; and small, with a capacity for supplying 60 to 125 men.

Supply Units and Supply Troops

The nitty-gritty work of the supply chain was undertaken by the *Nachschubtruppen*—the supply troops—whose leader, the *General der Nachschubtruppen*, reported to the *Generalquartiermeister*. The supply troops duties included loading, transshipment, and unloading, providing the *Nachschub-Kolonnenabteilungen* (supply columns, later renamed *Kraftfahr-bzw. Fahrabteilungen*—motorized transport divisions), as well as the supply battalions and companies. The MT regiments (later divisions) were used on a divisional basis. The field waterway divisions were also part of the supply troops' transport units. Not all the road transport was military: for instance, the civilian (NSKK) Transportkorps Speer.

The *Nachschubtruppen* provided the link between the *Armee* dumps and depots and the battalion or company distribution points. In autumn 1942, the *Heeresgruppen-*, *Armee-*, *Korps-* and *Divisionsnachschubführer* (army group, army, corps, and division supply commanders, the latter shortened to *DiNafü*) were renamed *Kommandeure der Nachschubtruppen* (commanders of the supply troops—the divisional commander

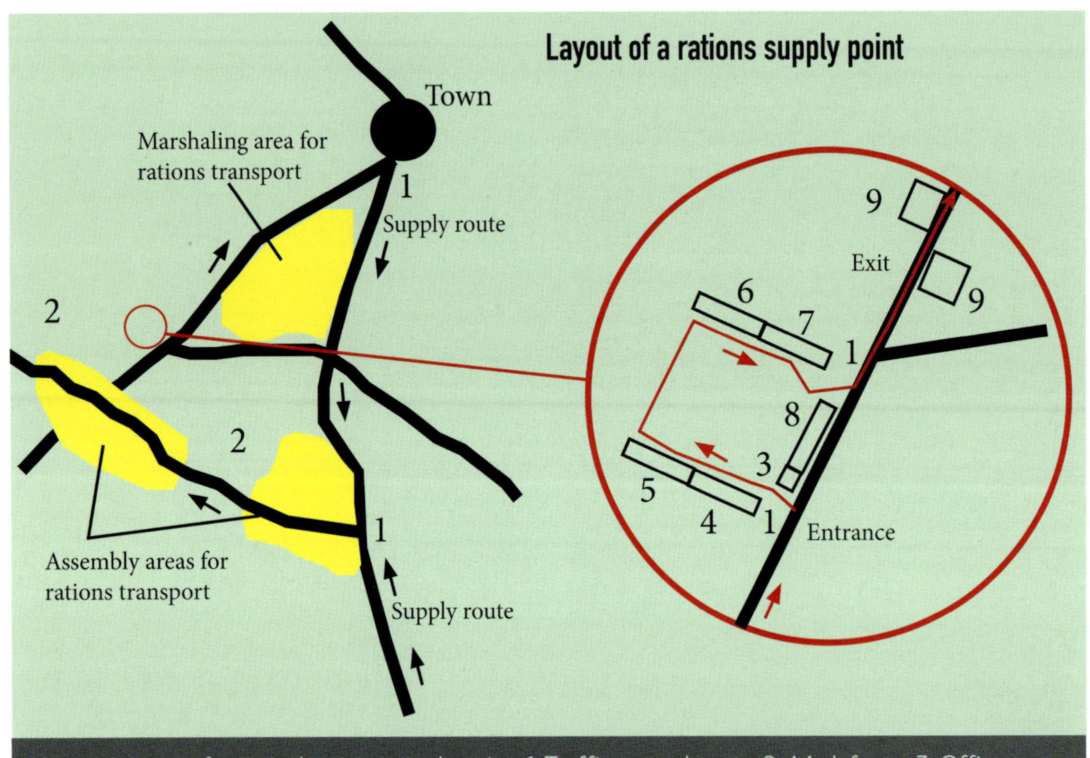

Above: Layout of a typical rations supply point: 1. Traffic control posts. 2. AA defense. 3. Office. 4. Oats. 5. Bread. 6. Vegetables and groceries. 7. Meat. 8. *Feldpost* office. 9. Forage. (Info from *Handbook of German Administration and Supply 1944*)

abbreviated to *Kodina*) and, for the *Heeresgruppe* area, *Höhere Kommandeure* (higher commander). On September 1, 1944, the supply units were then merged into the Divisional Supply Regiment.

Usually, the supplies were brought forward from the dumps by attached MT (or, more often, horse-drawn for the infantry) columns. The *Nachschub-Kolonnen-Abteilungen* (supply column detachments) were army troops and had a staff, several motorized columns, and a workshop platoon. The size of the motorized columns varied from unit to unit, as did the number and size of the vehicles. For example:

- Infantry light 30-tonne *Nachschubkolonne* (KstN 1225 of 1943) had 10 3-tonne trucks and an extra 3-tonne truck to carry fuel for them.

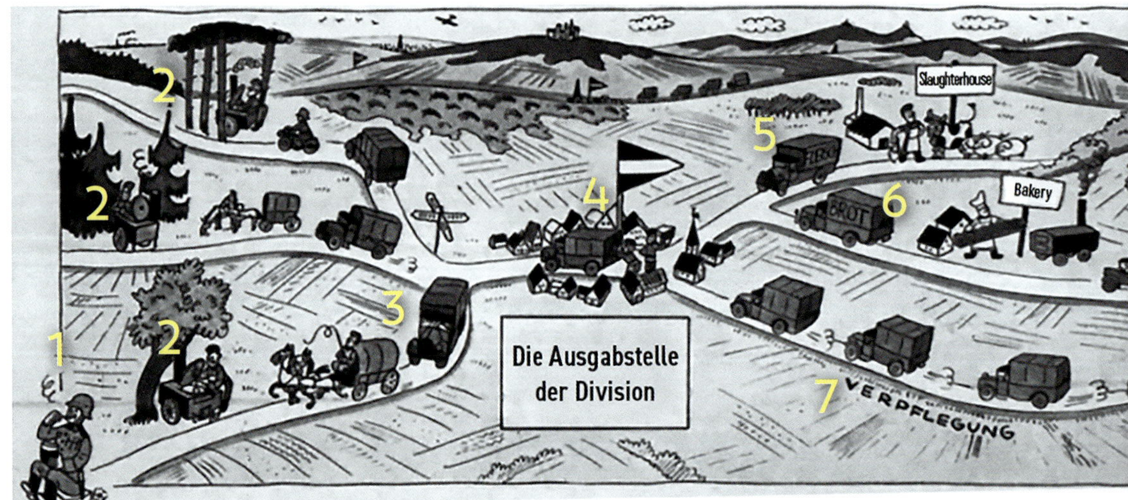

Supply of Rations

Transporting rations from home depots to the front used various transport media and collection points from the *Armee Verpflegungs Lager*—the individual armies' supply depots—through *Korps* depots to the divisions. Usually, they went by train to *Armee* dumps, trucks to division, and then horses.

Below, from left: 1. The end user: a happy *Landser.*

2. *Feldküchen*—field kitchens—well-camouflaged and as close to the front as possible, they planned to deliver hot food to the front line.

3. Each regiment initially had two *Verpflegungstroße*: supply trains I and II with supply officer and paymaster. Most were horse-drawn although vehicles were also used in motorized units.

4. The divisional ration supply point, the *Ausgabstelle.*

5. Trucks bring meat from the butcher/slaughterhouse (*Schlächterei*).

6. Bread en route to the *Ausgabstelle* from the bakery.

7. The supply of other provisions (*Verpflegung*) from *Korps* and *Armee* supply depots.

8. Flour en route to the bakery (*Bäckerei*).

9. The *Korps* supply camp. These weren't always inserted into the supply chain.

10. Railroads brought supplies from the *Wehrkreise.*

11. The AVL, *Armeeverpflegungslager*, *Armee* supply depot.

12. The AVLs were in front of the border between the operational zone and the home/*Wehrkreise.*

13. The inland waterways of Europe were usually big enough to make significant contributions to movement of goods and equipment.

14. The EVM, *Ersatzverpflegungsmagazin*, replacement supply center, was usually within the orbit of the *Wehrkreise.*

15. The *Wehrkreisverwaltung*, military district administration.

(*Die Wehrmacht* magazine)

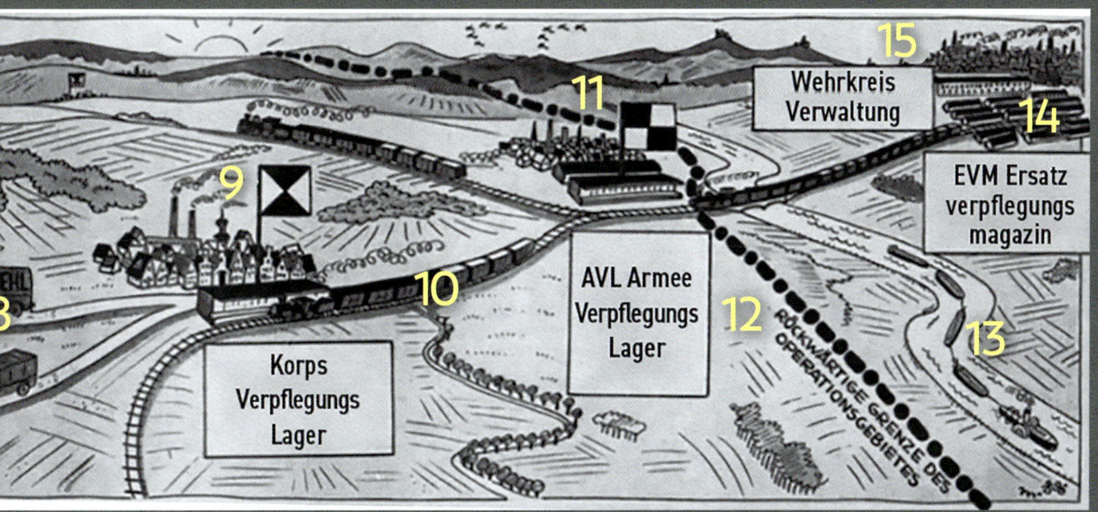

• Heavy 120-tonne *Kraftfahrkompanie* (KStN 1217b of 11/1943) had four *Züge* each of 10 3-tonne vehicles—plus six others: one 2 tonne for the *Kfz Instandsetzungstrupp* (maintenance troop) and five 3 tonne for the *Troß* (one for rations, two for fuel, one for luggage, and one for field kitchen.

• A *Versorgungskompanie* (service company) for a *StuG Abteilung* (KStN 1151c of 11/1944) had a more complicated organization with a staff unit that included a medical *Staffel*; five *Kfz-Instandsetzungsgruppen* (for the company, the staff, and three for the three *StuG Kompanien*), and one *Gruppe für Waffen und Nachrichtengeräteinstandsetzung* for weapons and signals equipment; *Betriebsstoffstaffel* (fuel) of six 4.5-tonne trucks to carry 200 l fuel drums; a *Munitionsstaffel* with 10 4.5-tonne trucks for ammunition; and a *Versorgungsstaffel* (service unit) with nine 3-tonne trucks for rations/cooking/tools, clothing and luggage.

There were several name and jurisdictional changes during wartime, as is exemplified in the divisional troops of 1. Panzer-Division (as quoted from *Lexikon der Wehrmacht*):

> Originally named Divisions-Nachschubtruppen 81, the staff was renamed Panzer-Divisions-Nachschubführer 81 at the beginning of 1940. The columns were reorganized in mid-1940. In 1940–1, 3. Werkstatt-Kompanie was added. In 1941, the number of columns was increased to 14 by the addition of the supply columns of the rifle regiments and the two columns of Panzer Regiment 1. In 1941 and 1941–2, the workshop companies were renamed Kraftwagen-Werkstatt-Kompanien. In 1942–3, the columns were reorganized again. In 1942–3, the staff was renamed Kommandeur der Panzer-Divisions-Nachschub-Truppen 81 [commander of Panzer Division Supply Troops 81]. In 1943, some columns were renamed Kraftfahr-Kompanien, while others were deleted. On October 7, 1943, the Nachschub-Staffel Ersatzteile 81 was registered. On March 15, 1944, Nachschub-Staffel Ersatzteile 81 was renamed Kfz.-Ersatzteil-Staffel 81 der 1. Panzer-Division. On July 3, 1944, 8. Kraftfahr-Kompanie was deleted. In November 1944, the Nachschub-Kompanie and Kraftfahr-Kompanien 4, 6, and 7 disappeared: the latter was renamed Fahrschwadron, the others were deleted. As a result, the former 5. Kraftfahr-Kompanie was renamed the 4.

At the end of January 1944, all units were deleted. The units were registered with new numbers by January 29, 1945. There were still some reorganizations of the subunits.

Railroad Distribution

Most of the supplies were transported as far as possible by rail. This meant that shortages could arise when there were problems with the railroads—whether from the elements, enemy action, or other causes—and this could mean military inaction. It is a constant story throughout the war that units—from battalions to armies—had to stop moving to await fuel consignments. This obviously hit motorized and *Panzer* units the most because the infantry and so many other parts of the army moved on foot (human and animal). The problem there came when fodder couldn't be brought forward for the horses, or ammunition, food, or such items as winter clothing couldn't reach the front.

In the main, small shipments—less than a railcar load—went to collecting stations (*Sammelbahnhöfe*) for combining with other requests to maximize efficient railroad usage. Next stop for shipments that were not unit-loaded were the forwarding stations (*Weiterleitungstattionen*). To ease congestion and improve organization, when many units were dependent upon a single railroad for their supply, distributing stations (*Verteilerbahnhöfe*) were sometimes set up to regulate the dispatch of supplies.

Important reserves of ammunition, fuel, and rations were kept loaded in trains in supply collecting areas (*Nachschubsammelgebiete*) and were the responsibility of the *Generalquartiermeister*.

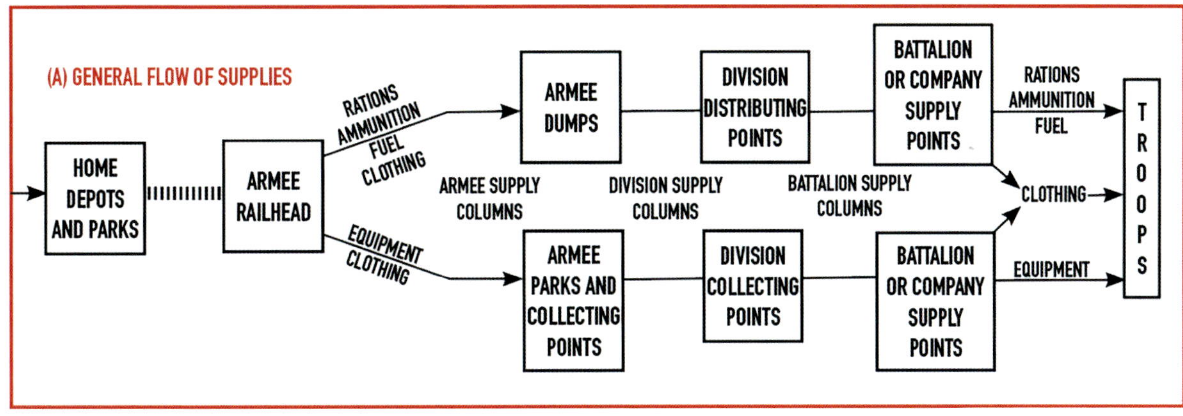

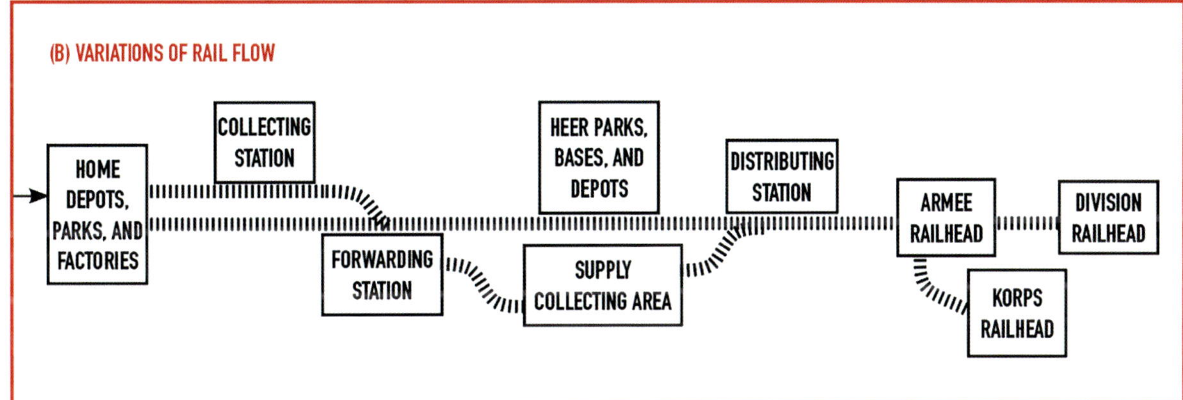

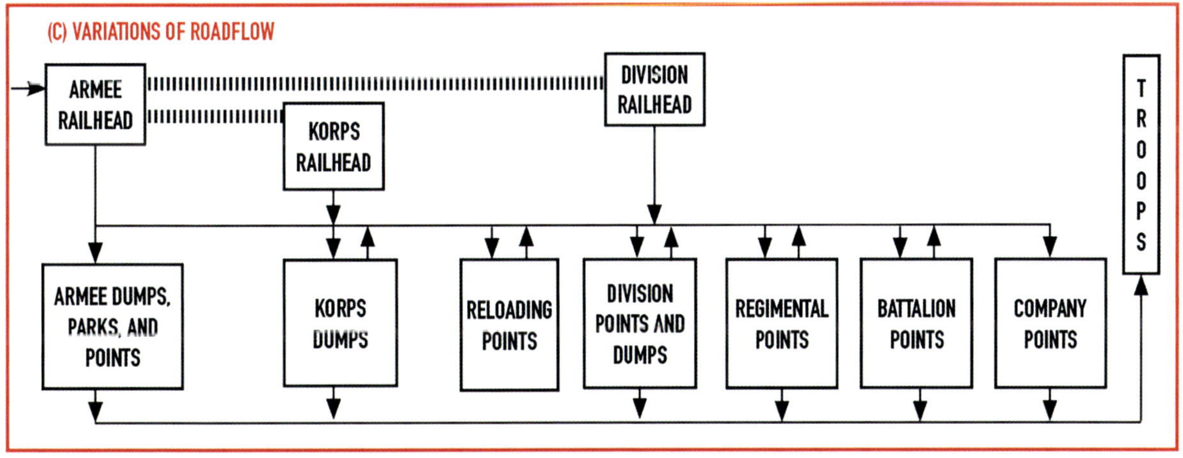

Synergy between railroads and roads in the supply chain: a) general flow of supplies; b) variations of rail flow; c) variations of road flow. (*TM-E 30-451*)

Rail transport of weapons to the front used a range of wagons. The flat goods *Rungenwagen* (stake wagons) were typified by the Rs Stuttgart R 10s. These are *Güterwagen* (goods wagon) with vertical stanchions and were used for transport of military vehicles and equipment. (RCT)

Railheads (*Kopfbahnhöfe*)

As far forward as possible, railheads could be commanded by *Armee* or *Korps* to supply several divisions. However, if possible, a division would set up its own railhead. This was more likely in the West where they were 10–50 miles from the front (and often the subject of RAF and USAAF bombing). During Operation *Barbarossa* they were often 100 miles behind the divisions and required significant onward transportation.

The NSKK was heavily involved in transport operations. Here a *Sturmmann* secures AA guns on flat cars in the West. Note his NSKK sleeve eagle and driver's sleeve insignia on the black lozenge. (Akira Takiguchi)

Supply Trains

TM-E 30-451 identifies the different types of supply train:

Type	No. of cars	Load
Rations supply trains (*Verpflegungszüge*)	40	(a) Iron rations: 300,000 full and 300,000 half iron rations, totaling 442 metric tons. (b) Full rations with fodder: 180,000 human and 40,000 animal rations, amounting to 454 metric tons. These may be loaded into three parts, each containing three days' supplies for 20,000 men and 4,000 animals. (c) Full human rations with no bread but only baking materials: 300,000 rations, totaling 450 metric tons. (d) Flour train (*Mehlzug*): 833,000 rations, amounting to 450 metric tons. (e) Oat train (*Hafersug*): 90,000 rations, totaling 450 metric tons. (f) Animal trains (*Viekzüge*): 360 cattle weighing 180 metric tons, 1,200 pigs weighing 120 metric tons, or 1,800 sheep weighing 72 metric tons.
Ammunition supply trains (*Munitionszüge*)	30	(a) Range of different types of ammunition needed by a particular division. (b) Various calibers of round.
Fuel supply trains (*Betriehstoffzüge*)	20–25	20 gasoline tank cars, holding between 340–440 cu m (around 89,800–116,200 gal) of fuel, or 25 cars, holding gasoline in 200 (53 gal) and 20 l (5 gal) cans and carrying 400 cu m (105,600 gal) of gasoline, and five cars with oil, engine oil, gear oil, paraffin, and (in winter) antifreeze barrels and cans.
Horse supply trains (*Pferdersatzzüge*)	55 cars	Each holding eight riding or light draft horses per car or 440 horses per train; six heavy draft horses per car or 330 horses per train; or four very heavy horses per car or 220 horses per train.
Signals and engineer construction materials trains (*Baustottzuge*)	40	39 are open cars, with a net tonnage of about 820 metric tons.

Supplies from home depots arrived at *Armee* railheads where they were picked up by *Armee* supply columns and transported to parks and dumps (*Armee Parke und Lager*). If these were too far to the rear, corps dumps (*Korps Lager*) could be set up to aid divisions' resupply. Occasionally, divisional dumps (*Divisions Lager*) were created. Division supply columns received rations, fuel, and ammunition from *Armee* dumps, and equipment from *Armee* parks. The divisional trains then carried their supplies to division distributing

Supply Columns

Above: Serried ranks of supply vehicles in Kharkov. The lack of uniformity is noticeable; surprisingly, there's no sign of maintenance. *Combat in the East*:

> As a result of the poor and extended supply routes, the condition of motor vehicles was a source of constant apprehension. Of those used in the supply service of the Eleventh Army a regular average of about only 40 to 60% of actual strength were in good repair. The large number of different types of motor vehicles greatly impeded their proper maintenance. During 1941–42 it was not possible to overcome the difficulties which thus arose in procuring automotive replacement parts. [NARA]

Below: "What is it this time?" A halted supply column of Renaults, 32,880 of which were produced for the German military. The white marking on the tailgate is for nighttime driving. The trucks will also have the Notek convoy lights (usually front and rear). There's obviously no fear of air attack and the road seems to be holding up well, so the delay may just be weight of traffic. (SF Collection)

Above: Unfortunately, for much of the time in the East the state of the roads didn't compare with the West: "Because of bad roads, fuel consumption was considerably higher in Russia than in European theaters. For wheeled vehicles it was about 150 to 200% of the normal rate, while it was frequently still higher for track-laying vehicles. Cold-resistant lubricants were necessary for winter driving. The large number of overstrained engines increased the general oil consumption." (*Combat in the East*/ SF Collection)

Below: A convoy advancing with caution—the frozen conditions solved the problem of mud but brought their own difficulties. Note the 12-ton SdKfz 8 towing what looks like a 15 cm sFH 18 heavy field howitzer with its crew of seven on board, all of them traveling in the open air. There are many stories about how difficult it was to fight in frozen conditions. One crewman of a Wespe remembered:

> For us on the gun platform the journey was a nightmare of freezing cold. The platform was open at the top, the wind howled through the many apertures and slits in the armor plating, the snow was pouring down and all through the night one man of us had to be standing up helping the driver to keep in contact with the rest of the column. The maximum period of time that any of us could stand up facing into the wind was a quarter of an hour. Quite literally we turned blue in the face from the freezing cold. The whole body then became an aching mass of pain ... We thought the night would never end." (James Lucas, *War on the Eastern Front*)

As well as the effects on people, the cold degraded the accuracy of large-caliber weapons, made conventional flash and sound ranging more difficult, increased fuel consumption—partly because it forced longer warm-up and engine-idling periods—and led to optical instruments and weapons becoming covered with ice as condensation froze. (SF Collection)

As early as the time of Field Marshal Helmuth von Moltke the Elder it was obvious that military operations would suffer if a railhead were more than 60 miles (100 km) from the front lines. There was little choice in the Soviet Union. The far-ranging armored units drove the Soviets before them and then encircled them far ahead of their logistical railheads. (SF Collection)

points (*Ausgabestellen*), and equipment to division collecting points (*Sammelstellen*)—these supplied both new and repaired equipment as well as being collecting points for damaged and captured equipment. At these points, supplies were transferred to battalion supply columns and carried to battalion or company supply points or *Umschlagstellen* (reloading points) where the supplies were turned over to the troops.

Ammunition resupply followed a similar chain: *Armee* ammunition dumps (*Armeemunitionslager*) or *Korps* ammunition dumps (*Korpsmunitionslager*) handled distribution to divisions' ammunition distributing points (*Divisionsausgabestellen*), although divisional ammunition dumps (*Divisionsmunitionslager*) were also sometimes set up. Particular attention was paid at every level to the return of faulty ammunition and the various packing materials back to *Armee* dumps for reuse.

However, it's important to remember that few things on a battlefield work exactly as laid down by the planners. Battlefield exigencies, lack of vehicles: these sorts of problems sometimes meant that resupply had to be handled more flexibly—something the Germans proved adept at.

Ammunition dumps had to be carefully sited. There was a huge variety of caliber and type of round requiring precise labeling and stock control. The usual practice was to stack shells up to 10.5 cm in caliber in six to seven layers, up to 15 cm in four to five layers, and over 15 cm in two to three layers, although the *Handbook of German Administration and Supply 1944* allows one or two extra layers if essential. A four-layer stack of 15 cm shells had dimensions of 3 m in length, nearly 1 m in height, and 90 cm depth. (Dutch Archives)

Ammunition

Ammunition was replaced as it was expended, each formation's allowance based on the weapons in its TO&E. Each weapon has an ammunition quota—a unit of issue. If possible, two units of issue are carried within the division, and another unit is held by the relevant army as a reserve.

Ammunition Issues (Rounds) for a Volksgrenadier Division (*TM-E 30-451*)			
Weapon*	Forward issue	Division reserve	Probable army reserve (unit of issue)
9 mm automatic pistol	18	16	17
9 mm machine pistol	690	512	601
7.92 mm machine pistol	720	540	630
7.92 mm rifle	99	75	87
7.92 mm rifle (troops other than infantry)	25	20	22
7.92 mm semi-auto rifle	159	135	147
Rifle grenade launcher	75	70	70
7.92 mm LMG	3,450	2,505	2,977
7.92 mm LMG (for arty)	1,350	1,020	1,185
7.92 mm HMG	6,300	4,750	5,525
8.8 cm bazooka	5	5	5
8.1 cm mortar	150	126	138
12 cm mortar	150	90	120
3.7 cm AA	1,200	none**	?**
7.5 cm inf howitzer	192	151	171
7.5 cm AT (mtz)	150	100	125
7.5 cm AT	255	—	—
10.5 cm gun howitzer	225	126	175
15 cm howitzer	150	60	105

Units of Issue for Artillery Units	
Weapon	Number of Rounds
3.7 cm AA	1,500
7.5 cm AA	300
8.8 cm AA	300
10.5 cm gun	125
15 cm howitzer	125
15 cm gun	75
21 cm howitzer	50

* Not included are 7.5 cm gun and flamethrower.

** AA ammunition reserves are usually kept by army and not by division.

Above: Where possible, troops made use of local facilities. Here, an Organization Todt vehicle operating in occupied Norway. The spring 1944 photograph was taken in the vicinity of Bergen. (Akira Takiguchi)

Fuel

Refueling stop. Note the empty cans stacked at the rear of the vehicle. If they were full, they would be upright. (SF Collection)

Jerrycans being filled with fuel by hand pump. Note pontoons in the background. (RCT)

POL

Distribution of POL—petrol, oil, and lubricants—was very strictly controlled because of its strategic value. Fuel was a commodity in short supply throughout the war but particularly after the Allied bombing campaign targeted fuel production and distribution.

At the very top of the fuel distribution ladder was the Central Petroleum Office of the Reichswirtschaftsministerium (Reich Ministry of Economy); beneath that, fuel reached the Wehrmacht through the Wirtschaftliche Forschungsgesellschaft mbh—WIFO (Economic Research Company) charged with the construction and operation of liquid fuel (natural and synthetic) storage depots distributed mainly to the air force and minimally to the army. The army's fuel dumps were administered by the OKW: army high command fuel supply depots (*OKH Nachschubtanklager*) and subsidiary army fuel supply depots (*Heeresnachschubtanklager*). Fuel usually went from depots to railheads to army fuel dumps (*Armeebetriebesstofflager*) where it was stored in 20 l and 200 l containers. From there it went forward to division fuel distributing points (*Divisionsbetriebsstoffausgabestellen*) or to division fuel dumps (*Divisionsbetriebsstofflager*). The divisions provided fuel to the lower echelon supply points/fuel points for single vehicles (*Tankstellen für Einzelkraftfahrzeuge*).

As with ammunition, fuel amounts were based on a consumption unit (*Verbrauchssatz*)—the amount of fuel that would move a vehicle in a formation 100 km or 62 mi. Army dumps held three consumption units for their formations; armored formations carried four units, reconnaissance carried six and a half, other formations five.

Road Columns

As there were fewer cars and trucks on German roads than in other industrial nations, driver instruction and training was an important element in the road transport logistical system. The Nationalsozialistisches Kraftfahrkorps (NSKK—National Socialist Motor Corps) was the main training organization prewar—some 200,000 men had passed through its 21 training facilities by 1939. On January 27, 1939, Hitler made the NSKK the sole authority for motor vehicle-related military training. When war began, its members were immediately involved, either called up into the Wehrmacht or as members of several transport brigades which helped either transport troops and supplies or provided support. These included various units controlled by Albert Speer. Between 1941 and the end of the war there were 10 *Kraftwagen-Transport-Regimenter (Speer) der Luftwaffe*; from 1942 the Legion Speer recruited over 7,000 non-German citizens for Legion Speer which served with the Organization Todt. In late 1944 it became part of Transportkorps Speer, still mainly serving the OT (using four-fifths of the *korps'* 50,000 vehicles) but now incorporating the NSKK groups. Nine NSKK companies were involved in Russia and Ukraine.

Armee supply columns—where possible of motorized vehicles—moved stores from the railheads to the divisional depots in the rear of the lines. Where possible, that distance wasn't too far so that the vehicles didn't use too much fuel or damage the equipment—although as already mentioned, lack of fuel led to the reduction in training time for drivers and as the war went on, driver quality reduced, leading to more accidents and greater vehicle attrition.

As an example, an Opel Blitz had a range of 400 km (250 mi), so a sensible radius of action was roughly 150 km (90 mi), a trip of 12 hours. From railhead to army dumps, parks, and collecting points was the realm of the *Grosstransportraum*. Each of the *Heeresgruppen* that took part in *Barbarossa* had a *Grosstransportraum* regiment—one of Kraftwagen-Transport-Regimenter 602, 605, and 616—that could deliver some 45,000 tons

The Germans used many different trucks, but the mainstay was the Opel Blitz. The Kfz 305 (4 × 2) 3-ton Blitz was used in many forms: about 100,000 were delivered to the Heer. The wicker sheaths were used to protect artillery shells. They were supposed to be returned to the army dumps for reuse. (SF Collection)

a day (up from 20,000 tons a day during the campaign in the West). They were directly subordinate to the general of the supply troops. Equipped with mainly 4-ton trucks with 4-ton trailers, nominally Regiment 602 had 2,200 vehicles with a load capacity of 4,500 tons although this was rarely the case. The other two regiments carried more: larger trucks—6- to 10-ton trucks with trailers saw Regiment 605 capable of carrying 6,000 tons and Regiment 616 9,000 tons. Reinhard Frank states, "Marching speed in daylight and in good weather was 30 kph, at night 10 to 15 kph. The regiment had a marching depth of 40 km when opened up, and up to 120 km on the march. A day's marching including loading and unloading of goods, stops and rests, averaged 300 km."

Of course, most of the German supply columns weren't motorized and were animal-drawn, usually by horses. The range of such wagons was usually 12 to 15 miles per day. Additionally, regular rest days were needed. In mountains, mules were used.

Supply Columns and Trains (*TM-E 30-451*)		
Type	Capacity (metric tons)	Capacity (short tons)
Very large motorized column	120	132
Large motorized column	60	66
Small motorized column	30	33
Large animal-drawn column	30	33
Small animal-drawn column	17	18.5
Mountain animal-drawn column	15	16.5
Mountain motorized column	10	11
Pack train	5	
Type	Minimum amount (cu m)	Minimum amount (gal)
Large motorized fuel column	50	13,200
Small motorized fuel column	25	6,600

German supply troops in the mountains of Norway, May 31, 1940. The mules' loads are covered suggesting poor weather to come. Note the mounted troops following at the rear. The Edelweiß badge on the right arm of the leading man shows that he is a *Gebirgsjäger*. (NAC)

Whenever possible, the planners allocated *Rollbahnen*—essentially supply roads along the main line of attack—for each unit from division up. Traffic control was crucial, as was keeping them up to standard and ensuring *Tankstellen* (fuel points) were available en route. This didn't always work. The *Rollbahnen* identified for the Ardennes campaign in 1944 were all well and good, but that for the most powerful unit, Joachim Peiper's 1. SS-Panzer-Division Leibstandarte, was stymied by Rollbahn D. Peiper who said before the operation that his route was unsuitable for tanks, and only good for bicycles. He was right. The nature of the terrain, the narrow roads and steep inclines, the size and weight of some of the heavy tanks, and above all the lack of bridging material meant that U.S. Army engineers were able to blow bridges and cut off Peiper's advance. In the end, his vaunted Tiger IIs had to be abandoned around La Gleize, out of fuel.

Fighting in the mountains is hard work. These mules are carrying ammunition to the 5. Gebirgsdivision who have redeployed to Italy's Gustav Line in December 1943. They had to defend Cassino to begin with and the *Gebirgsjäger* fought out the rest of the war defending up the Italian peninsula into the Western Alps. (NAC)

A cycle unit takes a break in muddy conditions. Note the ammunition box attached to the crossbar of the bike at left and the blankets attached to the crossbars. (NAC)

M42 *Truppenfahrrad*

The German Army bicycle was manufactured in millions, part of the reason being that the Treaty of Versailles severely limited the Army's mobility. There aren't many records but at least 1.2 million were made in 1943 alone. Cheap to produce and maintain, the *Truppenfahrrad* was constructed by several manufacturers to a common standard with special fittings, clips, and brackets designed to carry a variety of equipment including the MG 34/42, its AA tripod, the *Panzerbüchse* antitank rifle, the K98k rifle, mortars, mines, etc. Later in the war even *Panzerfäuste* were clipped either side of the front wheel. Most bicycles included an ammunition pouch under the crossbar and a mounting at back above the rear wheel. At first, rolled blankets were attached in front of the handlebars, soon discontinued for stability reasons. There was a *Fallschirmjäger* version that folded and fitted into a drop canister.

German infantry marching past dozens of abandoned Soviet trucks and cars at Kiev, 1941. The cycle has a briefcase hanging from the crossbar, two helmets, water canteen, entrenching shovel, gas mask container, rolled poncho, and other assorted items on or hanging from the rear carrying frame. (NAC)

Raised duckboards allow movement in wet or uneven terrain—and Finland has a lot of boggy ground. The leading soldier has rubber-soled soft hi-boots and is carrying boxes while the rear man has rolled topboots and is carrying a bundle of clothing. The two cycles carry churns. (SA-Kuva, Finnish Archives)

"Scoff" break. The cycle at left has a Panzerbüchse 38/39 (early antitank rifle) strapped to the crossbar. It weighed in at 16.2 kg (35.71 lb) and must have made peddling a strenuous task. A cycle pump is on the bar underneath and a haversack and gas mask are strapped to the rear. (Bundesarchiv, Bild 101I-213-0291-35/Gebauer/CC-BY-SA 3.0)

Is that envy? Cycle troops look on as an SdKfz 250 hurries past. Note the angle of the barrel of the MG 34 attached to the bicycle at A and the ammunition boxes carried at B and C. (Bundesarchiv, Bild 101I-009-0870-04A/CC-BY-SA 3.0)

From Heimat to the Front: By Land

In Western Europe, the excellent roads and railroads meant that communications and movement of troops and equipment was straightforward until Allied bombing and the exigencies of war impacted. However, in the East the immensity of the Soviet Union and its extremes of weather and terrain all militated against an invader. The farther the German front line advanced from the border, the greater the need for good supplies and good logistics.

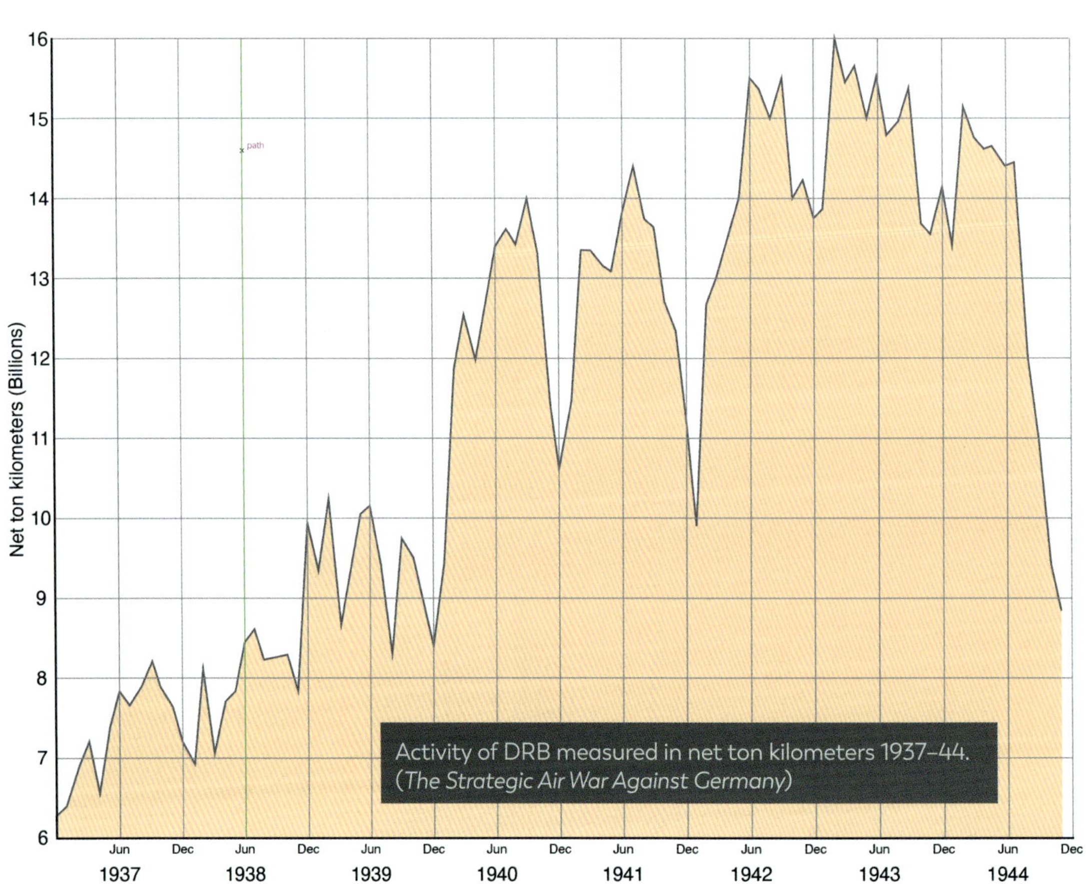

Activity of DRB measured in net ton kilometers 1937–44. (*The Strategic Air War Against Germany*)

The Germans would have liked to use the railroads but couldn't do so immediately because the Soviet rail and loading gauges were different to the German equivalents, and because the Soviets had effectively rescued most of the stock and motive power while sabotaging the infrastructure. They would have liked to have used large numbers of trucks, but motor transport was always a problem for the German Army whose dependence on horses to pull not only supply wagons but also artillery caused immeasurable difficulties.

Chef des Transportwesens im OKH (Transport Chief in the OKH)

Moving men, supplies, munitions, and all the paraphernalia of war to the front was a complicated and problematic job that never was the province of just one man, although the OKW's *Chef des Feldtransportwesens*—chief of transport—was as close to that as could be, as he was in charge of railroad and inland waterway transport.

For the period of the war the position was held by Generalleutnant Rudolf Gercke, an extremely competent man who was able to maintain his position despite the problems he encountered—and despite considerable friction between the Deutsche Reichsbahn and General Eduard Wagner, the OKH's *Generalquartiermeister*. Halder rated him highly and suggested he would make a future Reich transport minister.

Gercke's job got more difficult as lands were conquered and had to be assimilated into the Reich's transport system and when Allied bombing and battlefronts affected the transport systems and routes, although he wasn't responsible for coastal shipping (which came under the Kriegsmarine) and air transport (Luftwaffe).

Beneath Gercke, was a selection of staff officers—the *Bevollmächtigter Transportoffiziere* (plenipotentiary transport officers)—who were attached to the commands of *Heeresgruppen* and *Armeen*. Their role was to "harmonize the demands of the front with the efficiency of the means of transport," provide the army commands with the necessary routes, organize movements, loading/unloading, security, and the repair—and, latterly, destruction—of railroads, liaising with the railroad engineers. They were, Gercke said, the "diplomatic

A good road system determines how swiftly armies can move. Poor roads mean a hard slog no matter how good their mechanized vehicles are. And when the *Rasputitsa* takes hold ... (Ian Spring/Pixpast.com)

Among the many tasks of the RAD was road building and repair, a useful skill that they put to good use when the war began. RAD units were incorporated into the Bautruppen (construction troops). Often supported by infantry engineers, their work was essential to keep the German armies moving and to allow logistical follow-up. (NARA)

representatives of the transport system in the Armeen." (*Lexikon*)

The number of BvTOs increased from 11 in 1939 to 27 in 1944 (and as many as four more in the liaison staffs of cobelligerents). After the problems of winter 1941/42, from February 1, 1942, the BvTOs' role was changed as the *Generale des Transportwesen* (generals of transport) were created above them. The *Generale* were supposed to promote even closer links between the units, to make cooperation as smooth as possible, and not just to look after the HG in which they were based but all troops that were active in that railroad sector to improve the overall control of operations and construction. Initially, there were 13 of them (A, B, Italien, Mitte, Nord, Nordukraine, Nordwest, Süd, Südost, Südrußland, Südukraine, West, and zbV). The number of troops under the staff varied considerably.

After the winter of 1939/40, the *Eisenbahnpioniere* were also placed under Gercke's control and renamed *Eisenbahntruppen.*

Despite the chained rear wheels for extra grip, this 4 × 4 Horch Kfz 17 has come to grief, one of the problems of travelling "*ohne Weg und Steg*"—without fixed paths in a wild landscape. All vehicles carried an assortment of tools for almost every occasion, in this case an axe wielded by a crewmember. (NARA)

Railroad companies in the early and mid-20th century had large fleets of trucks and the DRB was no exception. Here are examples, a Hansa Lloyd Merkur and trailer in Poland. (Akira Takiguchi)

Railroads in German-occupied Europe

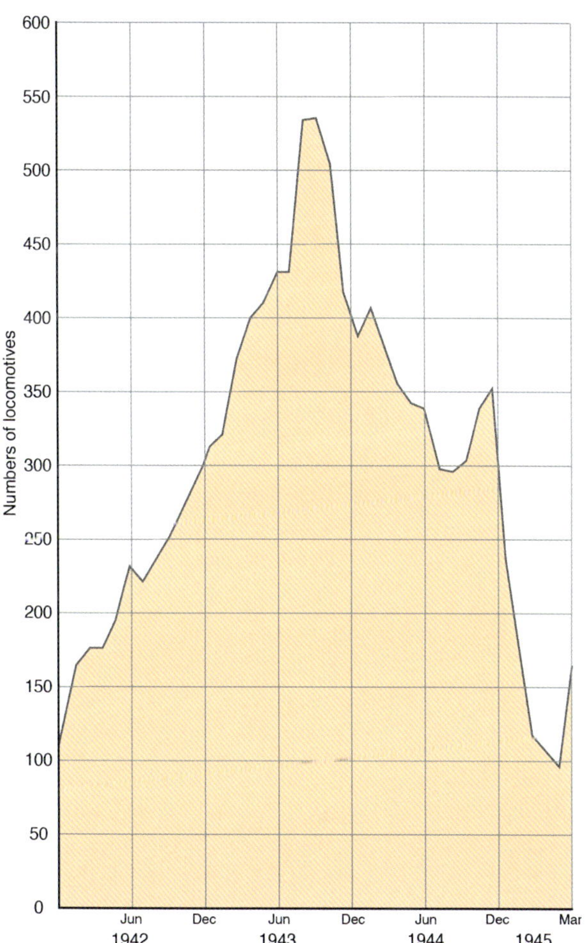

Production of locomotives in Germany 1942–44. (*The Strategic Air War against Germany*)

Railroads have been vital to troop movements since the American Civil War. They played a significant role in World War I and, if anything, would play a more important part in World War II. As a major coal producer, Germany had a well-developed rail network, but the Reichsbahn entered World War II without having enjoyed the investment of the military industries. It had a pivotal and central role but most of the locomotives and rolling stock were old and it would only be later in the war that new classes came in. In 1936 the German Four-Year Plan had readied the country for war: tanks, aircraft, ships—the hardware was under construction as part of the plan. What was missing from that list was railroads. When the war began in 1939, the Deutsche Reichsbahn (DRB) had 23,000 locomotives—fewer than at the start World War I—plus 1,892 railcars, 69,000 passenger coaches, and 605,000 freight wagons.

Adam Tooze highlights the problems this lack of investment caused. In its most basic form, the German economy was dependent on coal and the railroad system was how it was moved around the country: "On any given day, at least a third of the tonnage shipped on the German

Logistics mean hard work: as here, with soldiers loading sacks into railroad cars—note the official stamp on the front sack. On the left is a Wehrmacht noncommissioned officer, in the center a senior sergeant major. The DRB had a range of goods wagons and acquired many others through conquest. The classes or types were given *Gattungszeichen*—class references—and the names of German cities. The first letter of the reference indicated type (e.g., G = *gedeckt* = covered, O = *offen* = open); second and subsequent identified characteristics such as weight. For example, the 15-tonne *gedeckter Güterwagen* (covered goods wagons) were given the "Gr" reference and named "Kassel"; the 20-tonne open wagons were "Om Königsberg"; and the four-axled 40-tonne-carrying wagons "SSl Köln." Some wagons were converted to run on Soviet rails and their *Gattungszeichen* would contain the letter "r"—so the "Ommr" wagons were O = open; mm = more than 20-tonne loaded weight, and r = capable of using the Russian broad gauge. (waralbum.ru)

railroad system consisted of coal and coal derivatives." The problems on DRB in 1939 and 1940—undercapacity for the volume of traffic—led to massive traffic jams, disastrous crashes, and coal shortages in both industry and civilian life. The acquisition of the rolling stock of the defeated countries of Western Europe helped—200,000 freight wagons were taken—but German railroads were problematic, and the problems would only get worse when the bombing started.

As the Germans acquired and conquered territory, so the size of the DRB expanded considerably from 54,000 km of track in 1937, to over 150,000 at the end of 1942, by which time it employed some 1.6 million workers. The first stage of this was the assimilation of Austrian railroads (ÖBB) and then those of Czechoslovakia—the new Protectorate of Bohemia-Moravia.

The man with his hand on the controls of the DRB was Julius Dorpmüller, and he oversaw the integration of Austrian and Czech railroads directly into the DRB. The acquisition of Poland saw a new increase of responsibilities. The railroads in territories that had been German until the end of World War I were reintegrated into the DRB: Danzig–W Prussia went into the West Prussian Gau and Posen (Poznan) into Warthe Gau.

The rest of Germany's share of Poland became the Generalgouvernement under Governor General Hans Frank, and a new organization was created: the Generaldirektion der Ostbahn (General Directorate of the Eastern Railway)—better known as Gedob. Gedob was a company outside the DRB, financially and economically responsible to Hans Frank although the DRB had to provide rolling stock and technical supervision. The new company's president was Adolf Gerteis. There was considerable friction between the DRB and Gedob. There

No coal, no industry. The German economy depended on coal and the Nazis used slave labor from Polish concentration camps, forced labor from other countries, Allied prisoners of war, and the local population to ensure that the rich coalfields of Silesia kept producing coal until the very end. These coal wagons at a marshaling yard in Upper Silesia await onward transit. (NAC)

were added complications when the Wehrmacht got involved, the two key players being Generalleutnant Rudolf Gercke, the transport chief (*Chef des Transportwesens*) of the Wehrmacht, and General Eduard Wagner, the OKH's *Generalquartiermeister*.

There had been some criticism of the DRB during the Polish campaign and there were rumors that Dorpmüller would be replaced by Gercke. There were also delays handing over the French railroads to the DRB, but Hitler was pleased enough with the DRB's performance to award Dorpmüller the War Merit Cross I. Klasse in September 1940, the Golden Party Badge of the NSDAP in December, and he went on to become a member of the NSDAP on January 28, 1941. The delays in France came because of the work of the *Eisenbahnpioniere* (railroad engineers—EBP) who had to make good the lines before handing them over to the DRB. The EBP were understaffed and to compensate, in March 1942 Gercke called up 50,000 DRB staff. These *feldgrauen Eisenbahnern* (field-gray railroad workers) would operate the *Feldeisenbahn Kommandos*, which worked in the area behind the front line.

The railroad logistics problems facing the Germans in the preparations for *Barbarossa* were immense. First, they had to convey the army, much of which was in the West, to their eastern jump-off points in secret. Second, they had to bridge the area of Poland they had taken and then the area under Soviet control. While the Soviet border defenses were still a long way from being finished, the rail lines from Poland into the Soviet Union weren't numerous and weren't in top condition. Third, they would have to combat increasing partisan resistance that rose from an attack a month in 1940 to 600 in 1942–43 and 800 between January and June 1944. All in all, Poland would prove a problem.

The first thing to do was to improve the trans-Polish lines and roads. This was accomplished by a secret rebuilding program codenamed *Otto*. It was ordered on August 9, 1940, for completion by May 10, 1941. This program took three months' steel from weapons production (300,000 tonnes) and 30,000 workers but it made a big difference. Before *Otto*, the lines through East Prussia and the Gedob could handle 198 pairs of trains a day—at 70–90 trains per division that's not much better than two divisions a day. After *Otto*, the new arrangements allowed for 468 pairs of trains to the River Vistula, and 396 to the Soviet border. These broke down into:

Otto Delivery Improvements		
Heeresgruppe	Pairs of trains daily	Extras
Nord	192	Plus Baltic shipping
Mitte	168	—
Süd	108	Plus more through Hungary and Romania

The new lines worked well for deployment of the attacking troops—every day there was an average of 2,500 military transports on the tracks. When June 21, 1941 dawned, most units and equipment were in place—although the attack on Yugoslavia and the Balkans disrupted the 24 divisions of the fourth attack wave. The logistical problems came after the operation commenced: as the German armored divisions attacked deep into the Soviet Union, resupply required more trains and stock than the Gedob could supply.

From the border, railroad operations became the province of the Wehrmacht under the department of Chef des Transportwesens Rudolf Gercke. It had officers with the armies, in the field, and at railroad stations. The speed of the German advances meant that they soon had a great deal of territory to control. In the first four weeks HG Nord advanced 600 km, Mitte 400 km, and Süd 400 km. The EBP (railroad engineers) once again had to come to the fore. They had to convert the Soviet broad gauge of 5 ft to European standard gauge

Julius Heinrich Dorpmüller (1869–1945)

Director general of the DRB from 1926, and Reich transport minister from 1937, Dorpmüller was well traveled and well respected internationally. The elder statesman of the Nazi cabinet, this international standing helped him keep his position despite heavy criticism at times and the usual Nazi ministerial infighting that saw attempts by many other Nazi leaders—particularly Speer—to take over his ministry. Indeed, Dorpmüller proved an adept player of the political games until the very end when, suffering from terminal cancer, he had to spend increasing amounts of time hospitalized. His prewar international standing meant that the Allies would have used him to reconstruct the Reichsbahn postwar had his cancer not finished him off. His reputation lasted intact until historians looked more closely at his and the Reichsbahn's relationship with antisemitism and involvement in furthering the Holocaust.

Dorpmuller (left) visits Krakow in 1942. At right, Hans Frank's deputy, Josef Bühler. The latter took part in the Wannsee Conference and was heavily implicated in the Holocaust. He was executed in 1947. The railway "special movements" (*Sonderzüge*) saw 2,000 trains move some three million people to the death camps—but the two trains a day only impinged slightly on the DRB's massive daily movements about the Reich, some 23,000 trains a day in 1944. (NAC)

(4 ft 8.5 in) and keep within 75 mi of the front line—something made more pressing thanks to the adroitness of the Soviets, which meant that the Germans were unable to capture much by way of rolling stock or locos. So, as well as regauging, the DRB soon had to hand over increasing numbers of its own locomotives and wagons to the East. On September 25, 1941, there were 1,885 DRB locomotives in the Soviet Union; on October 7, 1941, 2,915; on June 23, 1942, 5,307. These were mainly old freight locomotives, and they were controlled by the transport directorates (originally *Haupteisenbahndirektionen*, later *Reichsverkehrsdirektionen*):

Location of *Haupteisenbahndirektionen*, later *Reichsverkehrsdirektionen*		
Location	Subsequent moves	Disbanded
Riga	Bromberg (July 1944), Reppen (February 1945)	Reppen (end of war)
Minsk	Biyalystok (July 1944), Berent (July)	Berent (September 1944)
Lemberg	Kiev, Vinnitsa (September 1943), Lemberg (December 1943)	Krakow (July 1944).
Poltava	Dnepropetrovsk, Dolgintsevo (September 1943), Nikolayev (October), Uman (November), Birsula (February 1944), Odessa (March), Radom (April)	Berent (July 1944)

Supply problems were noticeable from the start. Halder noted in his diary on August 3, 1941:

> Gen Gercke report on railroad position.
>
> The chronic critical situation seems to be due to the following factors:
> 1.) Shortage in Russian rolling stock. We have captured very little, and that mostly in unserviceable condition. Shortage particularly acute in locomotives, almost all of which are in need of repairs.
>
> 2.) Conflicting demands of the troops and of the Gen Qu.
> In view of the appallingly bad roads, the troops want the railroads built to follow them as closely as practicable (the same need is felt on the Russian side). The result are long lines, i.e, railheads close to the front, but a low capacity of the lines, which at best meet only current requirements of the troops.

Most long-distance troop transport to and from the battlefield was by rail. The ability to rotate units or to move them to trouble spots would have proved impossible without rail, and despite all the problems the Germans proved adept at keeping the railroads running until close to the end: rebuilding bridges, relaying track, regauging rolling stock. The rail system wasn't, of course, just important for transportation of fighting men but of the many sick and wounded to hospitals. (Bundesarchiv, Bild 121-0650/CC-BY-SA 3.0)

But the Gen Qu. must stockpile i.e., he must assemble supplies in excess of current demands, and not too far from the troops. Such a program is predicated on railroad lines of high capacity. If then the railheads are farther behind the troops, the gap must be bridged by the 60-ton Truck Clms.

These divergent claims, i.e., long lines with lower capacity, which fill only troop requirements, versus shorter lines with higher capacity, which make it possible also to accumulate stores, can be reconciled only by Army Gp.

3.) Shortcomings of the German operating personnel, who are too slow and lack resourcefulness. Just as we saw in France, we now see in Latvia, that the State railroads are run more flexibly and efficiently than our railroads.

Shortcomings of signal communications. With the cooperation of the Army Gps, this situation will be remedied.

Unfortunately for the Wehrmacht, the problems weren't sorted out, leading to crisis in December. In fact, the EBP had few problems with track conversion: by August they had already converted 16,000 km. But they hadn't increased capacity, and they hadn't worked on the infrastructure. In August Halder said:

Clothing: Troops had been refitted; at beginning of the campaign they had a 5% clothing and 10% shoe reserve. Position now tight. Economies necessary in units in the West. Replacement units and newly activated units must now be equipped with lace boots and leggings instead of shaft boots. Winter clothing: Results of drive to return of winter clothing issued last winter, which had to be turned in by May, was very disappointing.

The West will have to shift for itself. For the East, sufficient stocks will arrive in depots of the Chief of Army Equipment before October. Problem of distribution. (Each man: two woolen vests, toques, earmuffs, gloves, scarves, chest warmers.)

Quarters: Now available 150,000 wooden barracks; like number can be supplied again by fall. 255 trains needed to bring them to the front. The transport problem to move such quantities make it desirable to build log cabins on the spot wherever possible. Organization Todt has been out on the job. Sample cabins are being erected; leading construction specialist have been assigned to the Armies and tools and fittings are issued in large quantities, later on, Organization Todt will carry out bigger projects on its own, e.g,. troop, training-centers in the Rear Area. Woolen blankets (up to three each man), bed linen, straw ticks, stoves, incidental furnishings (wash basins, jugs etc.) are held ready in large quantities; also kitchen kettles to save our field-kitchens, and lighting fixtures, lamps etc.

As the Soviets retreated, they made sure that little railroad infrastructure was available to the Germans. Rails, trackbeds, engine sheds, water towers—the Germans found most lines destroyed and most of the rolling stock and locomotives had been spirited away. (NAC)

Troop Trains

TM-E 30-451 identifies five types of troop train used by the Germans although it prefaces its remarks with the caveat that conditions (e.g., the mountainous regions of Europe such as Norway, Italy, and the Balkans) saw many variations.

Type	No. of cars	Load
K-trains (*Kraftfahrzüge* or motor vehicle trains)	51	250 men (or more depending on vehicle numbers), 20 heavy vehicles (up to 22 short tons each), 20 light vehicles, plus other equipment.
S-trains (*Sonderzüge* or special trains)	30–35	125 men, 4–6 Tiger tanks or similar heavy SP guns, 6–8 Panthers tanks, interspersed with lighter equipment.
Sp-trains (*Sonderpanzerzüge* or special tank trains)	33	20 medium tanks together with personnel and other equipment.
I-trains (*Infanteriezüge* or infantry trains)	55	350–800 men, 10 light vehicles, 10 heavy vehicles (up to 22 short tons each), and 70 horses, together with other equipment.[1]
Replacement troop trains	50–60	Over 2,000 replacements.[1]

[1] Allied airpower meant that latterly use of these types of train was discontinued.

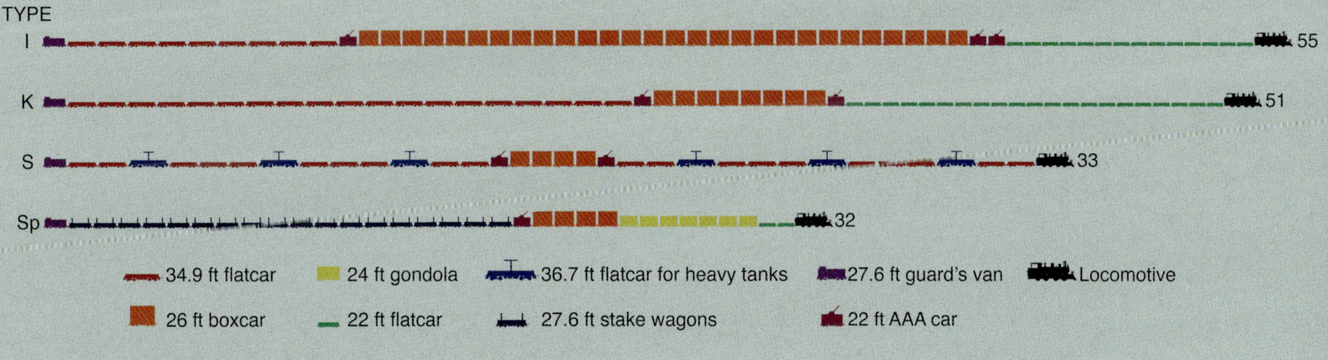

As we know, the winter clothing wasn't distributed on time. Frost and cold played havoc with German locomotives, and road transport was severely degraded. Halder again in his entry for December 4:

> Railroads:
> Construction of additional lines in Rear Area will increase elasticity but not capacity of system. The crux of the problem is in the railroad servicing installations (coal and water). Speed is dictated by bridges, strength of rails, railroad switching points, stations, signal network.

Soviet Railroads

In the sanitized, German-centric view of World War II promoted by the captured generals who wrote postwar, the travails of the German logistical system during *Barbarossa* were excused for a range of reasons: the low standard of the Soviet railroads, the need to regauge, the fact that German locomotives were bigger and heavier and couldn't be carried on Soviet tracks, the awful winter, and the poor state of the roads. While there may be elements of truth in this, most of these points are incorrect. Soviet railroads weren't as slick as the German, or as highly engineered, but they had a large enough workforce to cope with problems, could handle lots of long slow trains moving at 30 mph, and in the 1930s the Narodnyi Kommissariat Putei Soobshchenia (Narkomput or NKPS, People's Commissariat of Means of Communication, which was responsible for rail, road and waterways) moved almost as much freight as the United States and more passengers. Most—a third—of the traffic was carried by 10% of the tracks, the specially constructed lines for industrial traffic that carried 3,000-tonne trains and connected the Donets Basin, Moscow, Leningrad, and the Urals-Kuznetsk Combine.

The problem with the railroads in the Soviet Union wasn't the railroads, it was bad planning, the inefficiency of the German command structure, the conflicting infrastructure of command and control, and the interference of the military which meant the rail system never completely recovered from the way the Soviets had left it as they retreated.

> Centralized system of [German] not as easily managed as Russian decentralized organization. The signal installations are geared to the Russian system. Locomotive repair shops were completely wrecked by the Russians. Are operating again, but only in a makeshift fashion. We cannot increase number of engines, because we lack the requisite maintenance facilities, German engines are not built to withstand prevailing low temperatures. Transport of coal supply absorbs large volume of rolling stock.
>
> Not enough personnel (instead of 16 per km only 10, including one German); not accustomed to work under war conditions.

On December 15, 1941, Gercke met Reichsmarschall Göring and on December 16 the Führer. After these meetings a solution was put in place: from the beginning of 1942 the railroads behind the front were put under the control of the *Reichsminister* of Transport. Julius Dorpmüller set up an "Eastern Branch" in Warsaw, which took over the organization and operation of the railroads behind the Eastern Front with four main railroad directorates in Kiev, Minsk, Riga, and Dnepropetrovsk.

Three programs of work were put into effect by Dorpmüller in 1942–43:

- the initial Ostbau program employed 68,000 Soviet and 21,000 German workers to upgrade track and junctions;
- the winter 1942/43 program saw 40,000 workers used to upgrade the all-important infrastructure of depots and engine sheds;
- finally, the Ostbau 1943 program prepared the railroads for the Kursk campaign using 77,000 workers.

The reorganization could not solve all the transport problems, especially as there continued to be fierce disputes over authority between the ministry and Gercke. Additionally, Albert Speer did everything in his power to replace Dorpmüller. He didn't succeed, but Speer did get the responsibility for locomotive procurement and development moved from March 1942 to a newly founded Main Committee for Rail Vehicles under the former DEMAG company manager, Gerhard Degenkolb, who took over responsibility for the design and production of the new Class 52 *Kriegslokomotiven* (war locomotives) which would arrive in the fall.

Snowplows were essential in central Europe and the Soviet Union. (Bundesarchiv, Bild 101I-107-1311-33/CC-BY-SA 3.0)

In May 1942, Speer succeeded in having Deputy General Director of the DRB and State Secretary at the Reich Transport Ministry Wilhelm Kleinmann replaced by his appointee Albert Ganzenmüller, who was closely involved with the DRB's part in the Holocaust. From fall 1942, Dorpmüller whose cancer was worsening, was increasingly replaced by Ganzenmüller.

For *Fall Blau*, the summer campaign toward the Caucasus and its oilfields, there was a major effort to make good the anticipated destruction that retreating Soviet troops would leave behind. EBP, construction workers, Organization Todt: all were readied but they couldn't cope with the level of work needed, including rebuilding major bridges. They were able to restore the lines in places but never with enough capacity. This led to backlogs, with trains standing waiting for unloading. The captured Maikop oilfields, so important for the future—Konti Öl hoped for an output of 70,000 tonnes per month within six months of the oilfields reopening and had ordered the building of rail tankers to transport the oil in fall 1941—were in German hands from August 1942 to January 1943. During that time, the specialist team sent to restore the oilfields was so handicapped by lack of materials that no oil made it out. The retreat from the Kuban bridgehead in 1943 also stopped work on a railroad bridge over the Kerch Strait to replace a ropeway. The work had to be abandoned and destroyed: a permanent structure had to wait until 2014.

In October 1942, Dorpmüller was given sole administration of the entire transport system on railroads, roads, and waterways in the eastern territories. The previous branch office of the RVM in Warsaw became the

Operational Locomotives 1942–45

Date	RVDs	FEKdos
July 31, 1942	3,223	863
September 1942	3,545	1,176
December 31, 1942	4,047	1,464
March 31, 1943	4,399	704
June 30, 1943	4,472	1,075
September 30, 1943	4,381	443
June 30, 1944	1,664	93

General Verkehrsdirektion Osten (GVD Osten—General Traffic Directorate East). In January 1943 it was five times as large as the Gedob, employed a significantly greater workforce (over 100,000 Germans and over half a million Soviets as compared to the Gedob's 7,000/120,000) and more than twice the number of locos (over 4,500). GVD Osten was divided into the forward area operated by the *Feldeisenbahn Kommandos* and the rear area *Haupteisenbahndirektionen* became *Reichsverkehrsdirektion* which roughly matched the *Reichskommissariate*.

There were definite improvements as the DRB adapted its operational procedures and traffic management measures. In 1943, it recorded its highest ever freight transport performance with 178.6 billion tonne-km, and its highest passenger transport performance with 107.3 billion passenger-km. But there were clouds on the horizon: the Allied bombing campaign would only get worse, particularly in Italy and France as the invasion of Normandy neared. Soon transport figures fell significantly. Hitler honored Dorpmüller with the Knight's Cross of the War Merit Cross and on designated December 7 the Day of the German Railwayman (the first German railroad between Nürnberg and Fürth had been opened on that day in 1835).

In the West, 1944 saw significant air attacks on railroad infrastructure in northern France: the transportation plan saw railroad bridges, sidings, marshaling yards, and repair shops heavily bombed. Ground-attack aircraft knocked out as many locomotives as they could. The effect on German logistics was major. A German Air Ministry report of June 13, 1944, pointed out:

> The raids … have caused the breakdown of all main lines; the coast defenses have been cut off from the supply bases in the interior ... producing a situation which threatens to have serious consequences [and that] … large scale strategic movement of German troops by rail is practically impossible at the present time and must remain so while attacks are maintained at their present intensity. [Stephen Darlow, *D-Day Bombers, The Veteran's Story: RAF Bomber Command and the US Eighth Air Force Support to the Normandy Invasion, 1944.* Grub Street, 2004]

On June 6, Kampfgruppe Heintz attempted to move some 4,000 men of 275. Infanterie-Division's reinforced 984. Grenadier-Regiment from the south coast of Brittany to the invasion coast—a 120-mile train journey. It took them five days as Allied interdiction cut railroad lines and destroyed locomotives. In the end, having made no more than 75 miles by train in two days and three nights, the bulk of the unit had to march and the first elements—II./984—only arrived on bicycles in the evening of June 11 while I./984 arrived on the 13th. *Cross-Channel Attack* told the story:

> The Kampfgruppe took only about ten hours to assemble but was delayed in entraining by air attacks which blocked tracks, damaged locomotives, and generally interfered with the assembling of cars. These delays continued through the night, and by 08:00 the following morning only three sections of the Kampfgruppe had been loaded. In the afternoon five trains were under way; three were still being loaded. The lead train made good progress to Avranches, where at 14:00 it was held up by undetermined trouble ahead. While this was being cleared up, the rails behind it were cut. Late in the afternoon the train passed through Avranches and reached Folligny a few miles to the north. At Folligny, however, air attack destroyed it with total loss of vehicles and equipment and very heavy casualties. The second train in the meantime reached Pontorson but was there halted by rail cuts to the east. Under heavy air attack which took severe toll of the men and equipment of the engineer unit aboard, the train was unloaded and the troops ordered to continue on foot.
>
> All other trains en route on June 7 had been attacked and so delayed that at 18:00 they were still all south of Rennes. At that time it was reported that bombs had cut the rails in three places between Rennes and Dol and the whole movement was ordered rerouted via La Brohinière–Dinan–Dol. Scarcely had this decision been made when it was discovered that between Dinan and Dol the tracks were broken in no fewer than nineteen places. All during June 8 seven trains languished on the rails south of Rennes. Two other trains meanwhile were struggling to load artillery units of the Kampfgruppe and were being continually interrupted by air attacks. It

Kriegslok

The Reichsbahn's Class BR 52 2-10-0 was one of several classes of *Kriegslokomotiv* (war locomotive). From September 1942 it was ordered and built in large numbers—15,000 were ordered and over 6,000 built—in 20 factories across Europe and was one of the largest class of steam locomotives ever. Michael Reimer gives wartime production figures of:

1942	192
1943	3,828
1944	2,156
1945	28
TOTAL	6,204

Designed by Richard Wagner, they featured enclosed cabs to make cold weather use easier and were to be painted in gray (RAL 7011). The BR 52 was a pared-down version of the reliable Class BR 50, with many parts eliminated (such as the smoke deflectors), saving construction time and raw materials. The official term was *Entfeinerung*—de-refinement. To ensure delivery of large numbers, the main locomotive builders were formed into the Gemeinschaft Großdeutscher Lokomotivfabrike (Association of Greater German Locomotive Manufacturers). Manufacturing accelerated when Speer brought in the ambitious Gerhard Degenkolb to help push. His success in doing so was rewarded in early 1943 when he became head of a special committee producing the V2 rocket. In fact, production never reached the level required to build 15,000 locomotives but the change in conditions on the Eastern Front—the retreat toward the Reich—meant that fewer were needed.

Other *Kriegsloks* included the heavier two-cylinder Class 42 of which 837 were built in 1943 and 1944. These would have struggled on the Eastern Front where limitations on axle loads were demanding, as would Adolf Wolff's 1943 proposal for a 2-6-8-0 compound Mallet. The idea came too late to be put into production.

A pristine preserved Class 52 No 52 4867 at Zwingenberger (Bergstraße) Bahnhof on June 23, 2012. In wartime the smoke deflectors would almost certainly not have been there. Although railroads were hugely important to German logistics, they were well down the pecking order when it came to investment in the 1930s. (WikiCommons/Jivee Blau)

was 19:15 on June 8 before the last train got under way. Since no progress had been made to clear the route beyond Rennes on June 7, it had been decided to reroute the trains through Fougères. On June 9 the Fougères line was cut. The transportation officers then gave up. The troops of Kampfgruppe Heintz were all unloaded and ordered to proceed by truck or foot. The bulk of the unit had thus in two days and three nights traveled less than thirty miles. Three to five more days were consumed in the road march to the final assembly areas where the Kampfgruppe was attached to the 17. SS Panzergrenadier Division and put at once into the line southeast of Carentan.

The Final Solution

While it doesn't come within the scope of this book, the part the DRB played in the genocide and in the deaths of millions of Soviet PoWs and others needs to be mentioned. Like all other ministries, the RVM had supported the measures that discriminated against and persecuted Jews. Most deportations were carried out by rail: DRB officials had to timetable them and operate them. The DRB received payment for every "passenger" they carried and made a handsome profit as many of the cars were overfilled.

Partisans

It's easy to overstate the importance of the partisans and resistance fighters in Eastern and Western Europe during World War II. Extreme retaliation, hostage taking, and the killing of civilians reduced the number of actions by partisans until late in the war. However, in the Soviet Union, where the speed of the German advance trapped so many Red Army soldiers behind enemy lines, the numbers of partisans, their armaments, and their anti-German actions were always a problem for the military and civilian administrators in the captured areas. They certainly influenced German logistics, not just because of actual sabotage but because of the protection that had to be afforded to rail and road traffic, and the efforts that had to be expended by the *Sicherungsdivisionen* and regular army units in anti-partisan sweeps.

The amount of help the partisans received differed widely. There are many stories about Lysander operations in Western Europe landing spies and munitions by moonlight. In the East, the Soviet command was initially ambivalent: first, because they felt soldiers who weren't fighting were deserters; second, because they were concerned that partisans would end up unsympathetic to the communist cause. However, their numbers and value eventually led to official assistance and the effectiveness of the partisans grew.

For example, the preparations for *Unternehmen Zitadelle* were well known to the Soviets and partisan raids were supported to disrupt supply lines and prevent the deployment of transports. On March 7/8, 1943, partisans led by Mikhail Petrovich Romashin, commander of the Briansk Partisan Detachment and later of the N. A. Shchorsa Brigade, destroyed the bridges over the River Navila and the Desna near Vygonichi. The bridge on the Gomel–Bryansk road was of strategic importance for troops and vehicles and was out of action for over two weeks. Between April and June 1943, partisan bands damaged 298 locomotives, 1,222 wagons, and 44 bridges.

Partisan operations led to a real feeling of fear in certain areas behind the front lines and played a large part in affecting the logistics of the Wehrmacht.

Retreat

The retreating German Army did what it could to destroy railroad infrastructure and stock in the same way the Soviets had done, wherever possible sending locos and wagons back to safety. Examples abound: Red Army troops reached the suburbs of Kharkov on August 4, 1943. It took them 18 days to capture the city, by which time the Wehrmacht had destroyed vast quantities of food, medicines, equipment, weapons, ammunition, etc.

In March 1943, the Rzhev–Vyazma front was attacked. The evacuation lasted for some three weeks, March 1–21. Around 200 trains transported away 100,000 tonnes of evacuated goods.

And despite the bombing, even a few weeks before the end of the war the railroads were able to move 6. SS-Panzerarmee from the Ardennes to Hungary. The units, loaded on icy roads, went back to the Reich for refreshment, before 290 trains took the *Panzerarmee* 1,200 km in 10 days—a journey that would have taken a day and a half in the past.

Road

Getting equipment, fuel, food, or anything to the front could be a problem, particularly in the East. By August 1941 the number of working trucks in the logistical network had dropped below 60%. As we have seen, the winter clothing and equipment that had been readied for the troops couldn't be moved forward because of lack of rail capacity. Tactically, *Unternehmen Barbarossa* didn't just fail because of transport and supply problems in the winter of 1941/42. The soldiers on the ground improvised brilliantly and the higher command learnt from its mistakes: by winter 1942/43 most of the cold weather issues had been rectified. But that doesn't get round the fact that a key reason for *Barbarossa*'s failure was that resupply of the troops in the field was compromised by lack of transport mainly caused by the lack of operational vehicles, because the planners had confidently expected to have won before winter. Strategically, the fact that the war in the East didn't end in 1941 meant that German supply issues would play an increasing part in the battle, and lack of adequate motor transport played a large part in this.

The knock-on effects caused problems everywhere. Müller-Hillebrand identified the difficulties for *Panzer* repair:

> The supply lines were overextended at the time when the muddy season set in. Most of the roads in Russia became impassable and truck columns were therefore unable to move up supplies. At the same time the railroads proved incapable of carrying the entire supply load. Damaged tanks could not be repaired for lack of spare parts and could not be evacuated to the zone of interior because of the transportation bottleneck.

The original caption to these photographs of corduroy road construction talks of the struggle of RAD men against swamp and sand at Fastow, today's Fastiv in Ukraine. Note the Hf. 7 iron transport wagon. (NARA)

Rasputitsa

The *Rasputitsa* turned roads into quagmires where all motor transport—and most horse-drawn—units struggled to move anywhere. The wagon shown is the Hf. 7 (*Heeresfahrzeug* = army vehicle) Stahlfeldwagen, a large steel field wagon with a deadweight of 1 ton which could carry a payload of 1.5 tons. The Hf. 7 became famous as the "horse murderer" in these conditions and this was eventually recognized. It was often towed by the attachment of a drawbar. (NAC)

Leibstandarte in Ukraine, December 1943: 13./SS-Panzer-Regiment 1's MAN ML 4500 fuel truck is stuck in the mud. Behind it, the regiment's Tigers await their fuel—note the 200 l (53 gal) drum. At right, an SS NCO—probably an *Oberscharführer*—wears a "crusher" *Schirmmütze*. (Dutch Archives)

Horse-drawn motorcycle—this photograph illustrates well the problem of the *rasputitsa*. (Dutch Archives)

Even a Schwimmwagen makes heavy going in the conditions. This one belongs to the Leibstandarte—as per the skeleton-key insignia below the driver's mirror. Note the Panthers in the background, the winter gear and camouflaged helmet covers of the men, and the paddle clipped to the side of the vehicle. It had a top speed of 50 mph on land and 6 mph on water. (Dutch Archives)

The problems were exacerbated using *Beutewaffen* (booty weapons—materiel taken from subjugated countries). While the weapons—often excellent equipment—went mainly to the Ersatzheer, or coastal defense in the case of the artillery, *Barbarossa* saw large numbers of foreign vehicles in service. Liedtke suggests nearly 5,000 Renault UE Chenillette tracked vehicles and at least 13,000 French trucks meant that "40 of the 151 divisions assigned to 'Barbarossa' were equipped with captured vehicles"—this was on top of "an unknown percentage of the truck fleet belonging to the army's vital supply services" also being of foreign design. These contributed to some 2,000 different types of vehicle—a spare-parts nightmare. In the short term, these vehicles were vital but after the Axis failed to achieve its aim of a short war, the road haulage fleet—and its maintenance—proved to be a continuing nightmare. Leidtke highlights the difficulties:

> Between June 1941 and the end of June 1942, the Wehrmacht had lost at least 127,731 motor vehicles and even larger numbers were in various stages of disrepair. On February 20, 1942, Heeresgruppe Süd reported that it had suffered the Totalausfalle of 23,526 of its motor vehicles since the start of operations in the East: even more disconcertingly, out of the 86,757 it still possessed, some 70,969 (81%) were not operational because they required some kind of significant overhaul or repair.

On the march, when contact with the enemy was not expected and road conditions allowed, service parties—particularly those dealing with fuel supply, repair, and rations—would be a part of the advance. Fuel was an omnipresent concern. Tanks were filled at every stop. (NAC)

This problem continued on every front. In Normandy Panzer Lehr recorded 60% of its trucks being of foreign origin.

The German supply chain required trucks to take supplies from dumps at the railheads to the front. They couldn't do that if they weren't working, or the roads were impassable—and the railheads needed to be as close to fronts as possible. The situation got worse as the war went on. Ziemcke:

> The motor vehicle industry was hard hit both by bomb damage to its plants and by the breakdown of the railroads. In October and November 1944, the assembly plants turned out 12,000 trucks by rebuilding all the disabled Army trucks that could be found in Germany. In December only 3,300 of the 6,000 new trucks needed were produced, and Hitler earmarked 70 percent for the offensive in the West. In January the truck strengths authorized for panzer and panzergrenadier divisions would have to be reduced 25 percent, and the Army would have to begin mounting the panzergrenadiers on bicycles. Hitler tried to console himself with thoughts that the armored divisions had too many vehicles anyway, that the time of the sweeping maneuver was past, and that, if it came down to cases, the infantry divisions could move faster than the so-called mobile divisions, which he said only created traffic jams.

Fuel consumption is difficult to gauge in peacetime, let alone in combat in the mud and poor terrain. This boosts considerably the amount of fuel and oil used as well as leading to track and automotive issues. On August 6, 1941, less than two months into *Barbarossa*, LVII. Panzerkorps identified vehicles using 20–30 l of oil per 100 km rather than the planned half-liter, thanks to driving in first gear over rough terrain. Lack of fuel (in late November 1941 2. Panzerarmee received only a third of its fuel requirements) and maintenance meant that by December 5, 1941, 4. Panzer-Division reported that they had but 15% of their *Panzer*, 34% of their transport, and 10% of their motorcycles operational.

Traffic Control

The movement of large units, especially those that involved heavy equipment—particularly tanks—needed to very carefully marshaled. Key to the smooth running was the *Feldgendarmerie*. Most were usually under the command of the division operations officer, although a small number were permanently assigned to the supply staff section.

The main traffic control functions were to:

- Post signs and mark routes.
- Control traffic at key points and reroute local traffic in emergencies or because of tactical exigencies.
- Control traffic at the division command post.
- Supervise movements to the rear along designated routes such as barrier and straggler lines.

The elements under the division supply staff were to:

- Post signs, mark routes, and direct traffic along the division supply roads.
- Control traffic at division supply installations to prevent congestion at ammunition, fuel, and ration distributing points.
- Direct traffic at division rear echelon headquarters.

Because MPs had other police functions, it was rare for the full detachment to be available for traffic control duties. A *Panzer* division traffic control post was normally composed of four MPs and a messenger using two light personnel carriers and a motorcycle (although *Kettenkrads* and other transport were also employed). At full strength, 12–15 traffic control posts could be established. But when you include sickness, combat losses, furloughs, or other vacancies, in practice usually no more than six to eight control posts could be established.

In unusual situations or under extremely critical circumstances traffic control elements of an MP battalion from a higher headquarters were sometimes placed at the disposal of a division in platoon or company strength for limited periods or within specific areas. Some personnel always had to be held in reserve to cope with emergency situations.

In many instances—during retrograde movements and especially river crossings—a suitable officer (often from the division replacement pool) was designated the staff officer for march supervision (*Stabsoffizier für Marschüberwachung—Stoma*). What began as an emergency improvisation soon became an established staff position throughout the Soviet theater.

Ensuring that the roads were up to scratch was another important factor and a job that was often performed by service troops.

One of the problems with the advance into the Soviet Union was the paucity of good maps. The German maps of Russia proved inadequate. Maps showing road widths and surfaces, bridge capacities, and the condition of potential traffic bottlenecks—

Above and Left: The SdKfz 2 Kleines Kettenkraftrad HK 101 (where *klein* = small, *Ketten* = chains or tracks, and *Kraftrad* = motorcycle), commonly known as the Kettenkrad, was a halftrack motorcycle with a single front wheel. Originally designed for airborne troops and able to fit inside a Ju 52 or glider, it was a versatile workhorse with offroad capability. With one driver it could carry two passengers, a 500 kg load, and was able to tow a small multipurpose trailer or a small gun such as a PaK 35/36. Its many capabilities included cable laying, weapons carrier, rations and water carrier, and scouting, to name but a few. (SF Collection/NAC)

A Vomag 7OR 660 carrying an 8.8 cm FlaK. Vomag was known for its heavy buses and trucks and the outstanding—on good roads—7OR 660 Omnibus with its 150 hp engine which was introduced in 1935. In early 1940, 20-odd chassis were rebuilt as Selbstfahrlafette auf Fahrgestell Vomag 7OR 660 mit 8.8 cm FlaK—SP AA guns armed with the 8.8 cm FlaK 36. Used exclusively by I./FlaK-Regiment 42, the vehicles proved less than capable of dealing with poor Soviet roads. Note extra armor protection over the hood. (Akira Takiguchi)

such as defiles, steep inclines, and major intersections—were seldom available. The onus of advance-route reconnaissance fell on military police and often took place during the march itself. Because road conditions were frequently influenced by recent demolitions and seasonal weather changes, reconnaissance during a march was necessary to check the validity of previously reported facts. That mobile warfare and the movement of armor in Russia could be conducted successfully only after thorough advance reconnaissance was one of the first lessons the Germans had to learn.

The Mercedes-Benz L3000 medium general-purpose 4 × 2 truck had a 3-ton load capacity. A versatile vehicle suitable for various roles—cargo, troops, and light artillery or AA guns. It was the second most common transport after the Opel Blitz, but more reliable. All transport needed regular maintenance as here. Note FFK7 on the car door. FFK = *Feld-Fern-Kabelbau* = field trunk wire construction. (SF Collection)

The Krupp Protze was a utility six-wheeled *Gelandewagen* (all-terrain vehicle) with various roles, the main being as the Kfz 69 PaK 36 tower and the Kfz 70 personnel carrier that transported 10 men plus driver and his "oppo." (SF Collection)

Signals line layer with backpack cable reel harness about to pass a static convoy in Grodno (today's Hrodna in Belarus), August 1941. In the background is the Church of the Discovery of the Holy Cross. The heavily laden 6 × 4 Tatra heavy cargo truck has drop sides for ease of loading/unloading and carries an eclectic mix of cargo. (Dutch Archives)

Hungarian Army 1.5-ton 6 × 4 all-terrain 38M Botond trucks with Hungarian-pattern camouflage covers make their way forward in August 1941. They could carry 1,500 kg or 14 personnel. They probably belong to the *Gyorshadtest*, the Rapid Corps, which was the most motorized of the Hungarian units that went reluctantly to war in June 1941. (Dutch Archives)

While the bulk of German infantry marched alongside horse-drawn carts, the exception was motorized infantry divisions. However, there were never enough trucks, even after locally manufactured vehicles were requisitioned from all occupied territories, the huge inventory adding complicated mechanical needs and leading to spares availability problems. Photo taken as German troops entered Lviv in 1941. Many residents hoped the Germans would back Ukrainian calls for independence. (NAC)

A column of 17. Panzer-Division vehicles in summer 1941. Note the tactical marking on the front of the Adler 12N 3G in left foreground. On the right is a Horch 901 staff car—Horch's variant of the Einheits-Pkw Kfz 12. (In German *Horch* = listen; today, Horch's parent company is Audi which means listen in Latin.) It also provided the standard signals vehicle (Kfz 15); the larger Horch 108 was issued to mechanize some antitank companies. This vehicle's mudguard identification marking has been censored. Note the air recognition flag over the hood. (NAC)

Horch 8 Type 40 staff car monitoring an offroad incident. Many accidents were caused by mechanical failures or the terrain, but tiredness was probably the most common reason, although poor training also contributed. There's not much room to pass stranded vehicles on these sorts of roads, so they were often pushed to one side until mechanics could repair them—a long lonely wait for a crew, especially in an area where partisans were present. (RCT)

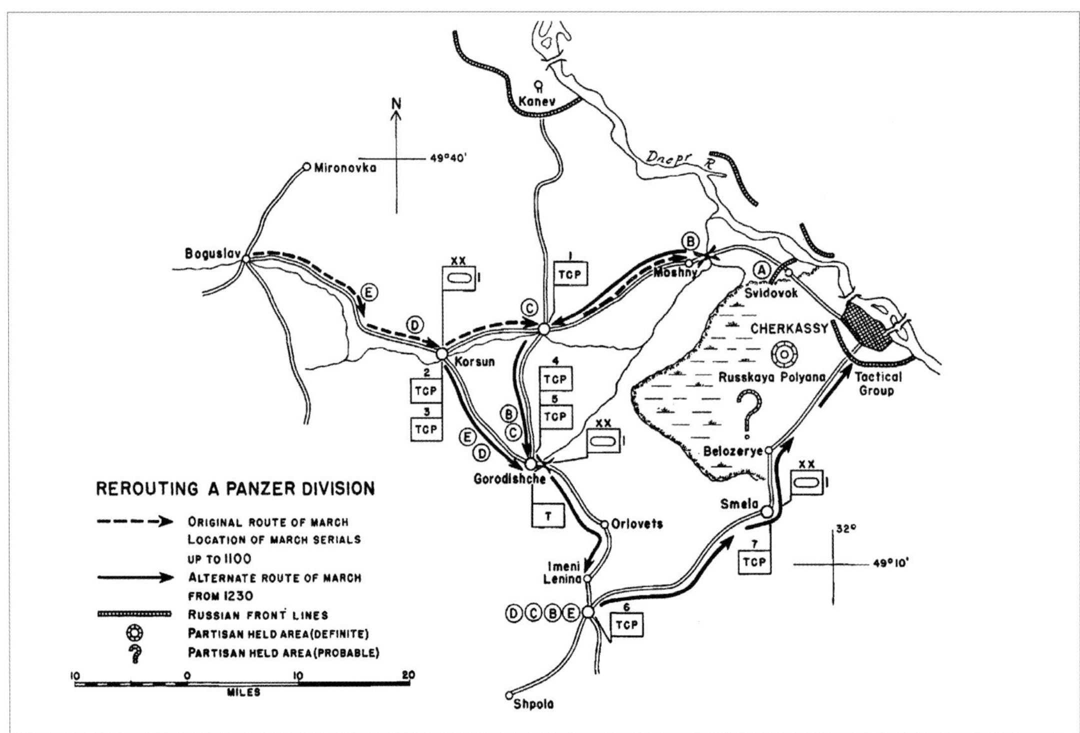

As an example, Müller-Hillebrand's *German Armored Traffic Control*, uses an incident during summer 1941. (See map above.) 1. Panzer-Division had been alerted to attack south of Kiev. 17. and 6. Armeen had thrown the Russians back across the Dnieper, although the Soviets still maintained bridgeheads at Kremenchug, Cherkassy, Kanev, and Kiev. A weak German tactical group had been fighting east of Cherkassy in an unsuccessful attempt to reduce the small enemy bridgehead. 1. Panzer-Division was ordered to eliminate this bridgehead.

On July 25, 1941, the division was formed into five march serials (A–E) and began its advance from Mironovka via Korsun and Moshny to Cherkassy. Elements of the division reconnaissance battalion, March Serial A, reached the northern outskirts of Svidovok, approximately six

The chronic lack of vehicles produced in Germany meant that requisition of transport from occupied territories was the norm. The downside was the ability to maintain them, especially over the vast distances covered during *Barbarossa*. The photo shows requisitioned vehicles being maintained. The pole with a "ball" on top is a guide for the driver to follow the edge of the road, something the author, as an inquisitive child living in Germany in the 1950s, remembers having explained to him. (SF Collection)

Just what isn't wanted during an advance: traffic jams the roads as the attack on Belgium—*Fall Gelb*—gets underway. Later in the war this sort of sight would be manna from heaven for Allied Typhoon or P-47 fighter-bombers, but the Germans had yet to learn to fear the *Jabos*. Note at right the Feldküche als Anhänger (einachsig) fahrbar (SdAh 401)—mobile field kitchen as a trailer (single-axle) as opposed to the Hf. 14 kleine Feldküche which was horse-drawn. (SF Collection)

miles northwest of Cherkassy. About 11:00 they reported that the northern section of the town was held by strong Soviet forces, and that the column had lost almost 50% of its men and materiel from mines, air attacks, and antitank weapons, and from artillery fire from emplacements on the east bank of the Dnieper.

On top of this, enemy prisoners, captured maps, and statements of local civilians confirmed the suspicion that a strong partisan band was concentrated in the wooded, swampy region around Russkaya Polyana. The division command post was in Korsun when this report was received. Meanwhile, March Serial B, consisting of tanks, had reached Moshny. It reported that the bridge east of the town had been destroyed and that, because of the steep embankment, the heavy vehicles were unable to cross the stream. The use of a ford was also precluded because heavy thunder showers had softened the approach roads, making them impassable. The remaining march serials—not including the trains—had meanwhile executed their respective movements according to the previously established march schedule. Thus, they were strung out along the Boguslav–Moshny road and offered an inviting target to enemy aircraft.

Had advance-route reconnaissance been properly conducted, considerable confusion and time-consuming rerouting of the division could have been saved.

Toward 12:00, division headquarters by radio ordered all march serials to halt the march in the direction of Moshny and await recall orders from the Stoma for rerouting via Imeni Lenina, and Smela to Belozerye. March Serial A, the reconnaissance battalion, had to remain at Svidovok to tie down the enemy forces there, and was not to fall back on Moshny except under severest Soviet pressure. March Serial B was to turn around and proceed to the intersection 10 miles east of Korsun, from where, upon receipt of radio orders, it was to resume the march in the new direction about 15:00. The Stoma was charged with the organization and execution of

March Speeds and Distances

(1) Divisional Marches (mph) (*TM-E 30-451*)		
Unit	By day	By night
Infantry division	3	3
Motorized division	16	10
Armored division	12	7

(2) March Columns (mph) (*TM-E 30-451*)	
Unit	Speed
Infantry (long marches)	3
Infantry (short marches)	4
Mounted troops	6
Cyclists	8
Motorcycles and cars	22
Trucks	22
Trucks with trailers	16
Half-track vehicles	16
Tanks	12

A Waffen-SS license-plated NSU 251 OSL (overhead valve, sport, luxury) scaffold-front-fork motorcycle struggles with the conditions: cloying mud that went on for miles, stopped engines from running, and exhausted men and horses. Two despatch riders (*Kradmelder*) struggle to release the bike from the mud—note rubberized coats and SS camouflaged helmet covers. (SF Collection)

(3) March Distances (*TM-E 30-451*)	
Unit	Distance
Infantry division	20 miles in a day; 10 miles a day adverse weather or road conditions
Motorized division	90–150 miles
Armored division	60–90 miles a day
Division by road without motor transport	10–15 miles a day
Movement by motor transport	30 miles a day

(4) Road Spaces (*TM-E 30-451*)		
Infantry division (at 3 mph)	Yards	Meters
Inf Regt (each of three)	6,234	5,700
Rcn Bn	3,116	2,850
AT Bn	2,734	2,500
Arty Regt	7,382	6,750
Sig Bn	3,193	2,920
Engr Bn	2,570	2,350
Div Serv	4,155	3,800
Div Hq	1,553	1,420
TOTAL	43,405 = 24.7 miles*	39,690
Armored division (at 12 mph)	Yards	Meters
Tank Regt	21,325	19,500
Pz Gren Regt (each of two)	13,145	12,020
Pz Rcn Bn	9,154	8,370
AT Bn	3,838	3,510
Pz Arty Regt	14,458	13,220
Pz Sig Bn	3,762	3,440
Pz Engr Bn	6,365	5,820
Div Serv	11,702	10,700
Div Hq	1,444	1,320
Others	5,468	5,000
TOTAL	103,806 = 59 miles*	94,920

* If distances between the individual units are included, the average length of the infantry division would be about 30 miles (at 3 mph), of the armored division 70 miles (at 12 mph), and of the motorized division 80 miles (at 16 mph).

A transport unit takes the opportunity to wash themselves and their vehicles. (SF Collection)

The *Feldgendarmerie Trupp* (military police detachment) came under the heading of service troops and among their responsibilities was traffic control: keeping the flow of troops and supplies, ammunition, food, fuel, spare parts, clothing, etc. moving. Their key identification features were their *Feldgendarmerie* cuff title (barely visible in this photo) and the *Ringkragen* (gorget) on a chain worn when on duty and giving them their nickname of "chained dogs." It had a dull matt silver finish; the bosses, eagle, and swastika emblems were finished in a luminous paint, and the scroll was dark field gray with lettering picked out in luminous paint. They weren't appreciated by the rank and file because law and order was also an MP responsibility. This MP points his field paddle in the direction the Audi must go. He's wearing a DRL sports badge and carries a torch and binos. Note the *Troddel* (tassel) hanging from his bayonet. Next to him is a Hungarian traffic controller wearing a white armband. (Dutch Archives)

the rerouting operation. The division MP detachment was placed under his direct command and was broken down into seven traffic control posts, each consisting of five men who had two light personnel carriers and one motorcycle at their disposal. This was the maximum number of control posts that could be established since the detachment was organized according to 1941 tables of organization. No radio equipment was available, and the motorcycle messengers were the only means of communication. When conditions permitted, the radio facilities of the march serials were used by the traffic control personnel. The division command post was temporarily located in Gorodishche, where the Stoma also established his central traffic regulation headquarters. The latter was staffed by one officer and five enlisted men, equipped with two light personnel carriers and two motorcycles. The Stoma issued the following instructions to the individual traffic control posts:

> Post 1: March Serial C will move out upon receipt of radio orders about 14:00 and is to be guided to Gorodishche along the Kanev–Gorodishche road. The intersection will, meanwhile, be blocked to all other traffic. About 16:00 March Serial B, upon receipt of radio orders, is to proceed behind Serial C and is to be conducted to Gorodishche along the Kanev–Gorodishche road. During this movement only limited traffic is permitted from south to north.
>
> Post 2: About 12:30 March Serial D is to be conducted from the southeast exit of Korsun to Gorodishche along the Korsun–Gorodishche road. This road is to be closed to vehicles of other march units. March Serial E will be called by radio and is to proceed behind Serial D, probably beginning at approximately 17:00.
>
> Post 3: This post will control the flow of traffic within Korsun in close coordination with the commanders of March Serials D and E.
>
> Posts 4 and 5: These posts will guide march serials through Gorodishche according to the following schedule: March Serial D from 13:00, while blocking north–south traffic. March Serial C from about 14:00, while blocking east–west traffic. March Serial B from approximately 16:30, while blocking east–west traffic. March Serial E from about 1800, while blocking north–south traffic.

The notice announces: *Wichtige Nachschubstrasse. Behandle Sie daher mit derselben Liebe wie deine Soldatenbraut*—Important supply route. So treat it with the same love that you give your soldier bride. (SF Collection)

Various directions to locations are given, but note *Nachschub* = supplies for the two indicated units 1. Panzerdivision (left) and 8. Panzerdivision (right). The motorcycle is a BMW R12. (SF Collection)

Post 6: Personnel will reconnoiter the road leading southeast from Gorodishche, as well as the bridge directly east of the town, and report their findings at once. After 1630 they will direct and guide all march serials through the intersection southeast of Imeni Lenina, while blocking the roads leading south and southwest from the intersection.

Post 7: This post will reconnoiter traffic facilities within Smela and guide march serials through the town and northeastward via Belozerye. Then, it will plainly mark the route through the town with divisional road signs and post control personnel near all potential traffic bottlenecks by 15:00.

Above: U.S. Army GIs of 83rd Infantry Division look at the signage at Place Poincaré in Paramé near Saint-Malo:

Platzkommandantur	Area command center
Standortkommandantur	Local command center
Feldgendarmerie	MPs
Ulla	Unknown
OT Frontleitstelle am Bahnhof	OT front control center at the railroad station
NSKK 64	National Socialist Motor Corps unit 64
Red Cross Bunker	Red Cross bunker
Hafenarzt und Revier	Harbor doctor and area
Haf-Überwachungsstelle	Port monitoring center
Ortskrankenstube	Local infirmary
Soldatenheim	Soldiers' home (R&R)
HKP 528	Heereskraftfahrpark 528 army MT park
Wehrmachttankstelle für feste Kraftstoffe	Wehrmacht filling station for solid fuels
Wehrmacht Nachschubstab KJ	Wehrmacht supply staff

(NARA)

Two German traffic controllers on a street in the occupied Soviet town of Opochka. Behind them the signs include AVL = *Armeeverpflegungslager* = army rations dump; a route identification toward *Newel über Pustosch* = Nevel via Pustoshka (a journey today of 113 km) and behind that Kfz Inst = *Kfz-Instandhaltung* = vehicle maintenance. (SF Collection)

The projected time schedule for rerouting the division could not be fully adhered to. Toward 13:30, Post 6 reported that the bridge near the eastern outskirts of Gorodishche was demolished. This meant that a ford had to be found as an alternate crossing point. The lead column, Serial D, was therefore unable to continue the march from Gorodishche until 14:30. As a result, the tail march serial failed to arrive in Smela until late in the evening, and the division—except for patrols—could not be committed against the Cherkassy bridgehead until the following day, 26 July.

From a purely tactical point of view, it was primarily the neglect of thorough route reconnaissance that led to the initial ill-fated advance via Moshny. The division had to be completely rerouted, a time-consuming operation which delayed its planned commitment by a whole day. Since March Serial A, the reconnaissance battalion, after having sustained heavy losses, had to remain at Svidovok and maintain contact with the enemy there, the division was at least temporarily deprived of some of its striking power. Fortunately, the speed with which the traffic control system was reorganized and the complete absence of enemy air activity over the alternate route of advance partially compensated for the disadvantages of the rerouting process.

German experience showed that centralized traffic control assumed particular importance during river crossings involving armored forces. In planning for such operations, the following points deserve special attention:

1. Defensive forces to protect the crossing sites and engineer elements to maintain the crossing facilities should be available in sufficient strength, at the right time, and at the right place.
2. The steady flow of traffic must not be interrupted by traffic jams of any sort. Traffic congestion, especially at the crossing sites, is an easy and a remunerative target for enemy aircraft and artillery and should be avoided at all costs.
3. Only those vehicles of weights below the maximum capacity of individual bridges and other crossing facilities should be permitted to approach the crossing sites.
4. Messenger vehicles must be able to always move freely in both directions.
5. It should always be possible to evacuate casualties, if necessary, even against crossing traffic.
6. When a river crossing is to be forced during an attack, the initial crossings should be restricted to those combat and support elements that are essential to the rapid seizure and buildup of the bridgehead on the far shore. The follow-up forces that remain behind must be well dispersed and camouflaged.

The intersection of Marx (then Kossuth Lajos) Street and Lenin (then Rákóczi) Street in Ostrogoshsk in 1942. As well as the location direction signs, note that to the AVL. (Fortepan/Hungarian Archives)

River Crossings and Bridging

The Soviet Union has big rivers. This one (above) is the Bug and the photograph comes from an album of Infanterie-Regiment (mot) 15, part of the 29. (Falke) Infanterie-Division, showing the regiment crossing the Bug during the thrust toward Kiev in September 1941. To cross a river like this, first a bridgehead needed to be established—usually by crossing the river in assault boats (opposite, center and below)—but often under fire. If the river were small enough a bridge would be improvised and a larger pontoon bridge would be built later. Later still, a larger more-permanent structure might also be constructed or an existing bridge repaired—as here (opposite, above) where German engineers are repairing the Varvarovsky bridge. The Ukrainian city of Nikolaev (today's Mykolaiv) can be seen on the far shore of the Bug. (NARA, above/NAC opposite, top/SF Collection opposite center and below)

Combat in the East emphasized:

> The route of advance of the Eleventh Army cut across the lower course of four great rivers, the Prut, Dniester, Southern Bug and Dnjepr [Dnieper]. The importance of these rivers for moving supplies was great. A considerable part of the army supply columns was continuously needed for transporting timber used in building emergency bridges to replace the military pontoon bridges and was thus temporarily unavailable for supply purposes. As many of the long bridges were one-way affairs, they formed bottlenecks which delayed the supply runs.
>
> In August the Dniester rose seven meters above its normal level and swept away all bridges. Ten days were required to rebuild them. During this period all supply movements from Romania were interrupted and had to be replaced by shipments from the north where railway construction had progressed to a further extent. The emergency bridge across the Dnjepr near Berislav became unusable during the winter because of drifting ice. The same was true of the railway ferries used in summer. Consequently, all supplies for the Eleventh Army fighting in the Crimea had to be transshipped across the frozen Dnjepr on trucks or horse-drawn sleighs. Various plans for the building of cable railways were not carried out as their capacity would not have sufficed to move eighty railway cars or so per day.

Bridging Equipment

The German Army had a range of bridges (*Brückengeräte*) and the bridging columns (*Brückenkolonnen*—shortened to *Brücko*) that erected them. There were several different bridge types, the Type A being Reichswehr material incorporating zinc-plated sheet steel pontoons that could construct bridges or rowed ferries. The Type B medium combat bridge could make 8-ton bridges (pontoon trestle bridges) up to 83 m in length, 16-ton bridges to 54 m, and 4-ton/8-ton/16-ton ferries. This combination could

sFH 18 prepares to cross a pontoon bridge over the Bug, 1941. (SF Collection)

carry 18-ton wheeled and 20–24-ton tracked vehicles (heavier because their footprint was reduced by tracks). Other bridging types included light recce bridges (Type D), light combat bridges (Type C), mountain bridges (Type G), and the medium combat Type T bridges, of Czech design, which were attached to many infantry divisions in both motorized and horse-drawn forms. The most important of the others was the Type K, a readymade box-girder bridge supported on pontoons and trestles (a heavier version, the J Type, was used by armored divisions). Used in assaults, it could bridge short gaps quickly and carry 27 tons. Other fixed bridges included leichte Z Brücke and the heavier H (Herbert) Type.

The basic transport tools of the *Brückenkolonnen* were the *Bockwagen* (Pf. 8, 10, or 14 support wagons), the *Pontonwagen* (Pf. 9, 11 or 15 pontoon wagons) and *Rampenwagen* (Pf. 12 ramp wagons) that carried the bridge parts. For example, a Brückegerät B had a nominal TOE (1 June 1944) of one officer, 20 NCOs, 104 men, 41 vehicles (trucks, motorcycles, SdKfz 7s, and a Schwimmwagen) and was carried by eight Pf. 8s, 16 Pf. 9s, two Pf. 12s, and had two trailers for assault dinghies (*Anhänger für Sturmboote*) and two for motorboats (*Anhänger für M-Boote*). Most of the bridging equipment was truck- or halftrack-drawn but a lot of it could be horse-drawn.

Bridging at the start of the war was the province of the engineer battalion, but they were sometimes grouped together and assigned from the army GHQ engineer pool, particularly if the division was operating in terrain where bridging was unnecessary. In 1942 this ad-hoc arrangement was confirmed, and the bridging columns became independent.

Troops queue to cross a damaged but usable bridge during the campaign in the West. In 1940 the Germans used *Fallschirmjäger* to capture key bridges before they could be blown. At the Corinth Canal in 1941 they did exactly that but then, while removing the charges, the stacked explosives exploded and destroyed the captured bridge. (RCT)

Improvisation was critical to ensure continuity of supply. This rickety crossing is testing the Krupp L3 H163 driver's skills. Some 2,000 of the L3 H63/L3 H163 models were produced up till 1938. They proved versatile in many forms by the Wehrmacht in the early war years. (SF Collection)

The German Army experimented with bridge-laying tanks based on the PzKpfw I, II, and IV chassis. Most had their turrets removed; some PKpfw IIs kept theirs. They were issued to the bridging units of the panzer divisions but the order for 60 was canceled after the French campaign. Crew was two or three, and much of the bridge-laying apparatus was manufactured by Magirus GmbH of Ulm.

In all 20 Brückenleger IVs were produced with a 9 m bridge that had a 28-ton capacity. Too heavy for its suspension, the tank was canceled. Most were converted back to regular gun tanks. In January 1941, Krupp built four of an improved Brückenleger IVc that saw service in 1941 in Russia with 3. Panzer-Division.

Built in parallel with the Brückenleger IV, the Infanterie-Sturmstegpanzer allowed foot soldiers to cross obstacles with extensible ladders.

The Canal d'Aire at Cuichy where Rommel drove his men on over an improvised bridge built by Pioneer-Bataillon 58. Later, a more sturdy 16-ton bridge was constructed. Here, PzKpfw IIIs, probably of 5. Panzer-Division cross. It was essential that bridging equipment and *Pioniere* were placed close enough to the front of an attack to be able to assist immediately. Later, more permenent structures could be erected. (NARA)

"Attention mines. Drive on stone surface only. Do not overtake." Landmines have an immediate impact on logistics, being strategically placed to block supply lines, troop movements, in fact anywhere vehicles are expected. Often, this necessitated finding alternative routes and raised issues of morale—particularly for crews of vehicles left to await repair or rescue. Clearing minefields required significant manpower, resources, and time. (RCT)

Bandenkampf—fighting the partisans in Yugoslavia—was a dirty war that disregarded most rules of warfare. This snowy group shows two more of the German motorcycle types, the BMW R12 of which over 36,000 were built and the DKW NZ 350—45,000 built, from 1941 exclusively for the Wehrmacht. They are elements of 14. Panzer-Division moving from Virovitica to Zagreb on April 10, 1941. The vehicle at far right is an SdKfz 254 *mittlere gepanzerte Beobachtungskraftwagen*, a wheeled/tracked armored vehicle whose wheels were lowered when it was used on roads and retracted for tracked movement cross-country. (SF Collection)

A Horse-drawn Army

(This section leans heavily on Mueller-Hillebrand (1951.)
The answer to the German transport and logistics problems during the *rasputitsa* in the fall and the later winter freeze was Russian: the *Panje* horse and sledge. These tough little native horses could survive and work in conditions that proved too much for the larger European horses. General Lothar Rendulic commanded XXXV. Korps at Kursk. He wrote:

> The light native carts (sleighs), and the small, strong, and undemanding native horses are absolutely indispensable for the trains of infantry units. They are equally indispensable for the supply of motorized troops during the muddy season and in the winter, whenever military operations grind to a halt. Before long, even the German motorized and armored divisions had such trains of horse-drawn vehicles at their disposal.
>
> I cannot imagine how the German Army could have fought and lived through four years of war against Russia if it had not made use of these carts, sleighs, and horses.

The lack of motor vehicles—and the difficulty in keeping them running—meant that all units used the *Panje* horses, so much so that some *Panzer* divisions were sarcastically nicknamed "*Panje* divisions."

> Report of Maj Mendrzyk, staff officer of 3. Panzergruppe
> Area: About 100 km W of Moscow
> Date: December 1941–January 1942
>
> The bringing of food and other supplies to our winter position was possible only with horses and sleds. This was particularly the case when, in the course of the various actions, the Russians temporarily gained control of the Smolensk–Vyazma highway. The supply line to the rear was cut and there were periods when no motor fuel whatsoever could be brought through.
>
> The Russians, accustomed to the severities of winter, were favored by this circumstance. The bulk of their troops moved forward on foot, some on snowshoes, accompanied by light vehicles, while our own clumsy, motorized mass in an area poor in roads but rich in forests could move forward only along the few good roads. Restricted to movement along the roads and hampered by the weather, action increasingly developed into close combat in which our various weapons, especially artillery, could not properly be brought into play. In close combat the Russians generally had the edge over us.
>
> In this winter position almost all motor vehicle traffic came to a dead stop. In part, as already mentioned, this was due to the lack of motor fuel, but it was also due to the fact that the few remaining vehicles were urgently in need of a complete overhaul if our forces were to become mobile again at the conclusion of winter.
>
> That our unit was still mobile, with the exception of a few prime movers, was entirely due to the use of Panje horses. These were accustomed to the adversities of the Russian winter and needed little care, fodder or shelter. These were our helpers and with their sleds were often the sole means of evacuating our numerous casualties, most of whom were frost-bite cases. [Mueller-Hillebrand, 1951]

Germany was less motorized than most major economies in the 1930s and much of its agriculture was still horse powered. Germany started the war in 1939 with 3.8 million horses, but the military requirement was voracious. In 1939, a first-wave infantry division's total requirement of horses was 4,842. The reserve for these horses comprised 35 cavalry mounts and 80 light and 15 heavy draft horses—130 in total.

Estimating the total horses employed during the war is difficult but 2.5 to 2.75 million is the figure given by Dorondo. In the conquered lands farmers were required to bring their horses to central locations for selection.

Horses selected by the Germans were immediately taken (including their equipment) and branded. Owners were not compensated. Requisitions and purchases by year were:

1939	600,000
1940	148,000
1941	282,000
1942	400,000
1943	380,000

By the start of *Barbarossa* in June 1941 the army on the eastern border had assembled 625,000 horses.

Origin of Wehrmacht Horses during World War II		
Procurement	Origin	Number
Stock	Peacetime army	180,000
Drafted	Old imperial territory	660,000
Youngsters	Remount offices	15,000
Booty	Red Army	310,000
	Other armies	125,000
Drafted	Russia	70,000
	France	330,000
	Poland	70,000
	Other	350,000
Purchases	Neutral, friendly states	10,000
TOTAL		2,750,000

While both vehicles and horses need fuel, the problem with horses is they need looking after and that isn't always easy in wartime. The assistant chief of staff 9. Armee (later Heeresgruppe Mitte) said:

> Regulations provided that each horse should receive 4 kg of oats and hay daily. It was thought at the beginning of the Eastern campaign that a large part of the requirements could be taken from the land. At the most it was considered that oats might have to be carried in.
>
> This was hardly the case, for even in such fertile regions as the Ukraine requirements could not be fully met. In the sectors of Army Groups Center and North, characterized by swamps, forests and steppes, not only oats but, even more important, hay was lacking. In summer and fall green forage offered a partial substitute for oats in the central sector, where horses fed well on grass and clover and occasionally even on green grain … Ninth Army was forced to issue only a portion of the authorized oats ration, at times only one half kilogram, and to use roof thatch as green fodder.

During the winter of 1941/42 horse losses were running at 1,000 a day. Mange was a problem. By November 1941, horse losses reached 102,910 killed and 33,000 sick or unfit. The army lost 180,000 horses in the winter of 1941/42 but they kept proving their worth:

> Report of Maj Richert, Operations Officer of 134. Infanterie-Division, Yalets–Orel, December 1941
>
> On December 5 the Soviets launched their offensive from the Voronezh area and forced the evacuation of Yelets between December 7 and 8. On December 9 the division was cut off from its already woefully inadequate supply base at Livni. Strong Soviet cavalry units with light, partially mounted artillery, motorized

Packhorses and mules were used extensively in mountain regions. Note the pack frame and the *Edelweiß* badge on the *Gebirgsjäger's Bergmütze.* (SF Collection)

infantry and for the first time light, mobile multiple-type rocket projectors (Stalinorgel) pushed through behind us from the south deep into the rear of the adjoining German division on the north. Some of the Russian elements also veered back toward the east. The 45th Infantry Division, adjacent to us on the south, and our own division were separated and surrounded. To add to our troubles, the combat trains which had been organized from our sorely needed supply troops, two ammunition trains, a few trucks with motor fuel and a bakery company were intercepted by Cossacks and captured. All but a few of the men were killed.

The division now fought its way back toward the northwest in a shifting pocket, using the Yelets–Orel rail line as a guide. If any aid could reach us at all it had to come by the railroad. While the infantry and the horse-drawn elements—with normal losses in horses—fought and marched on, each motor vehicle was burned when its fuel ran out. …

Catastrophe threatened during the evening of December 13 when the units were caught in an ovrag, one of those long, extended ravines which cut across the Russian steppes. Because of the icy roads our tired

Horses must be looked after. They had to be rested every 10 days or so because a week's worth of pulling equipment 25–30 miles a day was as much as most could do. After a short rest they'd be refreshed for further duties. (Dutch Archives/SF Collection)

Types of Horse

There are three types of horse: hot-blooded, cold-blooded, and warm-blooded. Hot-blooded are intelligent light-bodied horses that originate in the Middle East and North Africa. Crossing these Arabs with cold-blooded horses leads to warm-bloods. Cold-blooded are the heavy horses—bred originally to carry knights, they became draft horses and today are bred for size and strength. In the German Army they provided the motive power for heavy haulage such as artillery. Easygoing and with a docile temperament, although they can be stubborn, they have a thicker coat and are better suited to cooler conditions. Warm-blooded horses vary in size but tend to be middleweights and generally have lively and excitable natures. They make excellent riding horses and, therefore, excellent cavalry horses.

Around 1.5 million horses died in Wehrmacht service and, unlike vehicles, many of them ended up in the cooking pot. (SF Collection/Tanis)

The Germans eventually formed three divisions of cavalry: 1. Kavallerie was disbanded in 1941 and converted to tanks; 3. and 4. Divisionen were later war creations. There were three Waffen-SS divisions (8. Florian Geyer, 22. Maria Theresa, and the 37. which was unnamed). (Leo Marriott)

The *Panje* horse was able to work and survive in weather conditions that the larger German/European horses just couldn't deal with. *Panje* columns brought the ammunition to the front, fuel from the railheads, the wounded to the aid stations, and much more. In the swamps of the Pripet Marshes along the corduroy (wooden) roads they could move forward silently. (SF Collection)

Judging from the drooped neck of the horse center left, the help the infantrymen are about to give is timely. They're using a makeshift harness to pull a wagon. There were designated times to rest horses but sometimes this wasn't possible. Note the gas cape pouches on their chests. (RCT)

This is one of Georg Sluyterman's prints that shows in detail a cavalryman's gear. The quote is from Schiller's 1797 *Wallensteins Lager*, the "Reiterlied" (Rider's Song): "In the field, a man is still worthy, There shall the heart be weighed. None can stand in for him, there he himself stands quite alone." (SF Collection)

> teams were unable to climb out on the far side. Taking advantage of the fact that the German troops were concentrated within this ravine, the Russians fired on us from all sides with light artillery and multiple-rocket projectors. But in the early dawn of December 14 the 446. Infanterie-Regiment (IR) stood ready to attack in a westerly direction with all light antitank and infantry guns hauled by enlisted personnel into the forward line and with each rifle company accompanied by a horse-drawn light field howitzer. As the sun rose fiery red over the snowy landscape, the reinforced regiment and its supporting elements began to attack with the last of the ammunition in its rifles, the last shells distributed among the guns and the last piece of frozen bread in the packs. With the 445. IR as rearguard, and the 439. IR acting as a screen against strong enemy forces in the north, although some elements of the latter were supporting the attack of the 446., the 446. IR broke through the Russian encirclement and destroyed a Cossack brigade. The 439. IR likewise smashed and scattered a Russian brigade. The attack of the 446. IR was the most vigorous attack in which I ever participated. Commanders and company leaders either fought with gun in hand in the foremost line, or directed the action from horseback close behind, along with the horse-drawn batteries. The cavalry squadron, which had received new mounts since the episode of late November, was drawn up ready to be thrown in as a final trump against the Russian cavalry. Everything was staked on this final effort: to fail to break the encirclement would mean capture and Siberia.
>
> In the first onslaught the ridge dominating the area was carried by an attack across the frozen Lyubovska River. With the exception of three heavily damaged pieces of artillery, the division got all of its heavy weapons across, all of its wounded—over 400 of them stowed on Russian sleds and carts—but only a very small number of motor vehicles. Many wounded owed their lives to the horse-drawn Sanitäts-Kompanie 1 of the 134. IR, but the motorized Sanitäts-Kompanie 2 and the remnants of the motor ambulance trains had to withdraw as weak medical units, without any motor vehicles whatsoever, without medical equipment, and without any medical supplies other than the kit which the men carried on their backs. So once again the brave little Panje horses made possible the conduct of a successful operation, saving the lives of 15,000 German soldiers. [Mueller-Hillebrand, 1951]

The general revitalization of the Ostheer during 1942 applied to replacement horses as well as manpower. Some 200,000 were brought in from Germany and the occupied countries. Most went to Heeresgruppe Süd and

The hardy Russian *Panje* farm horse, was some 12–13 hands high at the withers, shaggy and short. They proved reliable and hard-working. Most were "requisitioned" although it was often more beneficial to hire the owner and the cart and harnesses that the horse was used to. (NAC)

feed was stockpiled for winter. However, the continuing losses, especially of motor transport and at Stalingrad, meant horses were even more important to the soldiers in the East. To get round the problem, the division strength was reduced and the number of horses in an infantry division was lowered. A QM report of January 18, 1942, shows LXXXI. Korps' 302., 332., and 336. Infanterie-Divisionen had an average strength of 3,300 horses (as compared to the 1939 division's near 5,000). There was also some juggling between the divisions. Those in the West reduced their number of horses: when 370. Infanterie-Division went to Russia, the 302. handed over 1,570 horses. When 371. went, 711. Infanterie-Division gave up 554.

Between 1940 and 1943 the German Army requisitioned 1.2 million horses from Germany and the occupied territories. They lost 1.5 million.

Horses Requisitioned	
Year	No. Requisitioned
1940	148,000
1941	282,000
1942	400,000
1943	380,000
1944	No figures
1945	No figures
TOTAL	1,210,000

The German Army requisitioned over 400,000 horses in 1944 but that wouldn't have covered the losses that Heeresgruppe Mitte suffered in late June 1944: 35 divisions were lost and—assuming even averaging 2,000 horses in each division that meant a loss of 70,000–80,000 horses. Replacements and requisitions ensured that the Wehrmacht on February 1, 1945, had 1,198,724 horses. During the war, an average of 865 horses died every day, meaning that over 2,076 days of war, some 1,785,740 horses died (out of 2.7 million).

Deployment of Horses on February 1, 1945	
Arm of Service	Number
Feldarmee	936,496
Ersatzarmee	123,610
Luftwaffe	37,072
Kriegsmarine	1,556
TOTAL	1,198,724

Toward the end of 1944 the veterinary companies of the infantry divisions were combined with the administrative and medical services into the administrative battalions of the new supply regiments—a measure occasioned by the shortage of personnel and motor vehicles. The veterinary officers so moved may have been better placed within a service unit than a line company, for they were largely reservists with little general military knowledge or training.

Soldiers made use of local equipment and horses wherever they could. In August 1942, to ensure that the next winter wouldn't be as bad the last, the official *Taschenbuch für den Winterkrieg (Handbook on Winter Warfare)* was circulated. Of sleds it said:

> The horse-drawn sleds used in central Europe, like the hand sleds of the same region, are too heavy and unwieldy for use on the Eastern Front. They cannot follow the troops, particularly ski troops cross-country, and they are not built to a standard track width. The panje sled generally used in Russia has proved to be the best for the transportation of light loads. Its carrying capacity is small, being commensurate with the draught strength of the panje horse. In midwinter the capacity is frequently not more than 100 lb.

It provided a "how to" section on making sleds, improvised wooden pack saddles, gun sled runners, and other useful means by which supplies could be transported. Note unusual facemask! (RCT)

***Veterinär-Kompanien* (Veterinary Companies)**

Sick and wounded horses were taken from the battlefield to a *Pferdeverbandplatz* (horse dressing station), where emergency cases were treated. From there they marched or were transported to a station set up by the division *Veterinär-Kompanie*. This station could treat 150 cases. If the horses required further treatment, they were moved to the *Armeepferdelazarett* (army horse hospital) or to the *Heerespferdelazarett* (Feldarmee horse hospital).

Pferdesammelplatz (horse collecting points) were formed to expedite the evacuation of horses to the rear. Normally there were those at army and divisional level. Horses needing special surgical operations and those not likely to be fit again for army use were moved by rail from the field hospitals to the *Wehrkreis Heimatpferdelazarette* (home horse hospitals). Horses that were cured here went to a home horse park (*Heimatpferdepark*).

At the beginning of the war there were three types of *Veterinär-Kompanien*:

Personnel and Horses in *Veterinär-Kompanien* in 1939

Type	Infanterie	Gebirgs	Bodenständig[1]
Veterinary officers	6	9	6
Civil servant	1	1	1
NCOs	24	52	24
Teams	203	203	196
Horses: regular	58	63	58
Horses: reserve	130	130	130
Horse-drawn vehicles[2]	21	7	21
Horse transport trucks	6	8	3
Catering trucks	3	3	1
Cars	1	1	1
Motorcycles	3	5	3

(www.lexikon-der-wehrmacht.de/Gliederungen/Sanitaets.htm)

[1] Infantry/mountain/static units.
[2] Incl. 2 × four-horse transport wagons.

During the war, the strength of the *Veterinär-Kompanien* was changed. One was assigned to each division which had horses. The unit's OC would be the senior veterinary officer on the divisional CO's staff. The company received and cared for all sick horses unlikely to recover quickly if left with their units, was responsible for collection and distribution of forage, and was responsible for all veterinary medical supplies and instruments.

The company consisted of an operations section, a collecting section with horse transportation trucks, a hospital section, a supply section, and a forage and stabling section. It was expected to care for horses held in reserve and in an emergency to deal with 800 extra horses. There were minor differences between the units highlighted and those of the Luftwaffe field troops (altogether a smaller organization) and the cavalry divisions.

Other veterinary service units were attached troops under *Armee* command: there were three or four vet hospitals, one or two remount depots for horses held in reserve, a vet supply depot (for medical and horseshoeing equipment) and a veterinary laboratory to handle blood tests, diagnoses and food research.

Artillery

So much of the German Army's artillery was horse-drawn. KStN 171 of December 1943 shows an *Infanteriegeschützkompanie (n.A.)*—new form infantry gun company—had six horse-drawn guns and required 54 light and two heavy draft horses. KStN 433 of January 1945 outlines the four-gun battery of le FH 18s for an *Infanterie-Division 1945* needed 25 horses for riders, and 40 light and 30 heavy draft horses. Heavy batteries would have needed even more.

Opposite, above: 168. Infanterie's Artillerie-Regiment 248 assembled on the Don, its camouflaged 10.5 cm le FH 18s horse drawn. (Akira Takiguchi)

Right: This 7.5 cm Gebirgsgeschütz 36 is mule-drawn . (NAC)

Top: A heavy load—eight horses are needed for this s FH 18 mount (the barrel traveling separately). Note the steel wheels. With rubber wheels, the gun could be towed by vehicles in one piece. (Dutch Archives)

Above and Below: Two more views of horse-drawn le FH 18s using six horses. (SF Collection/NAC)

A collection of cold-weather transport near the Don River: sledges, *Akjas*, and—of course—horses. Note the fodder in the front of the lines of *Akjas*. Introduced in winter 1942/43, the *Akjas* could be made by the troops to a pattern supplied in the *Taschenbuch*. (NAC)

At *Wehrkreis* level there was a veterinary replacement battalion for each. Remount depots in the zone of the interior were under the commander of the Ersatzheer.

One key responsibility of veterinary officers was the supervision of food supplies from animal origins—one of the problems of living off the land:

> Very frequently units stole cattle and slaughtered it themselves. The failure to examine the meat and a disregard of repeated instructions to the effect that the meat should be served only in small pieces and

Horses Released from Service, 1. *Kavallerie-Division* June 22–November 5, 1941

The great distances involved in the attack on the Soviet Union led to great attrition in horse numbers. Between June 22 and October 20, 1941, 5,726 of the division's original 13,580 horses were lost. The causes were death, straying, those turned over to veterinary services or left behind. Only 749 replacements were sent to cover these losses and of the first batch of 400 replacements, only 241 arrived fit for duty. They had had to walk 350 km. It's worth mentioning that on average a German Army horseshoe No 32 lasted around 600 km and another 300 km when repaired.

Reason for release from service	Number	Percentage*
Exhaustion	2,296	21.4
Lameness	656	5.7
Sores	228	2.0
Internal diseases	306	3.2
TOTAL released	3,712	32.33

* From total 11,481 horses on hand c. June 22, 1941.

> thoroughly cooked, resulted in numerous fatalities. Motorized units were particularly handicapped, since they were often unable to obtain a veterinary officer to inspect their meat. For this and other reasons, as the war went on, individual veterinary officers accompanied motorized and armored divisions insofar as they could be made available. ... Trichinosis ... was very common among their swine. Entire units became ill and were out of action for several months after consuming trichinous meat. The pork tapeworm, a parasite now very rare in Germany, was frequently present in Russian pigs and, when the meat was not properly inspected, its presence was overlooked by butchers. This resulted in a very considerable rise in the number of tapeworms among the personnel of units affected and, while it is not a serious infection in an individual frequently results in a serious case of cysticorcosis. [Mueller-Hillebrand 1951]

One factor that became apparent was that the two-wheeled carts used for luggage, ammunition, and infantry MGs had too little road clearance and the horse-drawn field vehicles, with the exceptions of the small No 3 and light No 1, were far too heavy for the Russian terrain which was usually unfavorable. Soviet carts were requisitioned wherever possible.

Transportation Facilities

Horse transport trains (*Pferdetransportzüge*) were composed of 55 cars, each carrying six sick or wounded horses, or a total of 350 horses per train. The standard horse transport road column could move 40 sick or wounded horses about 90 miles in one day.

A retouched photograph showing an animal transport train being loaded. (NAC)

Fodder

Horses need to eat and that's difficult if they can't graze. The typical European horse needed 12–20 lb of feed per day or needed to graze on grass for eight hours a day. No grass meant providing fodder, which had to be transported either on the cart the horse was pulling or in the baggage train. The farther the advance, the more required; a logistical nightmare. The assistant chief of staff 9. Armee said, "In the warm periods of the year it was relatively simple to provide adequate forage. Every opportunity for grazing was fully utilized. Horses which had grown emaciated during the winter soon recovered in the warm sun. ... After 1941 hay production was stimulated as much as possible in preparation for winter, and winter quarters with adequate forage stockpiles were established." Food bags, while widely used, were apt to rot or crack in the severe cold. Wooden racks wide enough for two horses were a good substitute. Horses were seldom fed forage from the ground. (SF Collection/RCT)

Russian farm carts came in different sizes; the smaller ones were ideal for hand-pulling on a firm surface. The two shown would most likely be carrying personal kit. All the troops wear the standard splinter camouflaged waterproof cape. (RCT)

The Wehrmacht made use of various trailers and trollies for diverse purposes—from transporting heavy equipment (usually vehicle-towed) to infantry supplies by horse or manhandled. The carts shown are the If. 8 *Infanteriekarren* infantry trailer, one with a towing adaption. Made of sheet steel and introduced in 1941, they were heavy but could carry a payload of 350 kg. They were widely used throughout the Heer but were an indictment of the German automotive industry's inability to produce sufficient light vehicles for these tasks. (NAC)

Casualty clearance was a multistage process. Initially, if the wounded couldn't walk, they'd be taken to a battalion aid post by *Krankenträger* (stretcher bearer) and then onward by ambulance. German motor ambulances were designated Kfz 31 and nicknamed "Sankas" or "Sankras." Common models were the Opel Blitz Type S, Phänomen-Granit 25H, and Steyr 640. Smaller models were Phänomen-Granit 1500A and Mercedes-Benz LE1100. Here a casualty from the 7. SS-Freiwilligen Gebirgs-Division Prinz Eugen is being placed in a Phänomen Granit 25H ambulance. (NARA)

Medical Logistics

Care for the wounded is a fundamental logistical requirement, and the Wehrmacht was well prepared for casualties. The battlefield evacuation procedure started (1) at the *Verwundetennest* (aid post) as this well-known but clear diagram shows. There a *Sanitätsunteroffizier* (usually a trained medical NCO who had six months' training at a *Sanitätsstaffel*) would provide the first dressing, splinting, or tourniquet. There was also usually a battalion aid post (*Truppenverbandplatz*) where the *Bataillonsarzt* (battalion MO) and his assistant (*Assistenzarzt* or *Hilfsarzt*) practiced.

Arriving by stretcher or under their own steam, the wounded were divided then into those who couldn't walk (2) and need to await an ambulance at the *Wagenhalteplatz* (ambulance post), from where they were taken (3) to the *Hauptverbandplatz* (field dressing station) or *Leichtverwundetensammelplatz* (collecting point for lightly wounded). The badly wounded were taken on (4) to the *Feldlazarett* (divisional field hospital). Divisional medical facilities—under the command of a *Divisionsarzt* (divisional MO)—usually comprised two medical companies, a motorized field hospital (with accommodation for

Casualty evacuation. (*Pocket Book of the German Army 1943*)

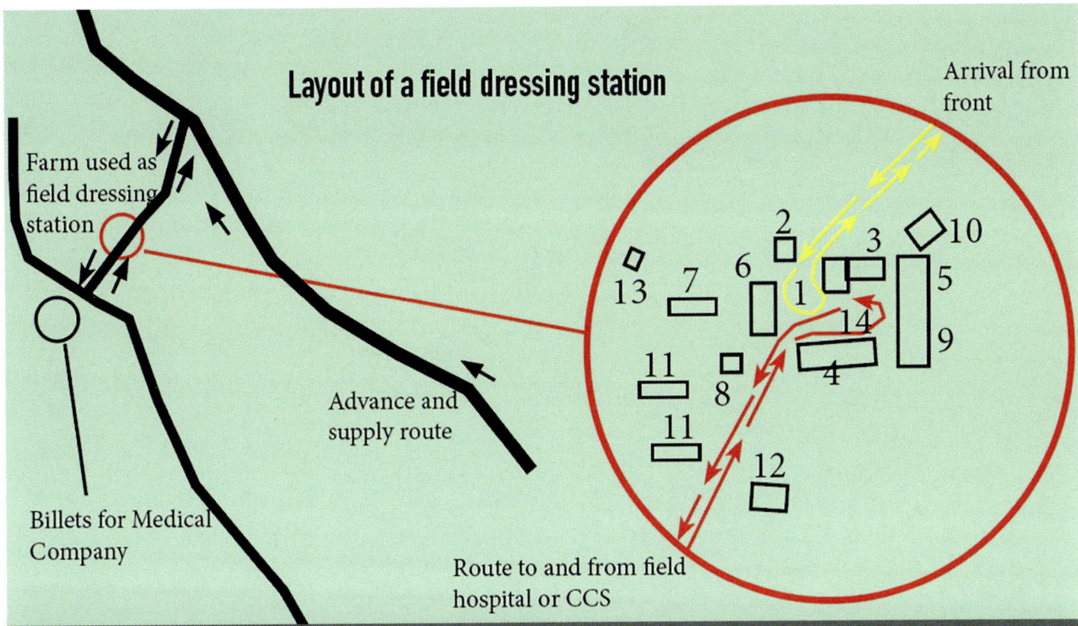

Typical layout of a field dressing station—often placed in farmyards using their barns, outbuildings, and well: 1. Ambulance unloading point. 2. Admin, reception, and dressing station. 3. Operating theater, dispensary, office. 4. Ward for mobile wounded. 5. Machine outhouse. 6. Ward for severely wounded. 7. Tent for medical personnel. 8. Cookhouse. 9. Stall for horses. 10. Shelter for vehicles. 11. Tent(s) for gas cases. 12. Tent for dead. 13. Lavatories. 14. Pickup to field hospital. (Info from *Handbook of German Administration and Supply 1944*)

200 patients), and two motor ambulance trains (each having 15 ambulances, sometimes with one motorized and one horse-drawn. Some mobile units had a third motorized ambulance train rather than a hospital). Walking wounded were taken/made their own way (5) to the *Krankensammelstelle* (casualty collection point). The next step after the *Feldlazarett* was (6) to either a *Kriegslazarett* (army field hospital) or a *Leichtkrankenkriegslazarett* (army field hospital for the lightly wounded).

Following treatment, the casualties were either sent home (7) to hospitals or to recuperate in Germany, while the lightly wounded return via an Ersatz (replacement) unit to the front. Those who had to return home used hospital trains (*Lazarettzüge*) that could carry around 375 lying or 920 sitting wounded.

The symbol (see also 3b in drawing opposite) and sign identifying a *Leichtverwundetensammelplatz*—collecting place for the lightly wounded. Note cycle medic. (RCT)

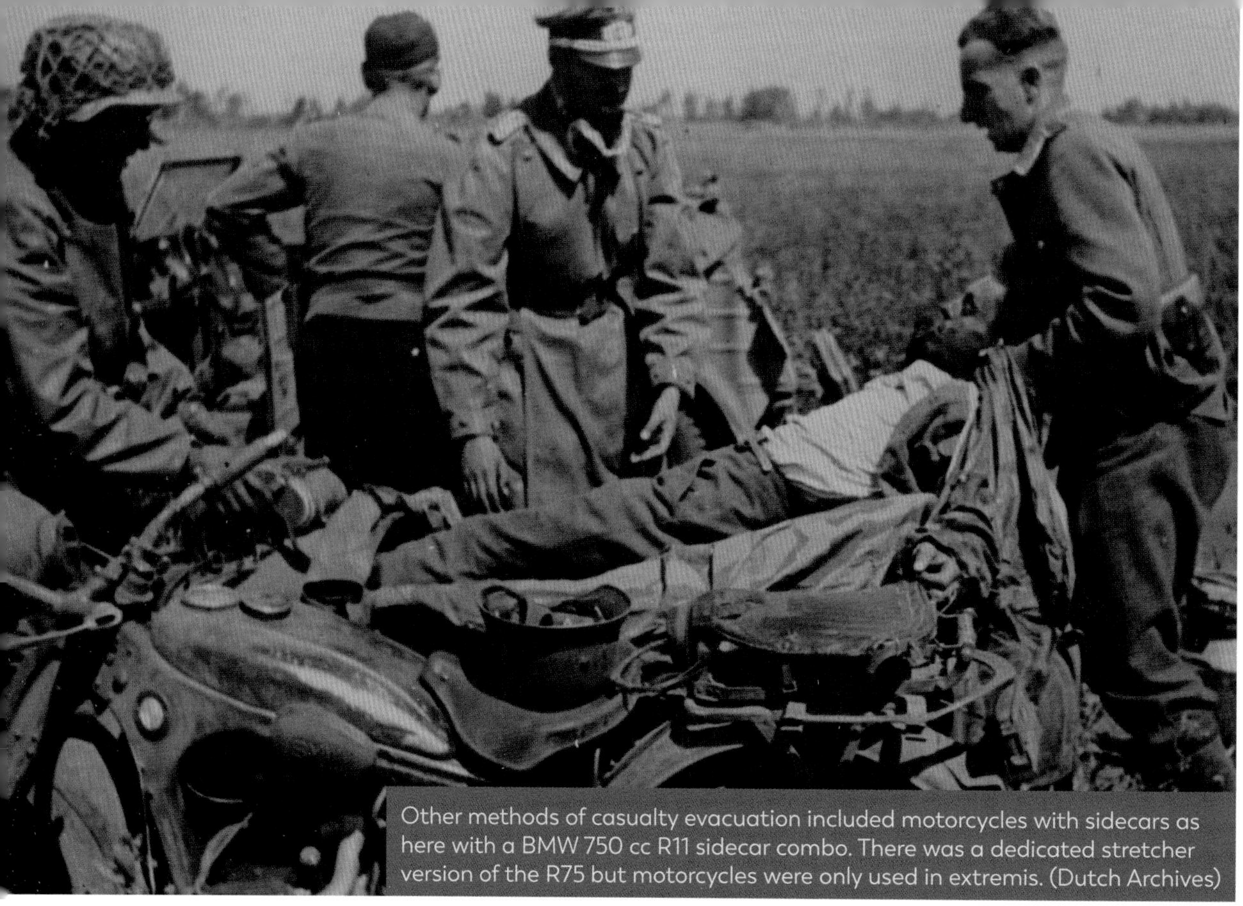

Other methods of casualty evacuation included motorcycles with sidecars as here with a BMW 750 cc R11 sidecar combo. There was a dedicated stretcher version of the R75 but motorcycles were only used in extremis. (Dutch Archives)

Air evacuation of the wounded became an important factor for all armies. This was especially true in pockets when surrounded by the enemy. In a postwar pamphlet produced by for the U.S. Army, this was emphasized:

> Every opportunity should be used to evacuate casualties by air. They must have priority on transport planes returning from a pocket, and this priority must be assured, if necessary, by force of arms. The desperate struggle for space aboard transport planes in the pocket of Stalingrad should serve as a warning for situations of this kind.

In extremis, the Fiesler Fi 156 Storch allowed quick air evacuation but could only officially take two severely injured. They'd land somewhere a larger aircraft, such as the Ju 52m/3, could continue the journey. (Dutch Archives)

From Heimat to the Front: By Air

After World War I and the restrictions of the Treaty of Versailles, the Luftwaffe developed clandestinely. Its emphasis was on army support rather than strategic warfare. The Nazis continued this approach, and its tough style was unleashed on the world during the Spanish Civil War: the bombing of Guernica resonated worldwide. By 1939, the Luftwaffe was a superb fighting machine, and its close support of the army helped defeat the Western powers.

Bombs being loaded onto a Ju 52 past stacked wooden ammunition boxes. Note the siren tubes on the bomb fins, designed to create terror when falling, Russia, 1942. (NAC)

North Africa, 1943: note the troops with stacked weapons waiting to board and fuel drums at right. (NAC)

Classic view of a parachute drop during *Unternehmen Merkur*, the invasion of Crete, with one of the Ju 52 transports about to crash in flames. (NAC)

However, the Luftwaffe had also developed another significant role: the delivery of troops to critical locations by air. It had been the Luftwaffe that carried the Spanish Army of Africa from Morocco to Spain in September 1936: 8,899 men, 44 field guns, and 90 heavy machine guns.

The transport of choice was the "Tante Ju," the Junkers Ju 52/3m, which was also used as a paratroop transport and glider tower. By the time war started, over 400 Ju 52s had been produced, and they had been formed into *Kampfgruppen zbV* (*zur besondern Vervendung*—battle groups for special purposes), the first, KGrzbV 1, was formed in October 1937 from IV./KG 152 "Hindenburg." It had four squadrons of Ju 52s. This *Gruppe* became the first *Geschwader* (lit. squadron—but the German *Geschwader* equates better with an RAF wing or USAAF group) in 1939. Other groups followed along with two *Luftlandesgeschwader* (air landing wings), LLG 1 (in 1940) and 2 (in 1942). These used Ju 52s as tractor aircraft and gliders.

Use for aerial resupply was recognized from the start. 10. Panzer-Division noted in divisional orders:

> Aircraft can, to a certain degree, assure the transmission of supplies in small quantities partially by parachute, partially by landing. This method of supply must only be used in cases of emergency. Application must be made to division either by telephone or wireless. In the case of supplying by parachute, a Ju 52 can carry, in addition to 1,500 kg of supplies, four containers to drop. The contents of a container can consist of fuel or ammunition to the following scale: 100 l of fuel or 250 kg of ammunition. Example—6,000 rounds of SAA or 500 rounds for the 2 cm tank gun or 150 rounds for the 3.7 cm antitank gun, 20 rounds for the 7.5 cm tank gun, 55 rounds for the 8 cm mortar.

This artwork is from Hauptmann Piehl's *Ganze Männer*. It glorified the life and experience of the German paratroopers and was published in 1943 when their exploits were still fresh in the minds of an adoring public. Photo shows well the position required by the Fallschirmjäger in exiting the Junkers Ju 52. Note the static line. The German parachutes were *Rückfallschirm, Zwangablösung* or "Backpack Parachute, Static Line Deployment." (RCT)

Interestingly, the orders included the instructions to save the parachutes and containers for return to ordnance depots.

Ju 52/3m Transport Units (KG = *Kampfgeschwader*; KGr = *Kampfgruppe*; zbV = *zur besonderen Verwendung* = for special duties)	
Unit	Fate
KGzbV 1	Formed August 1939. Used in Poland, Norway, Crete, Demyansk, and Stalingrad. Became TG 1 in May 1943 and used in the Crimea and, in 1944, in the Kamenets-Podolsky pocket. In 1945 it was used to resupply Courland.
KGzbV 172	Formed 1938 as TG 17 from Lufthansa's training Flugkommando Berlin. *Geschwaderstab* involved in Poland and then deactivated. Reactivated for *Weserübung*. Deactivated May 1940.

The Ju 52 could be used to airlift casualties, the air ambulance version taking 12 stretchers in theory—in practice, more were often carried. (SF Collection)

KGrzbV 2	Formed August 1938. Equipped with Me 321 gliders. Became I./TG 2 in May 1943.
KGrzbV 3	Formed September 1940. Used in *Marita* and *Merkur*, Italy and Southern Russia. Became Stab/TG 4 in May 1943.
KGrzbV 4	Formed early 1942; involved at Demyansk; probably disbanded August 1942.
KGrzbV 5	Cover name for glider units. Involved in Eben Emael and other 1940 operations. Became part of Luftlandegeschwader 1 in April 1940.
KGrzbV 6	Created February 1942 for use in Demyansk pocket; disbanded March 1942.
KGrzbV 7	Created February 1942 for use in Demyansk pocket; disbanded March 1942.
KGrzbV 8	Created February 1942 for use in Demyansk pocket; disbanded April 1942.
KGrzbV 9	Formed August 1939. Used in Poland, *Weserübung*, attack in West, Mediterranean, and North Africa. Also used in Russia: Demyansk, Stalingrad, and the Kuban bridgehead. Became I./TG 3 in May 1943.
KGrzbV 11	Formed May 1940. Used in attack on Holland, 1940; disbanded afterward.
KGrzbV 12	Formed May 1940. Used in attack on Holland, 1940; disbanded afterward.
KGrzbV 40	Formed March 1941. Used in attack on Crete, 1941; disbanded afterward.
KGrzbV 50	Formed March 1941. Used in *Marita*, Southern Russia, Crimea—including the Kuban bridgehead. Became II./TG 3 in May 1943.
KGrzbV 60	Formed March 1941. Used in attack on Crete, 1941; disbanded afterward.
KGrzbV 101	Formed March 1940. Used in *Weserübung*, attack on Low Countries, France, and Crete, 1940–41; disbanded afterward
KGrzbV 102	Formed March 1940. Used in *Weserübung*, *Marita*, Central Russia, Mediterranean, and North Africa, Stalingrad, and the Kuban bridgehead; became III./TG 3 in May 1943.
KGrzbV 103	Formed March 1940. Used in *Weserübung*, disbanded May 1940.
KGrzbV 104	Formed March 1940. Used in *Weserübung*, Holland, Mediterranean, and North Africa, Southern and Central Russia, and Ukraine. Became II./TG 5 in May 1943.
KGrzbV 105	Formed March 1940. Used in *Weserübung* and the West, *Marita*, Russia and at Demyansk; became IV./TG 4 in May 1943.
KGrzbV 106	Formed March 1940. Used in *Weserübung*, *Marita*, Northern and Central Russia, equipped with Go 244s April–November 1942; crews involved at Stalingrad. Reequipped with Ju 52s March 1943 and involved in North Africa. Became III./TG 2 in May 1943.

Examples of the German supply container (*Abwurfbehälter für Nachschub*). There were various types: the Mischlast Abwurfbehälter 250 was the early bullet-shaped version (250 = 250 kg); the wooden 700 carried 450 kg more but was prone to damage. The most common were steel versions with small wheels and a towbar to allow them to be moved. One end had a crash cushion, the other the parachute attachment. They contained either weapons, ammo, supplies or—as below—radio equipment. (RCT/SF Collection)

KGrzbV 107	Formed March 1940. Used in *Weserübung*; disbanded June 1940.
KGrzbV 108	Formed March 1940. Used in *Weserübung*, Norway and northern Finland; became TGr 20 in May 1943.
KGrzbV 172	Formed October 1941. Involved in Russia—including the Kuban bridgehead—and Mediterranean. I./became IV./TG 3 in May 1943; II./became Blindflugschule 6.
KGrzbV 200	Formed December 1942 with FW200s. Used in southern Russia, including Kuban bridgehead. Disbanded February 1943.
KGrzbV 300	Formed November 1941. Involved in Mediterranean and North Africa, Southern Russia; became an *Ergänzungsgruppe* (training unit and replacement pool for transport aircrew personnel) for the *Transportverbände* in July 1942. Officially renamed Ergänzungs-Transportfliegergruppe in May 1943.
KGrzbV 400	Formed December 1941. Used in Italy, Greece, Crete, North Africa, and Southern Russia; became III./TG 4 in May 1943.
KGrzbV 500	Formed December 1941. Involved in Italy, Greece, Crete and North Africa, at Demyansk and then in Southern Russia and the Kuban bridgehead; became I./TG 4 in May 1943.
KGrzbV 600	Formed December 1941. Involved at Demyansk and in Central and Northern Russia, Mediterranean; became I./TG 2 in May 1943.
KGrzbV 700	Formed December 1941. Involved at Demyansk, in Russia, and France; partially converted to LeO 451s 1943; disbanded summer 1944.
KGrzbV 800	Formed December 1941. Involved at Demyansk, in Russia, the Mediterranean, and North Africa; became II./TG 2 in May 1943.
KGrzbV 900	Formed December 1941. Involved at Demyansk, in Russia; reequipped with the Me 323 and renamed III./KGzbV 323 before being redesignated II./TG 5 in May 1943.
KGrzbV 999	Formed December 1941. Involved at Demyansk. Disbanded in April 1942.
KGrzbV S-7	Formed November 1942. The S in the designation refers to "Süd" i.e., the North African front where it was active. Disbanded in January 1943, remainder to KGrzbV 400.
KGrzbV S-11	Formed November 1942. Active in Mediterranean and North Africa. Disbanded December 1942.
KGrzbV Frankfurt	Formed November 1942. Active in Mediterranean and North Africa. Disbanded December 1943 in North Africa.
KGrzbV Naples	Formed November 1942. Involved in Mediterranean and Tunisia. Renamed Stab/TG 5 in April 1943.
KGrzbV Oels	Formed November 1942. Involved at Demyansk; disbanded in April 1942.
KGrzbV Posen	Involved at Demyansk and in Russia; disbanded in April 1942.
KGrzbV Wittstock	Formed November 1942. Active in Mediterranean and North Africa. Disbanded in April 1943.

Many of the Luftwaffe pilots had learnt to fly in gliders because the Treaty of Versailles had banned German military powered flight. One of the important designers, Alexander Lippisch, became chief designer of the Deutsche Forschungsanstalt für Segelflug (DFS—the German Research Society for Gliding) which was

When too far from the supply lines, aircraft could deliver essentials using "*Verpflegungsbomben*"—food bombs—air-dropped canisters. This photo is from the Polish campaign. (RCT)

responsible for designing the DFS 230 glider which was used to airland troops. At the beginning of December 1939, KGzbV 5 had 34 Ju 52s and 43 DFS 230s. It was in DFS 230 gliders that men of 7. Flieger Division's 22. Luftlande-Infanterie-Division dropped on Belgian Fort Eben-Emael in 1940 with such brilliant success.

The Ju 52s were used in Poland in September 1939, in over 2,500 sorties, carrying 1,600 tons of supplies and 20,000 troops to forward staging areas. More use was made of the transports during *Unternehmen Weserübung*, the attack on Denmark and Norway, on April 9, 1940. In Denmark, *Fallschirmjäger* dropped to secure the Storstrom bridge and the Aalborg airfields, and there was a surprise landing of infantry at Copenhagen. The Luftwaffe's transport aircraft saw more use transporting troops to Norway—including a dropping a parachute battalion that took the Oslo and Stavanger airfields—and resupplying Generalmajor Eduard Dietl's 3. Gebirgsjäger. In some 3,018 sorties, they transported 30,000 people and 2,376 tons of cargo.

Further successes came in the war in the West but the Achilles' heel of the *Transportverbände* was beginning to make itself known. The Ju 52 just wasn't very resilient. It was slow, easy to shoot down, and practically unarmored. Seven were lost in Spain during the German assistance to Franco's forces, 150 were lost in *Weserübung*, and nearly 300 in the battle for Holland. Indeed, in one day—May 10, 1940—278 Ju 52s were damaged or destroyed.

One of the fliers in 1940 was Oberstleutnant Joachim Gablenz who led KGzbV 172, which was based on the Lufthansa training unit. On May 5, 1940, Gablenz became *Lufttransportführer beim Generalquartiermeister der Luftwaffe* (air transport commander attached to the quartermaster general of the Air Force). Gabenz went on to become head of the Air Force Planning Office in November 1941 and then head of the Reich Aviation Ministry before dying in a plane crash in August 1942.

Gliders

The Germans were innovators in use of glider-borne troops to place well-trained men at key points in coup-de-main operations. In 1940 these took important bridges and eliminated important defensive locations. Later, the gliders were also used for carrying cargo, particularly into pockets or besieged locations. Their short-landing capabilities made them perfect for operations like this—although the downside was the loss of the glider if the pocket wasn't successfully reabsorbed into German lines.

German Gotha Go 242 transport glider in flight, Smolensk, May 1, 1942. Over 1,500 were built; of these, 133 were rebuilt as powered Go 244s. Occasionally given a boost with RATO attachments, the Go 242 could carry 23 troops or 3,500–4,000 kg (7,700–8,800 lb) of cargo. (waralbum.ru)

Various aircraft were used as glider-towing tugs, including the Ju 87—particularly the D-3 and R-3. This Ju 87R is towing a DFS 230 transport glider over Sicily. (waralbum.ru)

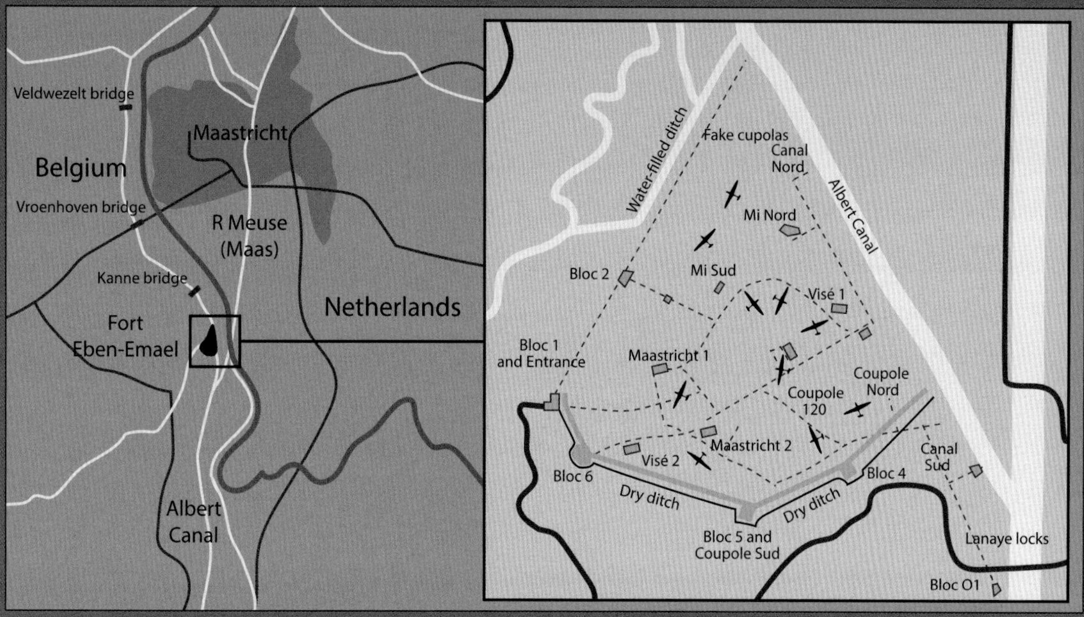

The glider-borne assault on Eben Emael on May 10, 1940, was a masterpiece of precision. Six months of training prepared the *Fallschirmjäger* for a remarkable coup de main. The spectacular success of Group Granit has overshadowed the other operations to take three strategic bridges to the north. The bridges at Veldwezelt and Vroenhoven were successfully taken, but the German armor reached Kanne too early and the defenders were able to destroy the bridge before the Fallschirmjäger landed.

Unternehmen Eiche (oak) was another carefully planned and brilliantly executed operation. SS-Hauptsturmführer Otto Skorzeny and his SS commandos took the credit, but the affair was in fact planned and executed by the *Fallschirmjäger* of 2. FJD under the command of Major Otto-Harald Mors. At the Campo Imperatore Hotel in Italy's Gran Sasso, high in the Apennines, on September 12, 1943, DFS 230 gliders (G4) carrying paratroopers of the Fallschirm-Lehr Battalion and SS commandos achieved complete surprise and rescued Italian ex-premier Benito Mussolini. (Bundesarchiv, Bild 101I-567-1503B-17/Toni Schneiders/CC-BY-SA 3.0)

The DFS 230 dropped its wheels when it was in the air and used a landing skid with a parachute brake to give it a very short landing length. That allied to the steep descent angle made it capable of very precise assaults. (Bundesarchiv, Bild 101I-568-1531-32/Stocker, Dr./CC-BY-SA 3.0)

DFS 230 gliders in flight before dropping the landing gear. Note the ventral MG 15 mounting aft of the cockpit. (SF Collection)

The 21.98 m (72 ft 1 in) wingspan of the DFS 230 is evident in this photograph taken in the North African desert. (NARA)

Cargo Gliders

The Germans made great use of their gliders for cargo drops—particularly later in the war when resupplying pockets or *Festungen*.

On April 1, 1937, the Lastenseglerkommando (cargo glider command) was set up in Darmstadt-Griesheim to train cargo glider pilots. The courses lasted six months. The *Kommando* was renamed, subordinated to Kampfgruppe zbV 1, disbanded and then finally was reconstituted by Generalmajor Kurt Student and renamed 17./Kampfgeschwader zbV 5 in November 1939. This unit led the cargo glider units until Luftlandegeschwader 1 was formed on July 27, 1940, finally ending up with three groups using Do 17, Ju 52, and Hs 126 tractors. It took part in the Corinth Canal and *Merkur* operations.

In the summer of 1942, four staffs—Verbindungskommando (S) 1, 2, 4, and V—were set up from personnel of Luftlandegeschwader 1. They were assigned to various air fleets and were planned to direct the deployment of the cargo glider squadrons there. After their establishment, the cargo glider squadrons were permanently assigned to these commands and renamed accordingly.

Verbindungskommando (S)	Notes
1	For Luftflotte 1 with 2 DFS 230 *Staffeln* and 1 Go 242 *Staffel*; served in Russia, flew missions to Stalingrad. Became Schleppgruppe 1, served in Balkans and took part in *Unternehmen Rösselsprung* and in 1945 supply missions to Breslau.
2	For Luftflotte 2 with 2 DFS 230 *Staffeln* and 2 Go 242 *Staffeln*; served in Mediterranean and North Africa. After surrender, the personnel who escaped went to a variety of units including Ergänzungsgruppe (S) 1, Schleppgruppe 1, and Luftlandegeschwader 1.
4	For Luftflotte 4 with 1 DFS 230 *Staffel* and 3 Go 242 *Staffenl*; served in Russia, flew missions into Stalingrad, in support of Kursk, Kuban bridgehead. Became Schleppgruppe 2, served in Russia in support of Crimea, and encircled 1. Panzerarmee.
V	For Luftwaffenkommando Ost with 1 DFS 230 *Staffel* and 1 Go 242 *Staffel*; served in Russia. Flew into Velikiye Luki and in support of Kursk. Became Schleppgruppe 3, served in Russia, and flew in support of Festung Kovel.

In November 1943 the *Verbindungskommandos (S)* were reformed as *Schleppgruppen*—towing groups. 2 and 3 were disbanded on September 9, 1944, while Schleppgruppe 1 remained in existence until the end of the war.

His role was taken over in September 1941 by Oberst Friedrich-Wilhelm Morzik. In 1943 the *Lufttransportführer* became first *Transportfliegerführer 1* and then *General der Transportflieger* in August 1943 at the same time that there was a major change in organization of the *Transportverbände*. A unified air-transport command—XIV. Fliegerkorps—was formed on April 30, 1943, in Tutow under General der Flieger Joachim Coeler. He held the position until February 1945 when Morzik, now a *Generalmajor*, took over and the designation changed to *Lufttransportchef der Wehrmacht* (air transport chief of the armed forces).

Unternehmen Marita—the invasion of Greece—saw a glider-borne attempt to capture the bridge over the Corinth Canal on April 25, 1941, which achieved its objective, but the bridge was blown. A month later, on May 20, the attack on Crete, *Unternehmen Merkur*, began with 100 gliders and 530 Ju 52s—of which 493 launched on 20 May. Just over 140 were lost in the battle. 7. Fliegerdivision landed by parachute and glider as Luftlandegeschwader 1 delivered troops by aircraft. At least 24 of the 69 glider pilots were killed during the operation.

Fuel availability—something that would become critical later in the war—was a significant problem in the attack on Crete. First, the fuel was delivered late by tanker and then, because the Greek ports did not support in-line fuel transfer, it had to be transferred to drums, offloaded onto trucks, and taken to the airfields. There were insufficient men put in place to handle this transfer. These problems led to the attack date being delayed from May 17 to 20, and the turn-round mission time being extended because of the lack of personnel at the airfields. The second wave of *Fallschirmjäger* was delivered three hours late and passed their escorts and close air support aircraft returning from Crete; nearly 50 Ju 52s were lost.

Further success—and attrition—took place in Russia in 1941. Several new *Kampfgruppen* were created, some having to be equipped with old bombers as there were insufficient Ju 52s. This was a story that would become more obvious as the war went on. German production of transport aircraft never kept pace with attrition and demand as the production figures show:

These containers were airdropped into the Demyansk pocket, 1942. (Dutch Archives)

Ju 52 Annual Production 1932–45														
1932	1933	1934	1935	1936	1937	1938	1939	1940	1941	1942	1943	1944	1945	TOTAL
1	17	175	347	293	260	300	578	423	502	573	897	447	0	4,813

Above and Below: Ju 52s deliver cargo into the Demyansk pocket. Sledges and handcarts carry assorted cargo from the winter-whitewashed aircraft. Note the forward and centrally mounted MGs and circular radio direction finder. (Dutch Archives)

A crashed German cargo glider—a Gotha Go 242—at an airfield near Kholm. 5,500 German soldiers held out for 105 days thanks to aerial resupply. (Bundesarchiv, Bild 101I-004-3635-27A/Muck, Richard/CC-BY-SA 3.0)

The Luftwaffe's transport aircraft were put to the test in spring 1942 when a Soviet counterattack surrounded German strongholds including Kholm and Demyansk. Generalmajor a. D. Fritz Morzik—at the time *Lufttransportführer beim Generalquartiermeister der Luftwaffe* and *Kommandeur der Blindflugschulen*—was told to organize resupply by air. However, the successful airlifts to these pockets had a knock-on effect, making planners believe the Luftwaffe was easily capable of this sort of mission, and ensured that Hitler expected other pockets to hold firm.

During the Demyansk operation, between February 20 and May 18, 1942, six trapped divisions were supplied entirely by the air (Ju 52s, He 111s, and cargo gliders): 24,303 tons were delivered, a daily average of 276 tons—sufficient food, weapons, and ammunition for the 100,000 trapped soldiers. Additionally, 5 million gallons of fuel were delivered and 15,446 replacement troops for the 22,093 wounded who were evacuated. The price was high: 165 aircraft lost, many thanks to the extreme cold that caused fuel and oil pipes to freeze, making engines difficult to start.

At Kholm things were rather different thanks to the proximity of the Soviets who, in the end, made landing supply aircraft impossible. Airdrops were used instead, along with transport gliders—Go 242s and DFS 230s.

Similarly, in December 1942, the German garrison surrounded in Velikiye Luki was resupplied by air: container-drops from He 111s, and glider operations from Orsha. In total 17 of the 25 gliders sent reached the defenders successfully but the supplies weren't enough to stop the garrison surrendering on January 16, 1943—and the gliders couldn't be retrieved.

The precedent set by the success of Demyansk led directly to the disaster at Stalingrad. Compounded by the assessment of the higher Luftwaffe command that resupply was possible—completely at variance to the

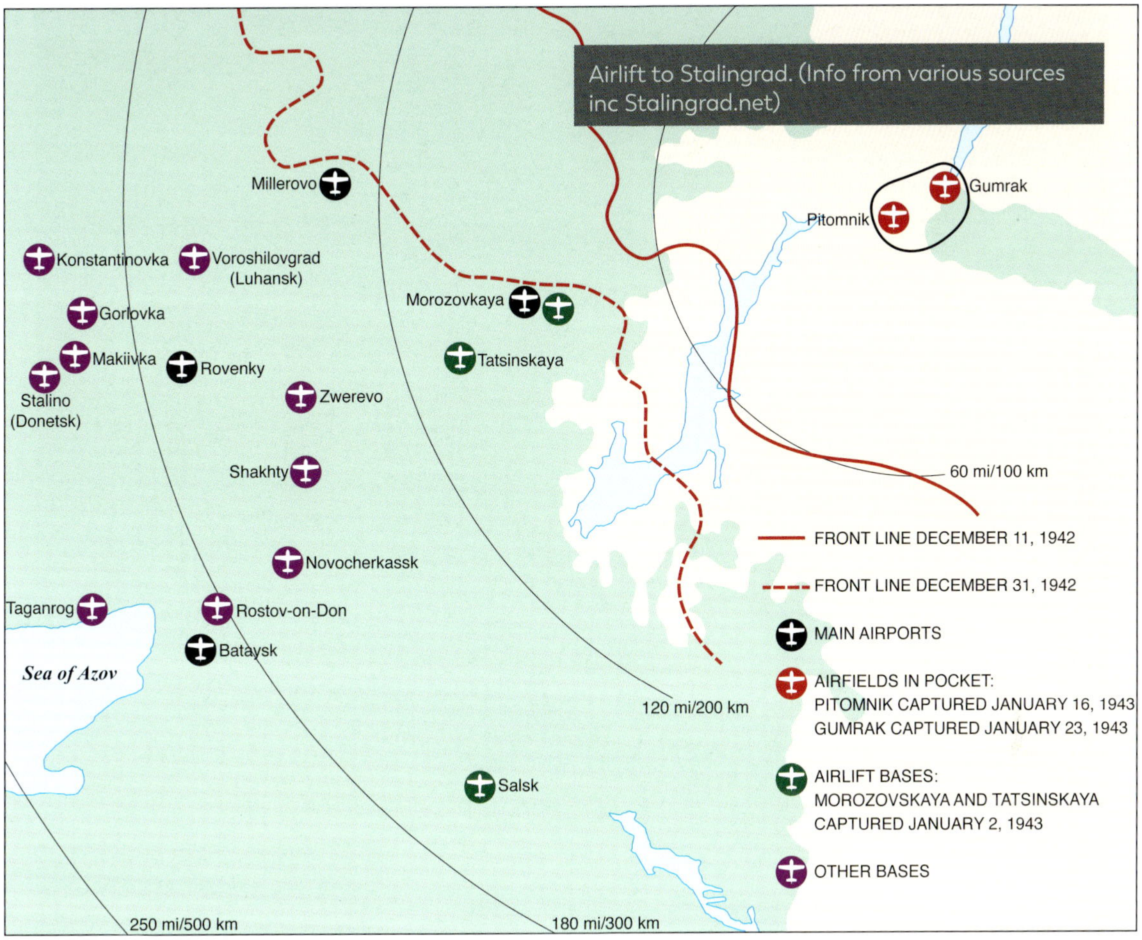

Airlift to Stalingrad. (Info from various sources inc Stalingrad.net)

Captured German aircraft at an airfield near Stalingrad: a Junkers Ju 87D dive-bomber, Heinkel He 111H bombers, and Junkers Ju 52/3m transport aircraft. (waralbum.ru)

Containers being prepared for dropping on Stalingrad. (SF Collection)

In 1943, Allied Operation *Flax* concentrated on severing the Axis resupply links and the Ju 52s were heavily predated. The "Tante Ju" had a dorsal-mounted 13 mm MG 131 and a pair of beam 7.92 mm MG 15s, the starboard one in evidence in this photograph. There are reports of soldiers firing their own machine guns through the windows when under attack. (Bild 101I-545-0614-21/Seeger, Erwin/CC-BY-SA 3.0)

more sober and professional view of the commander of Luftflotte 4, General Wolfram von Richthofen—the Luftwaffe could never get anywhere near the self-assessed figure of 750 tons a day, even when the target tonnage was reduced to 500.

They certainly gave it a go, pulling in aircraft from every establishment they could—not just Ju 52s but also Ju 86s, Fw 200s, Ju 90s, and He 111s. Denuding training establishments of both instructors and trainer aircraft, Luftflotte 4 scraped together some 600 aircraft. There were, however, obvious problems from the start. The two main airfields, Morozovskaya and Tatsinskaya, were 50 and 60 minutes flying time respectively from

The Messerschmitt Me 323D Gigant (giant) was a huge military transport, a six-engine version of the Me 321 cargo glider. The massive semi-cantilever, high-mounted wings were made of aluminum and doped fabric plywood to save weight. The fuselage was metal tube and wood also covered with doped fabric. The original load specification for the Me 321 glider was to lift and carry an 8.8 cm gun and its half-tracked tractor or a PzKpfw IV medium tank (around 20 tons). A typical load for the Me 323D could be a field howitzer and tractor (c. 15 tons), over 50 252 l (45 U.S. gal) fuel drums, 150 men, or 60 stretcher cases. It was the largest transport aircraft to fly in World War II and was first used to supply the Axis troops in Tunisia, delivering 15,000 tons of assorted cargo—including nearly 100 SP guns and assorted armor, almost 1,000 trucks and light vehicles, and radio stations. On one return trip to Sicily the aircraft found space for 340 troops including some traveling inside the hollow wings! Very slow and without the ability to maneuver, it could absorb a lot of damage but still took heavy losses doing the Mediterranean airbridge run—14 in one attack off the coast of Tunisia. This one (below) is under attack by a Martin B-26 Marauder off Corsica. (Fortepan/Hungarian Archives)

The heavyweight Me 232D-1 Gigant required hefty ground equipment to pull it—here two tractor units, an s. Zgkw 12t and Praga T6-SS. (Bundesarchiv, Bild 101I-552-0822-36/Pirath, Helmuth/CC-BY-SA 3.0)

Unloading a captured French tankette—a Renault UE Chenillette—from an Me 323. (Bundesarchiv, Bild 101I-554-0872-07/Pirath, Helmuth/CC-BY-SA 3.0)

the encircled airfield of Pitomnik. 6. Armee's logistical needs required around 250 missions a day, an unrealistic number, and reliability rates plummeted as the winter took hold: by late December, operational readiness was at less than 25%; by January 18, availability percentages were: Ju 52s, less than 7%, He 111s, 33%, and He 177s 35%. None of the Fw 200s were usable.

During the 72-day siege, the Luftwaffe averaged deliveries of 116 tons a day. Aircraft and crew losses were significant: nine Fw 200s, 169 He 111s, five He 177s, 269 Ju 52s, 42 Ju 86s, and a Ju 290 for a total of 495 aircraft.

Even before 6. Armee was encircled at Stalingrad, the British victory at El Alamein in November 1942 led to a helter-skelter German retreat that was compounded when Allied troops landed in Operation *Torch*. With their

North African armies at risk, the Germans rushed men and equipment to the Tunisian front, but Ultra intelligence reports allowed convoys to be intercepted. Airlift became the only option: 320 Ju 52s were made available in the Mediterranean theater. In the last two months of 1942, the transports delivered 41,768 personnel, 8,615 tons of equipment and supplies, and 1,470 tons of fuel—but in doing so lost over 150 Ju 52s by the end of January.

The two largest losses were because of Operation *Flax*: the Palm Sunday Massacre and the Cap Bon Massacre. On April 18, 1943, 24 Ju 52s, nine Bf 109s, and a Bf 110 were shot down at sea, and 35 Ju 52s crash-landed ashore during the attack by USAAF's Ninth Air Force's 57th FG and the RAF's No 92 Squadron. A few days later, on April 22, 1943, 10 Ju 52s of KGrzbV106 and 14 Me 323s of KGzbV 323, soon to be redesignated TG 5, flew a large resupply mission to Tunisia. Each of the 323s carried 12 tonnes of fuel. The Ju 52s reached Tunis safely. The 323s were intercepted by four squadrons of SAAF and RAF fighters and the Cap Bon Massacre resulted: all 14 Me 323s were shot down, loaded with fuel and 126 crew and passengers, including TG 5's commander.

The final toll—some 371 transport aircraft lost between November 1942 and May 1943—was over 30% of the Luftwaffe's total number of transports. Added to those lost at Stalingrad, the figure rises to over 50%. Almost as important as the loss of aircraft and aircrew—many of whom were from the training units—was the loss of maintenance equipment and spare parts. Many of the groundcrew managed to escape by jamming themselves into any aircraft they could—including single-seat fighters—but irreplaceable equipment was left behind in Tunisia and, later, in Sicily.

In May 1943 the *Transportverbände* was reorganized and the *Kampfgruppen* were renamed as *Transportgruppen*.

***Transport-Geschwader* (TG) and -*Gruppen* (TGr) Formed in May 1943**

Unit	Fate
TG 1	Formed from KGzbV 1. Deployed in Russia and the Reich. Most *Gruppen* converted to the SM.82 in 1944.
TG 2	Formed from KGrzbV 3, 600, 800, 106. Deployed in Southern Russia and Italy, saw action at Leros in 1943.
TG 3	Formed from KGrzbV 9, 50, 102, 172. Deployed at Stalingrad, in Russia and Germany.
TG 4	Formed from KGrzbV 3, 500, 600, 400. Deployed at Stalingrad and Italy (saw action at Leros in 1943).
TG 5	Formed from KGzbV 323, KGrzbV 104. Equipped with Me 323s and, later some Arado Ar 232s. Disbanded in 1944. Deployed in Mediterranean, North Africa, and Russia.
TGr 10	Formed in May 1943 from KGrzbV 5 with He 111s. Converted to Savoia-Marchetti SM.81 at the beginning of January 1944. Disbanded in October 1944.
TGr 20	Formed from KGrzbV 108 in Oslo. In November 1943, one squadron was converted to Seetransportstaffel 3.
TGr 30	Formed from KGrzbV 5 at Diepholz and Hildesheim, equipped with He 111s. Deployed France, Italy, Sardinia, and Corsica. (May–November 1943); Germany, Russia, and Romania (December 1943–May 1944); Germany and France (May 1944–May 1945).
TGr 110	Formed in March 1944 with three squadrons of Savoia-Marchetti SM.82s, disbanded in October 1944.
LVG Bronkow	Special emergency transport unit.
LVG Mobil	Special emergency transport unit.

In July 1943 the Western Allies invaded Sicily. The German transport fleet (Ju 52s and Me 323 Gigants) played an important role during Operation *Husky*. Three battalions—over 3,000 men—of 1. Fallschirmjäger-Division's FJR3 were parachuted into Lentini on July 12, 1943, in time to thwart General Montgomery's push toward Catania and Messina. The rest of the division was flown into Catania soon after. Again, transport crews paid heavily for their efforts—groundcrew too, although many were able to escape over the Strait of Messina. When the Germans withdrew, their equipment was left behind.

In fall 1943 XIV. Fliegerkorps was involved in two major evacuation operations: from Corsica—23,192 men and 618 tonnes of materiel—and the Kuban bridgehead. They had been supplying 17. Armee units in the bridgehead from February 4, 1943—using Ju 52s and Go 242 and Me 321 gliders until the thaw allowed resupply by sea. In the fall evacuation, they ferried 18,697 men and 1,156 tonnes of materiel across the Kerch Strait to the Crimea.

Another significant pocket resupplied by air was Korsun (also known as Cherkassy) in January 1944. Of the 60,000 men trapped there, there's dispute as to how many survived, Niklas Zetterling and Anders Frankson putting the figure of dead, wounded, and missing at 30,000. Degtev and Zubov's analysis of the resupply operations by TG3 indicates 1,500 sorties, 2,000 tons delivered, and 2,000 wounded evacuated for the loss of 32 Ju 52s.

From the end of March 1944 another huge pocket—200,000 strong under the command of 1. Panzerarmee—was surrounded at Kamenets-Podolsky in Ukraine. Unlike many of the other encirclements, this one was allowed to try to break out and began to do so almost immediately. The story of what became a moving pocket between March 27 and its linkup with the rescuing II. SS-Panzerkorps on April 4 was one of bitter fighting and highlights the logistical problems caused by such events: not just the resupply operations and the attrition to air forces but the major reduction in 1. Panzerarmee's fighting power. This was not just in manpower, but also through severe loss of heavy equipment: nearly 22,000 motor vehicles including over 10,000 trucks, 1,200 AFVs including 322 tanks and 39 StuGs, and significant amounts of artillery. Also devastating was the loss of repair, recovery, and other equipment of maintenance units: 661 repair and workshop vehicles, cranes, specialized trucks, and heavy machine sets. 1. Panzer-Division reported:

> The following no longer exist: the entire motor park units, the administrative units, the majority of supply units, the field post office, all repair and maintenance sections, tank workshop platoons, the majority of repair units, 50% of the field kitchens, all ration supply trains, 75% of the other supply trains; in addition, the majority of the signals equipment of the troops is missing.

7. Panzer-Division reported:

> In terms of motor vehicles, the division had to destroy the majority of its vehicles in accordance with orders. The Panzergrenadiers and Panzer Pioneers are therefore no longer motorized and mobile. Parts of the other units are also dependent on foot marches.
>
> The division has no supply and repair services (except for 1 repair unit in the armored artillery regiment). Furthermore, with the exception of a few field kitchens, rations and ammunition wagons, the majority of combat and rations supply trains are lost.

19. Panzer-Division reported:

> Due to the loss of the greater part of its motor vehicles in the battles of March 4–April 6, 1944, the division is almost immobile. The few remaining motor vehicles are almost all in need of major overhaul. Supply of the troops encounters the greatest difficulties from this.
>
> There is only one workshop company left. The Armored-Workshop-Company 27 is not operational due to a complete lack of equipment. … For the most part, the regiments and even battalions are no longer in possession of their repair and maintenance section.

The Gotha Go 242B-1 was a cargo version of the glider with jettisonable undercarriage; the B-2 was an improved version. This one was captured in North Africa. (NARA)

The aerial resupply missions started with supply aircraft—Ju 52s, He 111As, and Me 323s—landing at Proskuriv airfield, but as the pocket wandered west, temporary landing sites were used: Degtev and Zubov identify 30 different landing sites and container drop zones used between March 22 and April 11.

The Luftwaffe elements used to supply this wandering pocket and two others that formed around the same time at Kovel and Tarnopol were under Transportfliegerführer 2 commanded by Generalmajor Friedrich-Wilhelm Morzik. They included some 300 aircraft (150 Ju 52s, 100 He 111s, and around 50 other aircraft) flying out of airfields in Romania and Ukraine. Degtev and Zubov suggest around 8,000 flights to supply the Kamenets-Podolsky pocket, delivering 4,000 tons of cargo, much of it by container drop.

The pocket at Kovel was also resupplied by container as was Tarnopol, the latter also seeing the use of DFS 230 gliders until the landing ground was taken by the Soviets. Dropping containers reduced the per diem levels from 12–15 tons to eight. Unfortunately, dropping containers wasn't a precise science and Degtev and Zubov highlight the problems well: "On April 1, the garrison commander Generalmajor von Neidorf reported that only five of the ninety cargo containers dropped the previous night had ended up in the hands of German soldiers."

There were two other significant glider-borne assaults in 1944: that of Fallschirm-Kampfgruppe "Schäfer" on July 21–23, 1944 at Vassieux in the Vercors mountains of southeastern France. Part of *Unternehmen Bettina*, whose aim was to clear the area of Maquis, 220 men were landed by DFS 230 on the 21st, and 50 more on the 23rd. Supplies came in by Go 242A gliders. The other was *Unternehmen Rösselsprung* on May 25, 1944. This was an attempt to capture or kill Tito in his HQ complex at Drvar. Some 900 SS paras were dropped in three waves because of the lack of aircraft and gliders. The quick response of the partisans saw the SS contingent cut to pieces with 576 dead and 48 wounded.

In January 19–31, 1945, another "*Wandernden Kessel*" made its way back to German lines: Gruppe Nehring (elements of General Walther Nehring's XXIV. Panzerkorps) was resupplied from Sagan-Küpper as it headed toward Gruppe von Saucken (General Dietrich von Saucken of Panzerkorps Großdeutschland), the relief advancing toward Nehring. Both elements—Nehring and Saucken—received airdropped assistance. Among other drops, Gruppe Nehring received 82 canisters of fuel on January 21; Saucken 163 containers of ammunition from He 111s on January 25, and 91 fuel and 25 ammunition on the 26th.

Hitler created a range of strongpoints—*Festungen* and *feste Plätze*—to provide a bulwark against the advancing Allies. They ranged from the Channel Islands that were bypassed and surrendered only at the end of the war to cities such as Budapest and Breslau. These were regularly resupplied by air. They certainly needed to be. The idea proposed by Hitler in his Special Order for the Feste Plätze No 2 of December 22, 1944, that each should have stocks of food—600,000 mouthfuls of food, 200,000 of long-life bread or crispbread, and 400,000 daily rations of flour—was an illusion.

The Budapest pocket was another stern test of the Luftwaffe. Bravery aplenty was shown by pilots and aircrew, but a lack of aircraft meant that in the seven-week siege, only around 1,500 tons of cargo were delivered

The battle for Festung Budapest took place between November 1944 and February 1945. The loss of Ferihegy airport to the Soviets at the end of 1944 put the landing zones within range of Soviet artillery. The DFS 230 glider was used extensively. It carried up to 270 kg (600 lb) of assorted cargo. On February 5, 1945, the last glider resupply mission to Budapest took place. Six DFS 230s landed but one crashed into the top story of 35 Attila Street. (Fortepan/Hungarian Archives/Vörös Hadsereg)

Crashed and burnt gliders on Budapest's Bloody Meadow (in the background are houses on Attila Street). They were delivering food and ammunition to the German troops surrounded in the city. (NAC)

including 400 containers and 48 gliders. Losses were 36 Ju 52s and seven He 111s. The loss of the main airfield in the early days of the siege—it was lost on January 9—forced the garrison to use the Vermezo meadow near the Royal Castle in Buda. On February 5, 1945, the last glider resupply mission to Budapest took place. Six DFS 230s landed but one crashed into the top story of 31 Attila Road. The gliders delivered "97 tonnes of ammo, 10 tonnes of fuel, 28 tonnes of food, and four engine-oil drums and spare parts crates" (Ungváry, 2006). After the loss of the airfield 36 DFS 230s transported ammunition, fuel, food, medical supplies, and flour. The losses in the operation were severe: 48 gliders landed, but at a cost of 36 Ju 52s, seven He 111s, a Ju 87, and a Do 17. After the breakout, the fleeing troops were airdropped supplies on February 14 (by nine He 111s) and 15 (nine He 111s and three Ju 52s).

Breslau, on the other hand, was besieged from February 13 to May 6, 1945, surrendering after Hitler had committed suicide. The air bridge supplied some 7,000 tons of cargo—much by container and cargo glider—and evacuated 6,600 wounded and glider pilots. The last glider missions to Breslau took place on April 30. Hohenmauth (today's Vysoké Myto in the Czech Republic) was a prewar emergency landing ground which had been lengthened and used from August 1944. In the last months of the war various small units of Luftflotte 6 (under Generaloberst Otto Deßloch) flew from it, including Gruppe Herzog in April and May 1945. On April 25 the unit had 11 Do 17s, 15 He 111s, three Ju 87s, 13 DFS 230s, and six Go 242s stationed at Hohenmauth and at Königgrätz.

The map shows in red the airfields from which resupply missions flew to encircled Festungen in 1945: Stolp-Reitz to Elbing; Finow and Stettin-Altdamm to Arnswalde; Alt-Lönnewitz to Posen, Glogau, and Breslau.

Luftwaffe Training

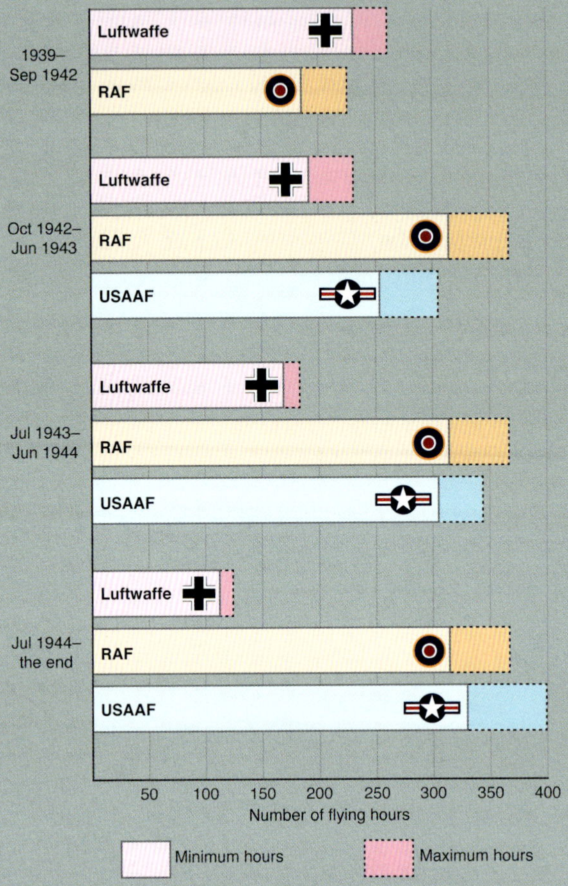

German military training was of the highest standard. The men who went to war in 1939 were the ultimate professionals: committed, well armed, and well trained. German pilots started their c. 100 hours of training in a *Flugzeugführerschule* with the 30 hours on a basic aircraft—although many of them would already have been involved with gliding clubs. Five of these 30 hours were dual control with an instructor; the rest were solo. If they passed that course, they went on to a further course, this one of 60 hours in more powerful aircraft. Their potential was assessed carefully, and they were directed toward piloting fighters or bombers, or other onboard or ground crew positions. Having passed these courses, the pilots would receive their license which entitled the holder to further training at flying weapon schools or at other establishments.

A further separate course instructed multi-engine aircraft use for bombers and long-distance reconnaissance. This training was mainly on Junkers Ju 52s, Dornier Do 17s, and Heinkel He 111s. Transport pilots would have learnt formation and low-level flying, landing techniques, forced landings, night and instrument flying, and personnel and equipment airdrops.

The trouble with training in wartime is that attrition always leads to reduction of training times. Initially, the training period was about a year, and the plan was to provide 30 trained pilots a month. The 100 hours of training—like the duration of Allied aviators' courses—was eroded from 1942 until by the end of the war it was down to less than 50 hours. Additionally, the aircraft and instructors were regularly pulled away from training to operational sorties—with all the losses that that entailed. In 1939 the Luftwaffe Training Command possessed two-thirds of the available Ju 52s. The paucity of transport aircraft led to temporary reassignment to the front. For example, 380 training Ju 52s were taken for use in the campaign in the West. They were away for 10 weeks, and 150 were destroyed.

When in December 1941, Hitler ordered the creation of five new transport groups for use on the Eastern Front, aircraft and personnel came from the training schools. Postwar, Generalmajor Paul Deichmann, chief of staff to the chief of Air Force Training in 1939–40, complained:

> It is a well-known fact that the practice of requisitioning Ju 52s from the training schools continued unabated and, in fact, became more and more common as the war progressed. As a result, of course, the schools were simply unable to fulfill their mission of providing trained replacement personnel for the bomber and long-range reconnaissance forces.

From Heimat to the Front: By Sea

The huge seaborne operations of the Allies in the West and the Pacific have overshadowed those undertaken by the Wehrmacht during the war. Things might have been different if *Unternehmen Seelöwe* or *Herkules* had taken place.

A German infantry unit boards ship. Note the horseboxes being loaded—a safe and secure method of travel where they could be looked after by crewmen responsible for their welfare. Many thousands were transported this way. (RCT)

The Kfz 69 Krupp Protze was a motorized munitions limber that usually towed an antitank company 3.7 cm PaK. This Kfz 69 is being loaded onto a transport ship. Note the horse fodder bags provide a barrier for the loading straps to stop fraying, the padding applied to the rear seat, and a plentiful assortment of extra cargo. (RCT)

10.5 cm leFH 18 light field howitzer being offloaded from a transport ship. Note the ship's "dazzle" paintwork, designed to break up its shape and size when operational. (RCT)

The Pionierlandungsfähre 41 and 42 (landing ferries—PiLF—41/42) were types of Siebel ferry that could carry 65 tonnes or 250 men—as here in the Aegean. Note the distinctive ribbed life jackets. (NAC)

The Germans placed much emphasis on their navy and expended a great deal of money, time, and precious materials on building a surface fleet and, of course, U-boats. The wisdom of this, the procurement of naval assets, the logistics of fleet operations and U-boat resupply, are not in the scope of this book but there were elements important to army use.

Deployment of troops and their equipment by sea played a significant part in many German operations during the war as well as being critical to the survival of the German forces in Africa, on bridgeheads such as the Taman Peninsula and, latterly, in the evacuations from the Baltic states and Crimea.

The German merchant fleet was very much smaller than those of its western opponents. Indeed, in the Mediterranean it was the Italian fleet that took on most of the Axis logistical movements—particularly to North Africa.

Unternehmen Weserübung saw the first major use of ships to carry German troops in the war. Norway's main ports north of Oslo, including Narvik, fell to German troops transported on destroyers. The attack on Oslo, however, saw the first major German reverse when the guns of the Oscarsborg fortress sank the German flagship *Blücher* and severely damaged other German ships. As many as 800 died when *Blücher* sank, but it didn't stop the Germans taking Oslo after an airdrop on Fornebu airport. It did, however, allow the Norwegian royal family to escape Nazi clutches and set up a government in exile in England.

It was *Unternehmen Seelöwe*—the projected invasion of Britain—that saw the Germans get to grips with seaborne operations and develop new equipment and techniques—submersible tanks, landing craft with ramps, seagoing Herbert and Siebel ferries, and heavy auxiliary gunboats. They particularly experimented with ramp modifications to barges and ferries to allow speedy egress on landings. The resulting *Marinefährprahme* (MFP) were initially powered by aero engines as were the early production Siebel ferries. Later versions used water screws powered by three Deutz truck engines.

The most important byproduct of *Seelöwe*, the MFP building program, started with a prototype in December 1940. Production began in February 1941. 700 MFPs were built of several types (A–D), initially

Escorting an invasion fleet could be a dangerous business. The Norwegian Oscarsborg Fortress in Oslofjord was under the command of Oberst Birger Eriksen on April 9, 1940, when the German invasion force steamed toward Oslo. The German heavy cruiser *Blücher* was engaged by three Norwegian batteries: Rauøy, Bolærne, and Oscarsborg whose 280 mm guns hit the *Blücher* twice before 533 mm torpedoes launched from North Kaholmen Island finished the job. 700 died when the ship sank. (SF Collection)

Unternehmen Weserübung

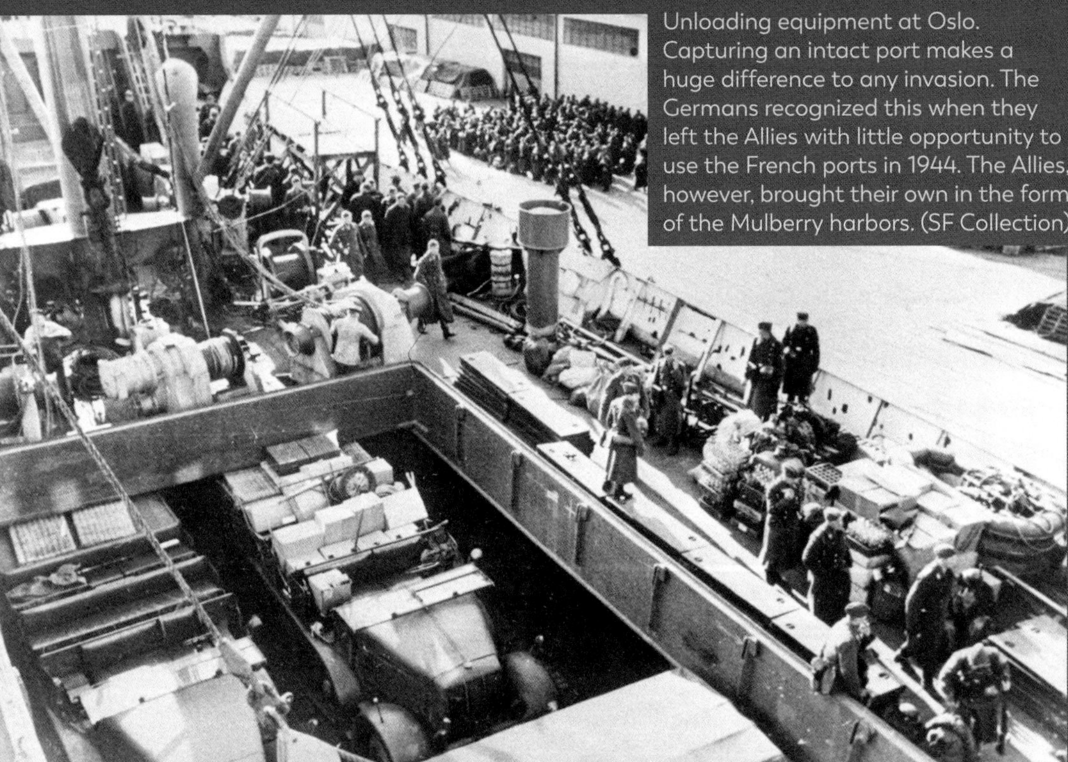

Unloading equipment at Oslo. Capturing an intact port makes a huge difference to any invasion. The Germans recognized this when they left the Allies with little opportunity to use the French ports in 1944. The Allies, however, brought their own in the form of the Mulberry harbors. (SF Collection)

German destroyers—in the foreground, *Diether von Roeder*; moored *Wolfgang Zenker*—at Narvik during *Unternehmen Weserübung.* Ten destroyers carried an invasion force of 1,900 *Gebirgsjäger* of Gebirgsjägerregiment 139 which arrived on April 9, 1940. The other boats are Norwegian patrol boats. (Bundesarchiv, Bild 101I-758-0056-35/Ehlert, Max/CC-BY-SA)

Unternehmen Blücher was the codename of the successful Axis assault on the Taman Peninsula between September 1 and 9, 1942, in support of *Fall Blau*, the 1942 German summer offensive to capture the oilfields of Baku. 46. Infanterie-Division was landed by 24 MFPs of 1. Landungs-Flottille in the North and XLIX. Gebirgskorps in the West, using a fleet of ferries, naval ferry barges, engineer ships, and assault boats. (SF Collection)

armed with 2 cm AA guns. The armament increased during the war and later versions carried four 2 cm AA guns in two mounts, two 3.7 cm AA guns, a 7.5 cm PaK, and two 8.6 cm rocket launchers.

Type A was 43 m long, 6.5 m wide, and had a draught of about a meter at the front and 1.5 m at the rear. Displacement was 220 tonnes and it carried 17 crew. The first combat use of an MFP was during *Unternehmen Beowulf II*, the occupation of the Estonian Islands of Saaremaa, Hiiumaa, Muhu, and Vormsi, in the mouth of the Gulf of Riga. A substantial joint German and Finnish task force of light cruisers and coastal defense ships provided protection for over 250 barges, ferries, and assault boats. The operation lasted from September 9 till October 21, 1941, when 19,000 Soviets surrendered. They had lost 5,000 in the fighting, the Germans almost 3,000 dead, wounded, and missing.

Types B and C only had minor differences (to loading space heights); Type D was 7 m longer, had improved draught, displaced 240 tonnes with a load capacity of 140 tonnes, and had a crew of 25.

There were three other versions: artillery, mine-laying, and tanker.

The *Artilleriefährprahm* was produced initially by conversion and later built as new. It was slower and less seaworthy but could provide landing support with its two quadruple 2 cm AAs, one 7.5 cm, and two 8.8 cm guns.

Mining

Sea mines are an important method of restricting enemy logistics and of protecting friendly sea lanes. Mines were an important factor in the German preparations for war, as the U.S. Navy's Ordnance Pamphlet 1673a *German Underwater Ordnance: Mines* of 1946 details:

> Beginning in the early 1920s, the German Navy developed an extensive marine mine research program, and by the outbreak of World War II possessed a number of revolutionary types ready for mass production. These included seven contact mines, eight influence mine cases, and three magnetic units. Among them were ground and moored mines suitable for laying by aircraft, surface vessels, and submarines.
>
> The German Navy had already perfected highly efficient contact mines during the first World War, but Allied countermeasures seriously limited their effectiveness. Consequently, in 1927, research began upon mines operating on non-contact principles and was first directed toward the development of a magnetic unit.
>
> The Germans assumed erroneously that the British, who had laid the first magnetic mine, would have developed sweeping techniques and established degaussing procedures to counter it. Consequently, in 1939, when the magnetic mine program was well advanced, they commenced research upon acoustic mine firing mechanisms. ...
>
> By 1941, British countermeasures against magnetic and acoustic mines were so effective that the Germans began a new research program to develop units using new firing principles, combined units, and auxiliary devices calculated to hinder or defeat British sweeping methods.

Fortunately for the Allies, the development and delivery of mines was split between the Kriegsmarine and Luftwaffe. While they made significant advances in every area of mine development—including the substitution of papier-mâché for aluminum in the casings to overcome supply problems—inter-service rivalry saw dual development that never received the level of commitment it needed. Quite simply, there was more propaganda value in the Luftwaffe bombing England and Kriegsmarine U-boats torpedoing merchant ships. By the time the need for mining became critical—1943 and 1944 and the huge Allied seaborne landings—the Luftwaffe didn't have the aircraft or crews and the Kriegsmarine had to use E-boats or MFPs rather than dedicated minelayers.

The first *Minenfährprahm*—minelayer version—was a hasty conversion in the field that could lay 36 mines but only in calm seas and while reversing as the mines were bow-launched. A comprehensive reworking led to more specialized versions that laid the mines from the stern from rails. These were designated Types AM (M for mines), CM, and DM (the Type B wasn't converted). The number of mines carried ranged from the Type AM's 36 to the Type DM's 54. The *Minenfährprahmen* could also be used to carry 16 assault boats on the mine rails.

MFPs were used extensively in wartime operations in the Baltic, Black Sea, and Mediterranean, and on some of the arterial rivers of Europe, mainly to carry supplies but also in such operations as *Unternehmen Eisbär* on Kos, October 3–4, 1943. Airborne landings of 1,500 paratroopers preceded the amphibious landing of a battlegroup made up of 22. Infanterie-Division (Luftlande) and Brandenburg special forces, a mixture of marine troops, 1./Küstenjägerabteilung and the 5. Fallschirmjäger-Bataillon, along with light artillery and

View of the *Unternehmen Tanne Ost* landing area after the fighting. Due to the air threat, the Germans did not dare send the cruiser *Prinz Eugen* to support the landing forces. The logistics of amphibious landings are always complicated by lack of air superiority and support from big guns. In the D-Day landings, naval gunfire proved significant—indeed, on Omaha Beach it was crucial. (SA-Kuva, Finnish Archives)

Amphibious Landings

Amphibious operations call for a range of specialists who—as the Allies found in 1943/44—iron out difficulties in operational procedure, timings, and logistics until the process becomes better organized and executed. One area that needs careful control is the beach over which troops land. Peter Schenk's excellent book on Operation *Sealion* outlines the German approach to beach organization:

> Beach parties were divided up into units each of which consisted of two officers (a harbour captain and a director of shipping), eight naval NCOs and 32 crew. Fourteen of these units were formed ... they were to lend technical assistance and advice to army and engineering troops in unloading and constructing landing bridges ... Every naval amphibious unit had ... lanterns to mark the landing zones so they could be seen at night.

However, it was events in the air that caused the main problems for the Germans on September 15, 1944. The island of Suursaari commands the Gulf of Finland and after the Finns had left the German side, it was important the Germans took it back under control. The mission was given to the Kriegsmarine, and the result was the botched *Unternehmen Tanne Ost* (Fir East). The German force made landings on the island, but they were contained by the Finns and then bombed by the Red Air Force. The rest of the force withdrew, leaving the men on the island stranded: some 1,230 became PoWs.

The Germans lost three MFPs. This 8.8 cm didn't even get off the landing craft. (SA-Kuva, Finnish Archives)

The Allied Dodecanese campaign of 1943 was designed to take Italian territory after their capitulation before the Germans could move in. It became a British-only event as the Americans thought it was unnecessary. The Germans, with air superiority and more troops available, crushed the British and Italian forces and went on to execute many of the Italian officers. Once the German garrison had taken Rhodes on September 9–11, the next target—*Unternehmen Eisbär*, Operation *Polar Bear*—was on Cos. It made use of paratroops and an amphibious landing on October 3. Here German troops exit an MFP Type C. (NAC)

The Dodecanese Campaign

After Cos fell, Leros was the next island attacked in *Unternehmen Leopard*. Delayed after the Royal Navy intercepted a reinforcing convoy of a cargo ship and seven MFPs, nearly 50 days of preparatory bombing heralded multiple landings. The island surrendered on November 16. (NAC)

Loading a barge on the River Berezina. There's a mixture of Germans (in caps with a bayonet) and others wearing Soviet greatcoats and *ushanka* hats made from artificial or real fur. These are *Hiwis*, auxiliary volunteers usually from Eastern European countries under German control. If caught by the Soviets, life expectancy was zero. A tributary of the Dnieper, the Berezina proved both a strategic barrier and an artery for logistics that didn't require vehicles. The major rivers of Russia have been heavily used throughout history. A Byzantine emperor had a Varangian (Viking) Guard who had made their way down the rivers to the Black Sea. For the Germans in 1944, assailed by Operation *Bagration*, it proved a major obstacle. 100,000 German soldiers were caught in a pocket from which there was no escape. *Bagration* was possibly the Germans' greatest defeat of the war. (Dutch Archives)

armored cars. The similar *Unternehmen Leopard* (November 12–16) saw British forces pushed off Leros by a mixture of air- and seaborne troops: III./Infanterie-Regiment 440, II./IR 16 and II./IR 65 of the 22. Infanterie-Division (Luftlande), parachutists from I./FJR 2, and 1./Küstenjägerabteilung of the Brandenburg Division.

The final German amphibious landings of the war were during *Unternehmen Tanne Ost* on September 14–15, 1944, when they attempted to seize the strategic island of Suursaari in the Gulf of Finland. A first wave landed 1,400 mixed army and navy troops from minesweepers and landing craft, but the second wave was canceled after heavy bombing by the Soviets and strong resistance from the Finns. The Germans lost three landing craft, three patrol boats, a minesweeper, and a tug along with 150 dead; over 1,200 surrendered.

The Siebel ferries, of which nearly 400 were built, were a joint army/air force production. They were used particularly on Lake Ladoga as part of the Luftwaffe's Einsatzstab Fähre Ost (lit. Ferry Operations Staff East) during the siege of Leningrad, and as floating FlaK platforms. An example of their use was during *Unternehmen Brazil* on October 22, 1942, against Sukho Island, part of the supply chain to Leningrad across Lake Ladoga. A raid on the island used 16 armed Siebel ferries and seven infantry boats protected by Italian MAS 526s of 12a Squadrigha MAS to take a 70-man landing group to the island. Alerted by a minesweeper, the Soviet garrison was able to beat off the raid but not before two of three land-based 100 mm B-24BM naval guns were knocked out. German losses were four ferries, an infantry boat, and 79 dead, missing, and wounded.

Latterly, the main use of the ferries and MFPs were for ferrying German troops away from difficult situations such as *Unternehmen Blücher* during 1943 when they helped ferry 17. Armee troops to Crimea from the Kuban bridgehead—the not inconsiderable numbers of 239,669 soldiers, 16,311 wounded, 27,456 civilians, and 115,477 tons of military equipment (primarily ammunition), 21,230 vehicles, 74 tanks, 1,815 guns, and 74,657 horses.

Ferries and Rafts

Ferries at work in the Soviet Union, 1942. (NAC)

Because the Kriegsmarine didn't have a dedicated amphibious arm, the Wehrmacht and Luftwaffe used many variations of ferries/rafts. Many of the designs came because of the preparatory work for *Unternehmen Seelöwe* (*Sealion*), the invasion of England, in August 1940. The Germans modified Dutch, Belgian, and French barges into landing craft that needed tugs to pull them. These barges were separated into types, A1 and A2. A1 could carry 360 tons of assorted cargo—fuel drums for example—or assorted vehicles such as three PzKpfw IIIs; the A2 620 tons or four PzKpfw IVs. Most of the bridging sets used by the Wehrmacht could provide rafts as well as bridges.

Fuel drums refuel Siebel ferries, 1943. (NAC)

The original propaganda caption suggests that the photograph shows "new weapons for the Eastern Front. An arms transport has reached its destination. The new weapons are loaded onto a ferry to be taken to their final position." The guns are mainly 10.5 cm leichte Feldhaubitze 18M and 18/40s, the latter with their characteristic muzzle brakes. (NAC)

The two Cossack cavalry divisions were transferred to the SS in 1944 to become XV. SS-Kosaken-Kavalleriekorps. This photograph shows men of 1. Kosaken-Kavallerie-Division while still operating under the Wehrmacht crossing the Sava River in Croatia. The Cossacks were used from October 1943 against Yugoslav partisans. (NAC)

The Siebel ferries were designed for *Unternehmen Seelöwe* by Luftwaffe Major Fritz Siebel. The result was a flat-bottomed catamaran, square in front with a wide cargo deck that made a perfect weapons platform, particularly for Flak or artillery (as seen here). Siebel ferries saw wide service. Luftwaffen-Fährenflottillen II and III (Luftwaffe ferry flotillas) had been formed in Antwerp but were moved to Lake Ladoga as Einsatzstab Fähre Ost (Task Force Ferry East). As well as heavy weapons, the Siebel ferries were equipped with dual-purpose machine-gun mounts for use against land or air targets. (SA-Kuva, Finnish Archives)

Over August 11–17, 1943, *Unternehmen Lehrgang* (training course) saw German forces evacuated from Sicily to the Italian mainland across the Strait of Messina. Planned and executed by Oberst Ernst Baade and Kapitän Gustav von Liebenstein of the Kriegsmarine, they used 10 ferries, seven barges and over 100 smaller boats, and sailed from a dozen separate evacuation points. The week before they refined the process during which they evacuated some 12,000 men, 4,500 vehicles, and 5,000 tons of supplies. By the time the main operation began the straits were heavily protected by two FlaK brigades, making Allied interdiction virtually impossible. In the end, some 40,000 German troops, 5,000 wounded, and a high proportion of their heavy equipment and weapons, including AFVs, artillery, ammunition, and fuel, were rescued. The Italians also separately evacuated over 60,000 men using a 932-ton train ferry, the *Villa*.

While there has been much criticism of the ease with which this evacuation was conducted, James Holland provides an interesting range of counter arguments:

• that many of those evacuated weren't the combat troops. The badly mauled units who did escape did not constitute a decisive force and would not have been able to play an immediate part in any counter to an Allied invasion of Italy;

• as the British evacuations of Dunkirk, Greece, and Crete, and the later German evacuations over the Seine and Scheldt after Normandy and through Operation *Hannibal* from East Prussia show, wartime sea-borne evacuations were very difficult to stop.

Other important evacuations included transporting 15. Armee over the Westerscheidt in September 1944—86,100 men, 616 artillery pieces, 6,200 vehicles and 6,200 horses, and 6,500 bicycles—and possibly the most difficult logistical problem the Germans had to undertake: *Unternehmen Hannibal*. Between January 13 and May 8, 1945, large numbers of civilians, government officials, and soldiers were taken from Königsberg and the Baltic states in front of the Red Army.

The Courland pocket developed in October 1944 and held out till the war's end when upward of 180,000 troops surrendered. They too could have been evacuated—one reason why the Soviets maintained pressure on the area, with six major battles. The pocket was partially evacuated in January 1945 when 4. Panzer-Division, 31., 32., 93., 218., 227., and 389. Infanterie-Divisionen, along with 11. SS-Division Nordland were extracted by ship which provided a dress rehearsal for *Hannibal*.

Rear Admiral Konrad Engelhardt, head of the Kriegsmarine's Transport Service, was ordered by Admiral Dönitz to begin the *Rettungsaktion* (evacuation operation) in January 1945. The main concern was troops, but civilian refugees were also taken. Engelhardt had 13 large liners, two dozen freighters, and hundreds of smaller merchant vessels, barges and fishing boats. Protection was provided by the Kriegsmarine warships still available, including the heavy cruisers *Prinz Eugen* and *Admiral Hipper*, the pocket battleships *Admiral Scheer* and *Lützow*, a handful of destroyers and large torpedo boats, several flotillas of minesweepers, and countless

Unloading an SdKfz 10/4 armed with a 2 cm FlaK 30 from a Pionierlandungsboot 39. In the foreground an NSU motorbike with sidecar. Developed from the late 1930s, the *Pionierlandungsboote* series started with the kl. Labo 39 (kl = *klein* = small, 15 m long) which entered service in September 1940 and was developed up to the larger s. Labo 43 version (s = *schwer* = heavy, 35 m long). Other than size, the major difference was the bow door/ramp setup which was altered from the double swinging doors plus internal ramp of the kl. Labo 39 (as here) to the bow front dropping system of the s. Labo 43. The 39/40/41 boats could be divided into two equal longitudinal halves for easier carriage (usually by rail); the s. Labo 43 divided into three. First deployment was in May 1941 with the Landungsbootzug Afrika (Landing Boat Platoon Africa), and they went on to be used in every theater, their last use probably being during *Unternehmen Hannibal*. (Bundesarchiv, Bild 101II-MN-2781-19/Peter/CC-BY-SA 3.0)

Wilhelm Gustloff in Hamburg harbor before the war. (RCT)

smaller auxiliaries and patrol boats. In all, more than 1,000 ships of all kinds were used to evacuate over two million people across the Baltic Sea to Germany and German-occupied Denmark over the next 15 weeks.

At least 250 of them were sunk, causing the deaths of at least 33,000 people, the greatest single loss being the liner *Wilhelm Gustloff*, torpedoed by a Soviet submarine on January 30, 1945, with almost 10,000 dead, the largest maritime disaster on record. On February 9, the 14,660-ton *Steuben* with over 5,200 passengers and crew was sunk with only 650 survivors. On April 16, the *Goya* was torpedoed and only 183 survived from the 6,000 on board. Despite the losses, some ships made multiple crossings to and from Gdynia to Kiel, evacuating many thousands of refugees and wounded soldiers.

Supplying the Deutsches Afrika Korps

The first logistical requirement was to transport supplies from Europe to Africa: by rail to Italian ports and then by ship to ports in North Africa. Initially, this wasn't a problem. In early 1941, convoys reached Tripoli regularly and losses were minimal. Coastal shipping was able to ferry supplies and as early as April 1941 Italian submarines transported fuel to Derna. Then things got worse.

There were a lot of reasons why supplying German forces in North Africa proved difficult. The first, and most important, was the nature of the DAK's original commander, Erwin Rommel. Sent to Africa to block the British in a subsidiary theater while the main event took place in the Soviet Union, Rommel was unwilling to perform such a minor role. His thrusting offensive style meant that his forces were always too few and always too far away from his supply depots. The second major problem was that the British had cracked the German

Opposite, top: An uparmored F-Lighter (British term for an MFP) in the Mediterranean. It has twin-barreled 20 mm guns amidships and a larger-caliber gun astern. (SF Collection)

Opposite, center: MFP F-935 on the Adriatic in summer 1944. This landing barge was built according to the MFP Type D design at the S.A. des Chantiers shipyard in Ateliers de Provence, Port-de-Bouc, France. It was commissioned into the Kriegsmarine on June 25, 1944, and was part of 4. Landungs-Flottille. The barge had a flat-bottomed hull and the cargo hold was covered by a superstructure. The bridge and engine room were protected by 25 mm of armor. Troops: 3 medium tanks, or 200 men, or 140 tonnes of cargo. (SF Collection)

Organization of MFP and Transport Flotillas

The two main organizational units for sea transport were the *Landungsflottillen* and *Transportflottillen.*

- The first of 20 *Landungsflottillen* was set up in 1941 for MFP operations in the Black Sea. LF 3., 5., 7., 22., and 23. were based in Kirkenes.
- 2., 4., and 10. LF were based in the Mediterranean.
- Norwegian-based *Landungsflottillen* were 6. which was set up in June 1944 on the Norwegian coast, 8. LF set up in 1942 in Bergen, and 9. LF in Narvik.
- 15. LF (originally set up in 1943 in Toulon) was based in the Aegean.
- 11. LF (originally Marinehafen-Abteilung Rotterdam) was on the Channel coast.
- 12. LF (originally Marine-Hafenabteilung Antwerpen) was based on the Scheldt but moved in late 1944 to the Baltic.
- 13. LF was based in the Baltic (and took part in *Tanne Ost*), as were 17., 21., 24., and 27. LF.

There were six transport flotillas established between May 1943 and March 1944:

1. TF was set up in France and moved to the Italian Riviera.
2. TF was based in Venice and served the Adriatic.
3. TF was employed in the Black Sea before moving to the Rhine.
4. TF commanded the Dardanelles and Aegean.
5. TF also was used in the Aegean.
6. TF was formed from 2. TF and employed in the Adriatic, Ligurian, and Ionian Seas—including the Corinth Canal.

German landing barges unload troops at Cape Kazantip in the Sea of Azov, September 1942. (SF Collection)

PzKpfw II being offloaded at Tripoli. A successful round trip from Naples or Palermo would take about 10 days. Thorough planning and organization were the key to rapid turnaround. At certain times, these journeys could be hazardous in the extreme—often depending on the amount of air cover which, in turn, dictated whether British naval vessels were able to attack the merchant shipping. The one constant was the British submarine menace. (NARA)

Enigma codes. Intelligence is only useful if the recipient has the means to exploit it and the British had. Thanks to the British hold on Malta, between the Axis ports and the destinations in North Africa there was a sea that was, if not dominated by the enemy, then certainly contested strongly enough to be a problem.

Enemy surface ships weren't always the main issue: after the fall of Greece and Crete they had been forced back toward Alexandria—but the Royal Navy out of Malta had a "happy time" between June and November 1941 exploiting their cracking of Axis codes and the fact that the focus of German attention was in the East. The peak of the success was Force K's demolition of a big Axis convoy on the night of November 8/9, 1941. Force K—light cruisers HMS *Aurora* and *Penelope* and destroyers *Lance* and *Lively*—combined with Force B (light cruisers HMS *Ajax* and *Neptune* and destroyers HMS *Kandahar* and *Jaguar*) sank 40,400 tons in the battle of the *Duisburg* Convoy. All good things come to an end: for Forces K and B that happened on December 19 when they ran into a minefield that saw *Neptune* and *Kandahar* sunk and *Aurora* damaged. The force withdrew and as more Luftwaffe assets were moved into action in the Mediterranean, so British surface ships were withdrawn.

With the surface ships withdrawn, Allied submarines took up the baton: in particular the British U class in the Sicilian channel and the larger T class in the Aegean. In all British and Allied submarines went on to sink four cruisers, eight destroyers, 21 submarines, nine other warships and over a million tons of merchant shipping—53% of the total loss with aircraft achieving 40%—between 1941 and 1943. However, at the end of 1941 with Force K crippled, in early 1942, the Luftwaffe made a concerted effort to bomb Malta into submission, and this further helped to reduce Royal Navy effectiveness.

The third major problem for DAK logistics was the lack of suitable ports in North Africa. The main port used by the DAK was Tripoli—about 1,000 miles from Alexandria. To put that into context, Moscow is about 750 miles from Warsaw. There were other ports—the best being Tobruk but that remained in British hands until 1942—the others were smaller and less suited to receiving large merchant ships. This meant that once the ships arrived, the personnel and equipment had to be loaded onto trucks and transported to the front—unlike the

Resupply column. Volkswagens, cross-country cars and lorries, belonging to 21. Panzerdivision, moving up towards the front line, January 1942. (British Official)

Convoy protection was essential. Losses to men and materiel were substantial from RAF and RN threats: in the air, on and below the surface. This convoy has protection from a *Staffel* of Messerschmitt Bf 110s which were more often used in the ground-attack role in the desert and as night-fighters in defense of the Reich. (SF Collection)

Reinforcements and supplies going on board a six-engine Blohm & Voss BV 222 flying boat. Only 13 of this large transport were built (it could carry as many as 92 troops or 72 wounded on stretchers). Between October 16 and November 6, 1941, a BV 222 made 17 resupply flights to North Africa. (Col. T. Bock)

advance into the Soviet Union, the DAK wasn't a horse-drawn army. As the Axis forces advanced eastward, so the supply lines expanded—and trucks found the hot and dusty African conditions difficult.

Oberquartiermeister Afrika was Oberstleutnant Graf Klinkowström, who organized his logistics support into three columns, each with a lift capacity of 360 tons. The main depot was established at the Arco dei Fileni, 20 miles outside Tripoli. However, as the distance to the front increased, so getting water and supplies (the light division, for example, needed 320 tons daily; after the arrival of 15. Panzer-Division in July, the monthly supply requirements for the German forces rose to 30,000 tons; the Luftwaffe needed 8,000 tons) took time. This could take up to six days for a round trip—and there were insufficient trucks available. Coastal traffic became important. Klinkowström trucked the supplies to Benghazi and then used coastal vessels to Derna. However, this traffic was very susceptible to British submarine and RAF activity. Some supplies were deliverable by submarine—the Italian submarines could bring 80 tons of tank main-gun ammunition or 140 tons of fuel—and this proved effective.

To assist the seaborne logistics, in September 1941 Schleppschwarm Afrika was set up. Based in Athens–Eleusis in Greece, it was composed of a few Go 242 gliders and Ju 52s from KGzbV 1, supported by Go-Kdo/X. Fliegerkorps. It operated between there and Derna with Heraklion, Crete, as a midpoint. The British Operation *Crusader* advance stopped the flights and the *Schleppswarm* was disbanded in December.

From the end of 1941 into early 1942, the balance of power shifted in the Mediterranean and supplies began reaching Africa. On January 5, 1942, a convoy brought Rommel 50 tanks and 26 armored cars. On January 19, more transport vessels arrived in Tripoli. Rommel's tanks increased in number to 111, with an extra 28 in reserve. These were followed by five more convoys from January 22 to 25. Once again, he was able to attack.

It was in spring 1942 that the plan to invade Malta—*Unternehmen Herkules*—was closest to being approved, but Hitler had been frightened by the *Fallschirmjäger* losses on Crete and doubted the ability and resolve of the Italians to fulfill their end of the operation. It was postponed, but by this stage Axis air superiority

German soldiers after leaving the troop transport at Tunis airport, January 1943. In the background, a Junkers Ju 52/3m and their discarded life jackets. Note the pith helmets and other equipment being distributed. (NAC)

Italian submarines proved an effective method of bringing supplies to Africa—albeit in small amounts. This photo shows an Italian submarine leaving Bardia (note the harbour defences). The second half of 1941 saw nearly 50 such missions. (NARA via Digital Archive)

seemed to have made it irrelevant. In April 1942 less than 200 tons of a total of 150,578 sent to Africa failed to arrive. Adequate supplies allowed stockpiles to be set up. Rommel had the supplies he needed and won his greatest victory of the desert war at Gazala in May–June 1942.

But the Allied position improved as convoys to Malta got through and the availability of Spitfires turned the tide in the air war. The DAK's supply position was once again threatened by air and submarine. Coastal shipping became dangerous. The supply lines were too long to be practicable. Toppe said:

> The British succeeded in bringing German convoy traffic to an almost complete standstill. The Italian battleships were in port at Taranto and La Spezia, unable to operate because of lack of fuel. Losses in materiel and fuel were so heavy that it was barely possible to obtain adequate supplies from Germany. The sea routes to Tripoli and Benghasi were completely severed. Air transportation from Crete now played the major role, but quite naturally, the volume was far too small to meet even the most urgent demands of the front.

Generalmajor Fritz Bayerlein, chief of staff of Panzerarmee Afrika, is said to have claimed, "We should have taken Alexandria and reached the Suez Canal had it not been for the work of your submarines." August 1942 saw 33% of Axis supplies and 41% of fuel lost. In September 1942, Rommel received only 12,000 of the 50,000 tons of supplies he needed to continue his offensive. In October, thanks to Ultra, a critical fuel resupply convoy was intercepted. Rommel lost 44% of his supplies that month. The result was defeat at El Alamein and the start of the long retreat.

Water in the Desert

German planning obviously took account of the issues of fighting in the desert. Each division had a water distilling company and corps supply services included a water supply company and geographical teams.

> In addition to assessing the terrain for armored vehicles, supplying water for Rommel's Afrika Korps was one of the main tasks of Military Geology Unit 12 (Wehrgeologenstelle 12), headed by geologist Leo Medard Kuckelkorn. The appropriate equipment for the groundwater investigations was transported in a geologists' heavy truck with a trailer. Lieutenant Werner Jessen was responsible for the underground geophysical measurements. [*Fuentes: Militärische Trinkwasserversorgung*]

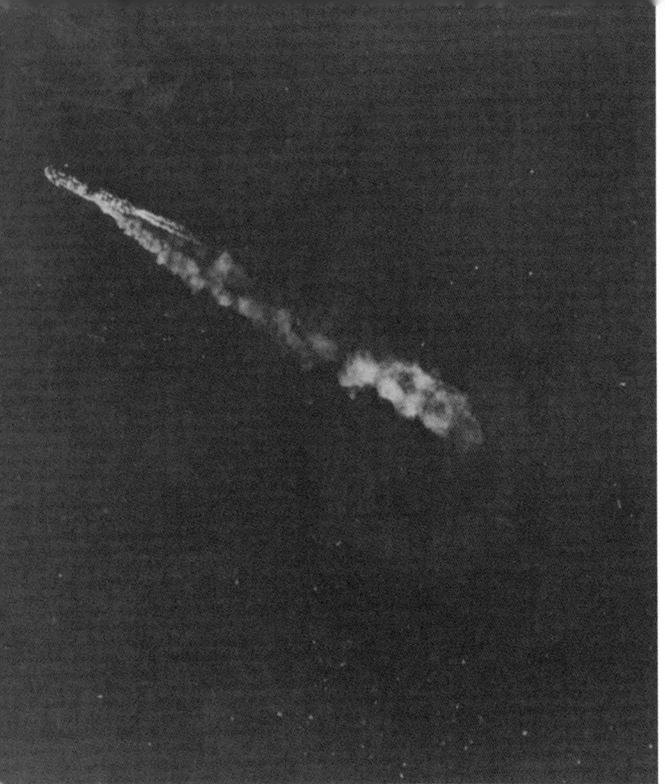

Allied interdiction of Axis shipping in the Mediterranean made life very difficult for surface vessels in the spring of 1943. This is a successful anti-shipping strike off Bizerte. (NARA)

Remarkably, the Italians had used dowsing to find water. The Germans were rather more scientific, and their water group included the corps geologist, the corps hygienist, the water engineer, and a water officer.

- The water group was responsible for the acquisition, testing, replenishment, and distribution of drinking and service water required.
- In addition to his other duties, the corps geologist was responsible for exploring and providing practical testing of the water.
- The hygienist of the corps ordered the first chemical and bacteriological examination of the water. He also arranged for hygienic control of all water transport and storage vehicles.
- The hydraulic engineer oversaw the technical repair, maintenance, expansion, and new construction of water points and water pipes, as well as the filtration of water where necessary.
- The water officer processed the instruction of the German and Italian divisions for the water distribution points and the load levels according to the type and strength of the vehicle and its distance from the distribution point. He proposed the use of the water columns and supervised their activity. (Fuentes: *Militärische Trinkwasserversorgung*)

As a result of this work, as Toppe points out:

> The water supply for the German troops in Africa was never a troublesome problem … In all combat operations, our chief concern was about motor fuel and not about the water supply. Only the garrison of Halfaya suffered severely from the lack of water after its well had been destroyed by gunfire … For example, a tank needs an average of 50 liters of motor fuel for 100 kilometers, whereas the three crew members need only an average of 12 to 15 liters of water per day. Added to this is the radiator water, averaging about seven liters. In a daily run of 100 kilometers, therefore, each vehicle requires 50 liters of motor fuel and 22 liters of water.

Rommel's forces would not have survived for as long as they did without captured supplies, fuel, and vehicles. This photograph shows British and Commonwealth rations appropriated at Tobruk where immense stocks had been accumulated around the port for Operation *Acrobat*, an intended attack on Tripoli. While Tobruk had withstood a seven-month siege in 1941 between April 10 and November 27, in June 1942 the second "siege" lasted four days. The dumps yielded significant amounts of supplies: some 7,000 tons of water, three million ration packs, 15 aircraft, thousands of assorted vehicles, and 30 serviceable tanks. (NARA)

German cans—jerrycans to the British—being filled with water ready for transportation up to the forward positions. The prominent white crosses painted on the containers distinguish them from cans carrying gasoline. (Battlefield Historian)

Water

Water was critical for maintaining troop morale (hot drinks), health and hygiene, and to maintain the operational capabilities of military equipment and, of course, animals. A reliable water supply was essential. Some locations—Africa and parts of the Eastern Front—created significant logistical challenges. Every soldier had a felt-covered aluminum canteen holding 750 ml of water and drank a gallon a day. If official sources weren't available, they would be supplemented with water sources in the field if safe to drink. Rationing was introduced in those areas with limited water recourses, vehicle needs being paramount. This drinking-water bowser has an interesting selection of hand-painted symbols: at bottom left is the Infanterie-Sturmabzeichen (infantry assault badge); at the top, the marching bear with a tank hanging from the barrel of a machine gun carried over his shoulder is linked to the Hs 129-flying 4./Schlacht-geschwader 1—the bear meaning Berlin where the Henschel works was and the tank is being hunted, which is what the *Staffel*'s role was. (Dutch Archives)

In North Africa, the arid desert environment meant water supplies were critical for the German military, troops and transport, both animal and mechanical. A significant proportion of logistical effort went toward specialized convoys of water tankers transporting water as well as the famous jerrycans which held 20 l or 5.3 U.S. gal. The cans for water always had a white stripe or cross—as here—to differentiate the type of liquid they contained. The original caption suggests this photograph shows either fuel or water resupply in 1941. (Battlefield Historian)

Water's also important in cold weather: field kitchens provided hot drinks as well as hydrating condensed rations, soups, and drink crystals. (Dutch Archives)

The FIAT 634 N II "Cisterna" provided water for the Regia Aeronautica and the DAK. It was based on a heavy truck nicknamed the "Elephant" because of its size. (Dutch Archives)

Sinking a new borehole in the desert. (Col. T. Bock)

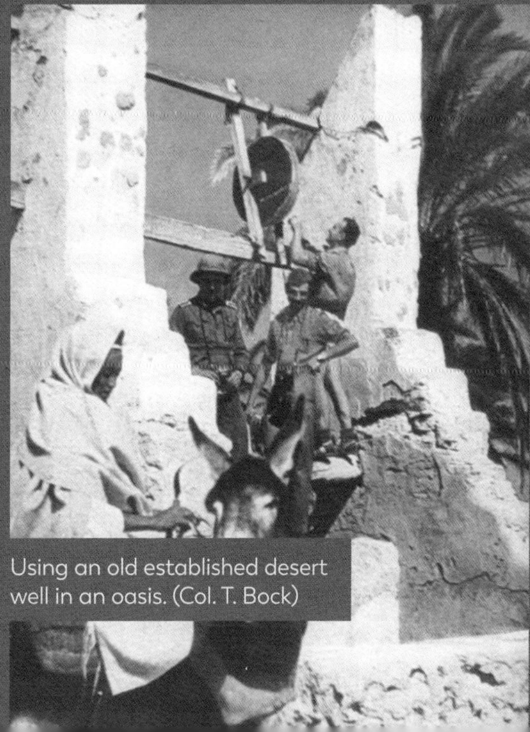

Using an old established desert well in an oasis. (Col. T. Bock)

| Conclusion

There are various modern interpretations of the principles of logistics, but the key areas are:

- Responsiveness—providing what's needed when it's needed and where it's needed. Reliability and speed are crucial.
- Simplicity—using straightforward systems: efficiency in planning and execution.
- Flexibility—improvisation allows for unpredictability and changes of needs, environments, and circumstances.
- Economy—providing what's needed without overusing scarce resources in a timely fashion and with the smallest risk.
- Attainability—realism is essential in logistics planning and execution.
- Sustainability—having the required supplies and being able to supply them for the duration of the operation.
- Survivability—prevailing in the face of threats.

How did the Wehrmacht's logistical systems stack up?

Responsiveness: strategic issues—lack of fuel, in particular—meant that German logistics were struggling from the start. In the main, the Germans could cope when they were winning but toward the end of the war, Allied bombing caused havoc. Normandy was cut off from supplies by rail and the Allied lodgment could only be contained rather than counterattacked.

Simplicity: there are few indications that the German systems were anything other than straightforward, although mechanics who had to cope with the problems of *Panzer* automotive reliability or had to clear frozen mud from *Schachtellaufwerk* might agree to disagree. The problems were caused by availability rather than systems, although the politics of interdepartmental rivalries and private armies (the Waffen-SS) and Hitler's propensity to micromanage complicated the procedures.

Flexibility—that the Wehrmacht was able to remain an effective fighting force well into 1945 in the face of overwhelming odds shows great flexibility. The way they were able to rescue troops from pockets (such as Falaise, the Taman Peninsula, Crimea) showed great resourcefulness. Their ad hoc *Kampfgruppen* usually gelled and did what was needed.

Economy—this was a problematic area for the Germans. The requirements at the front were for equipment that worked well: think M4 Sherman or T-34. Compare that to the problems the Panther faced entering service or the perennial problems the Panzer IV/70, whose massive gun meant too much weight over the front which led to suspension issues. The German response to the battlefield arms race was intricate and technological. When it worked, it worked very well; but too often it led to production complications which meant too few Tigers or

Fuel supplies from Europe to Africa, running the gauntlet through the Mediterranean. The trucks carrying the large drums of fuel are 8-tonne Tatras. Note the life rafts ready for speedy launching. (Brig. P. A. L. Vaux)

"Acht-Achts" were produced to allow the qualitative superiority to outweigh the quantitative superiority of the Allies. Look at the reaction of German industry to the Schell Plan. Continuous sniping and political moves led to a weakening of Schell's simple and practicable plans for standardization. The duplication of effort caused by the growth of the Waffen-SS didn't help.

Attainability—Göring, the Luftwaffe, and Stalingrad: enough said. The lack of winter clothing in the East in 1941/42 was caused more by the arrogant belief that the war would be over before the snows arrived than lack of equipment. Attainability is a realistic assessment of what is needed and then a realistic assessment of whether it can be achieved. Too often German logistics failed because of higher authorities meddling rather than system issues.

Sustainability—short term, the German logistics system worked brilliantly in 1939–41. Strategically, their lack of raw materials and mass production meant that they ran short of many important commodities: transport aircraft (Ju 52s or a replacement that meant aerial resupply as an option dwindled in size), trucks (which meant a dependence on large numbers of captured vehicles and weapons with all the spare parts' issues that caused), and, of course, fuel.

Survivability—in the end, the Germans logistics systems failed but the threats they faced and the length of time they survived showed great survivability. Other than for lack of fuel, there were few occasions when battles were lost because of equipment deficiencies—possibly, the battle of Britain could be cited as showing a lack of suitable aircraft but there were many other factors involved.

The overwhelming feeling one gets from a study of German procurement and logistical systems is that they worked well at first when the speed of the advance allowed flexibility to paper over the problems, but strategically they fell into the traps that a dictatorship will always create. Depending increasingly on the whims of the upper echelons rather than practicality, the procurement process depended too much on competition rather than compromise. Its industry only moved toward mass production as the war neared its end—and was only able to do so because of the levels of slave labor that were introduced.

In the field, manpower became a concern: the Nazi maltreatment of conquered populations—for example, the independence fighters in the Baltic states or Ukraine—meant that potential allies were treated as enemies. Security in rear areas had to be kept high because of the ill will engendered. The sensible idea that Luftwaffe troops should be moved over to the army was wasted when the *Luftwaffefelddivisionen* were created. Badly trained, they suffered high casualty rates and were wasted.

However, the key issue the Germans faced was lack of fuel. It didn't matter how good their logistics system was: if there was no fuel there wasn't much that could be done except use it sensibly. That's not logistics.

Glossary and Abbreviations

APCR: Armor-piercing composite rigid—a type of armor-piercing projectile.

AVL: *Armeeverpflegungslager—Armee* supply depot.

BvTO: *Bevollmächtigter Transportoffiziere*—plenipotentiary transport officers.

CBO: Combined Bomber Offensive—USAAF by day, RAF by night.

DRB: Deutsche Reichsbahn—German railroads under the Nazis.

EVM: *Ersatzverpflegungsmagazin*—replacement supply center.

***Fall Blau*:** The summer 1942 attack toward the Caucasus oilfields.

***Fall Gelb*:** The 1940 attack on the West.

FlaK: *Flugabwehrkanone*—antiaircraft gun.

Gedob: Generaldirektion der Ostbahn—General Directorate of the Eastern Railway.

If.: *Infanterieanhänger*—infantry trailer or *Infanteriekarre(n)* cart(s).

KStN: *Kriegsstärkenachweisungen*—authorized strengths of units.

KwK: *Kampfwagenkanone*—tank gun.

LKW: *Lastkraftwagen*—heavy goods vehicle (i.e., a truck).

MT: Motor transport.

n.A. *neuer Art*—new style/form/model

NSKK: Nationalsozialistisches Kraftfahrkorps—National Socialist Motor Corps.

OKH: Oberkommando des Heeres—High Command of the German Army.

OKW: Oberkommando der Wehrmacht—High Command of the German Armed Forces.

PaK: *Panzerabwehrkanone*—antitank gun.

Parks and depots: The top levels of these divide into those run by the Feldheer and those run by the individual *Armeen*. The latter was where repairs took place, but they also were supposed to have a reserve of 5–10% of the *Armee*'s arms and equipment. An *Armee* had the following parks: infantry park, artillery park, anti-gas equipment park (for gas masks, decontamination suits, anti-gas clothing, and smoke equipment), engineer stores park, signals park, motor transport park, army equipment park (for harnesses, horse carts, equipment for cooks, and general items), medical park (for medical equipment), veterinary park (for veterinary equipment), and horse park (for riding and draft horses).

PKW: *Personenkraftwagen*—passenger vehicle; the Einheits-Pkw der Wehrmacht program was an attempt to standardize these into three categories (light/medium/heavy).

POL: Petrol, oil, lubricants.

RAD: Reichsarbeitsdienst—Reich Labor Service.

SdAh: *Sonder Anhänger*—special trailer.

***Unternehmen*:** Operation.

***Wehrkreis* (pl *-e*):** Germany was divided into military districts after World War I. Initially, there were 13 (usually given Roman numerals I–XIII) under the Nazis, each linked to an *Armeekorps* and was commanded by the *Armeekorps* commander. After the *Anschluß*, the number increased to 15 and a further four were added after wartime conquests. The numbering sequence omits the numbers of the original motorized Korps (XIV, XV, XVI, XIX). The *Wehrkreise* were an extremely important link in the logistics chain and part of the process by which recruits were trained and garrisoned before being sent to their divisions. The *Wehrkreis* system supported the field commanders and supplied men to its linked army divisions providing a regional association. The final 19 *Wehrkreise* (and their centers) were I (Königsberg), II (Stettin), III (Dresden), IV (Stuttgart), V (Münster), VI (München/Munich), VII (Breslau), VIII, IX (Kassel), X (Hamburg), XI (Hannover), XII (Wiesbaden), XIII (Nürnberg); the two Austrian—XVII (Vienna) and XVIII (Salzburg); three created following the invasion of Poland—XX (Danzig, XXI (Posen), and General-Gouvernement (Warsaw—created in 1943); and the Protektorat Böhmen und Mähren (Protectorate of Bohemia and Moravia—created in 1942).

Further Reading

AAF Evaluation Board in the European Theater of Operations. *Effectiveness of Air Attack Against Rail Transportation in the Battle of France*, 1945.

Air Historical Branch: "A survey of Anglo-American air operations against the Reich and Western Europe 1942–1944." Translated studies prepared by the German Air Historical Branch (8th Abteilung), October, 1944, accessed via https://www.raf.mod.uk/what-we-do/our-history/air-historical-branch/ahb-german-translations/.

Akins, Maj Willard B., II. "The Ghosts of Stalingrad." MA thesis, U.S. Army Command and General Staff College, 1989, accessed via CARL.

Balsamo, Larry T. "Germany's Armed Forces in the Second World War: Manpower, Armaments, and Supply." From *The History Teacher*, Vol. 24, No. 3, May 1991, accessed via https://doi.org/10.2307/494616.

Boog, Horst. "Luftwaffe and Logistics in the Second World War." From *Aerospace Historian*, Vol. 35, No. 2, summer/June 1988, accessed via www.jstor.org/stable/44525411.

Boog, Horst. "German Air Intelligence in World War II." From *Aerospace Historian*, Vol. 33, No. 2, summer/June 1986, accessed via www.jstor.org/stable/44524196.

British Bombing Survey Unit. *The Strategic Air War Against Germany 1939–1945*.

Brookes, Andrew. *Air War Over Russia*. Ian Allan Publishing, 2003.

Caviggia, Lt. Col. John D. *British and German Logistics Support During the World War II North African Campaign*. U.S. Army War College study project, 1990, accessed via CARL.

Collingham, Lizzie. *The Taste of War: World War Two and the Battle for Food*. Penguin, 2013.

Corum, James S. "The Luftwaffe and its Allied Air Forces in World War II: Parallel War and the Failure of Strategic and Economic Cooperation." From *Air Power History*, Vol. 51. No. 2, summer 2004, accessed via www.jstor.org/stable/26274547.

Czerny, Val. *Das Truppenfahrrad*. Accessed online at https://www.scribd.com/document/421402794/Das-Truppenfahrrad.

Davie, H. G. W. "The Influence of Railways on Military Operations in the Russo-German War 1941–1945." From *The Journal of Slavic Military Studies*, Vol. 30, Issue 2, 2017, accessed via https://doi.org/10.1080/13518046.2017.1308120.

Degtev, Dmitry, and Dmitry Zubov. *Hitler's Air Bridges: The Luftwaffe's Supply Operations of the Second World War*. Air World, 2022.

Dinardo, R. L. *Mechanized Juggernaut or Military Anachronism? Horses and the German Army of WWII*. Stackpole, 2008.

Donges, Alexander. "Import Dependence and Strategic War Planning: The German Iron and Steel Industry, 1933–1945." From *The International History Review*, Vol. 46, 2024, accessed via https://doi.org/10.1080/07075332.2024.2323490.

Department of the Army Pamphlet No. 20-234. *Historical Study: Operations of Encircled Forces German Experiences in Russia*. January 1952.

Department of the Army Pamphlet No. 20-242. *Historical Study: German Armored Traffic Control During the Russian Campaign*. June 1952.

Department of the Army Pamphlet No. 20-244. *The Soviet Partisan Movement 1941–1944*. Edgar M. Howell, Washington, D.C., 1956.

Ehlers, Robert S., Jr. BDA. "Anglo-American Air Intelligence, Bomb Damage Assessment and the Bombing Campaigns Against Germany,1914–1945." Doctorate dissertation, Ohio State University, 2005, accessed via https://apps.dtic.mil/sti/citations/ADA433892.

Harrison, Mark. "Industrial mobilisation for World War II: A German comparison." From *The Soviet Defence Industry Complex from Stalin to Khrushchev*. Macmillan Press, 2000.

Harrison, Mark. "Resource Mobilization for World War II: The U.S.A., U.K., U.S.S.R., and Germany, 1938–1945." From *The Economic History Review*, Vol. 41, No. 2, May 1988, accessed via https://doi.org/10.2307/2596054.

Hart, Russell A. "Feeding Mars: The Role of Logistics in the German Defeat in Normandy, 1944." From *War in History*, Vol. 3, No. 4, November 1996, accessed via www.jstor.org/stable/26004473.

Historical Division European Command. *Combat in the East: Experiences of German Tactical and Logistical Units in Russia*. Foreign Military Studies Vol. 1 No. 10, 1952.

Holland, James. *Sicily '43*. Penguin, 2020.

Jersak, Tobias. "Blitzkrieg Revisited: A New Look at Nazi War and Extermination Planning." From *The Historical Journal*, Vol. 43, No. 2, June 2000, accessed via https://www.jstor.org/stable/3021042.

Jessen, Morten. *The Junkers Ju 52 The Luftwaffe's Workhorse.* Greenhill Books, 2002.

Kalthoff, Jürgen, and Martin Werner. *Die Händler des Zyklon B.* VSA-Verlag, 1998.

Keller, Maj. Shawn P., USAF. "Turning Point: A History of German Petroleum in World War II and its Lessons for the Role of Oil in Modern Air Warfare." Air Command and Staff College dissertation, 2011, accessed via https://apps.dtic.mil/sti/citations/AD1020261.

Kennedy, Maj. James L., Jr. "The Failure of German Logistics during the Ardennes Offensive of 1944." MA thesis, U.S. Army Command and General Staff College, 1988, accessed via CARL.

Kershaw, Robert. *War Without Garlands.* Ian Allan Publishing, 2000.

Kurowski, Franz. *Das Afrika Korps: Erwin Rommel and the Germans in Africa, 1941–43.* Stackpole, 2010.

Liedtke, Gregory. *Enduring the Whirlwind: The German Army and the Russo-German War 1941–1943.* Helion & Co Ltd, 2016.

Maiwald, Barbara. *Feldküche und Co. Verpflegung und Ausrüstung im Deutschen Heer.* Motorbuch Verlag, 2018.

Ministry of Defence. *Oil as a Factor in the German War Effort, 1933–1945.* Chiefs of Staff Technical Subcommittee on Axis Oil, 1946.

Müller, Rolf-Dieter. *Hitler's Wehrmacht, 1935–1945.* University Press of Kentucky, 2016.

Müller-Hillebrand, Generalmajor Burkhart. *Horses in the German Army (1941–1945).* Historical Division, USAREUR, 1966.

Overy, Richard. *Why the Allies Won.* Pimlico, 2006.

Reimer, Michael. *Lokomotiven für die Ostfront Menschen und Maschinen im Zweiten Weltkrieg.* GeraMond Verlag, 1999.

Reinhard, Frank (trans. Dr. Edward Force). *Lastkraftwagen der Wehrmacht.* Schiffer Publishing Ltd., 1994.

Roba, Jean-Louis. *Casemate Illustrated: The Luftwaffe in Africa 1941–1943.* Casemate Publishers, 2019.

Schenk, Peter: *Operation Sealion: The Invasion of England 1940.* Greenhill Books, 2019.

Scherner, Jonas. "Preparing for the Next Blockade: Non-ferrous Metals and the Strategic Economic Policy of the Third Reich." From *The English Historical Review,* Vol. 137, Issue 585, April 2022, accessed via https://doi.org/10.1093/ehr/ceac063.

Schreiber, Paul K. "Rommel's Desert War: The Impact of Logistics on Operational Art." Naval War College, 1998.

Smith, J. Richard. Profile 177, *The Junkers Ju 52 Series.* Profile Publications, 1967.

Stolfi, R. H. S. "Barbarossa Revisited: A Critical Reappraisal of the Opening Stages of the Russo-German Campaign (June–December 1941)." From *The Journal of Modern History* Vol. 54, No. 1, March 1982, accessed via https://www.jstor.org/stable/1906049.

Thomas, Joan Maria. "Tungsten in the Second World War: China, Japan, Germany, the Allies and Iberia." From *Comillas Journal of International Relations,* Sep–Dec 2017, accessed via www.researchgate.net/publication/321972324_Tungsten_in_the_Second_World_War_China_Japan_Germany_the_Allies_and_Iberia.

Tooze, Adam. *The Wages of Destruction: The Making and Breaking of the Nazi Economy.* Penguin, 2006.

Toppe, Generalmajor Alfred. *Desert Warfare: German Experiences in World War II.* U.S. Army Command and General Staff College, 1991.

Weinberg, Gerhard L. "Hitler's Memorandum on the Four-Year Plan: A Note." From *German Studies Review,* Vol. 11, No. 1 February 1988, accessed via https://www.jstor.org/stable/i262373.

Wheatley, Maj. William G. "German Airborne Operations in the Battle of Crete, 1941." MA dissertation USMC University, 2020, accessed via CARL.

U.S. War Department. Technical Manual *TM-E 30-451 Handbook on German Armed Forces.* March 15, 1945.

U.S. War Department. Special Series No. 18 *German Winter Warfare.* December 15, 1943, accessed via https://doi.org/10.2307/1430838.

Van Crevald, Martin. *Supplying War: Logistics from Wallenstein to Patton.* Cambridge University Press, 2007.

War Office. *Handbook of German Administration and Supply 1944.* Reprinted by Naval & Military Press Ltd.

War Office. *Pocket Book of the German Army 1943,* September 1943.

www.stalingrad.net/german-hq/the-stalingrad-airlift/map_airlift.htm.

www.geldscheine-online.com/post/führergeschenk-beschaffungsgeld-und-goebbels-spende.

War Office. *Handbook of German Administration and Supply 1944.* 1944, reprinted by Naval & Military Press Ltd.

Index